THE LAW OF PRIVATE NUISANCE

It is said that a nuisance is an interference with the use and enjoyment of land. This definition is typically unhelpful. While a nuisance must fit this account, it is plain that not all such interferences are legal nuisances. Thus, analysis of this area of the law begins with a definition far too broad for its subject matter, forcing the analyst to find more or less arbitrary ways of cutting back on potential liability. Tort law is plagued by this kind of approach.

In the law of nuisance, today's preferred method of cutting back is to employ the notion of reasonableness. No one seems to know quite what 'reasonableness' means in this context, however. This is because, in fact, it does not mean anything. The notion is no more than the immediately recognisable symptom of our inadequate comprehension of the law.

This book expounds a new understanding of the law of nuisance, an understand-ing that presents the law in a coherent and systematic fashion. It advances a single, central suggestion: that the law of nuisance is the method that the common law utilises for prioritising property rights so that conflicts between uses of property can be resolved.

Volume 10 in the series Hart Studies in Private Law

The Law of Private Nuisance

Allan Beever

·HART·
PUBLISHING
OXFORD AND PORTLAND, OREGON
2013

Published in the United Kingdom by Hart Publishing Ltd
16C Worcester Place, Oxford, OX1 2JW
Telephone: +44 (0)1865 517530
Fax: +44 (0)1865 510710
E-mail: mail@hartpub.co.uk
Website: http://www.hartpub.co.uk

Published in North America (US and Canada) by
Hart Publishing
c/o International Specialized Book Services
920 NE 58th Avenue, Suite 300
Portland, OR 97213-3786
USA
Tel: +1 503 287 3093 or toll-free: (1) 800 944 6190
Fax: +1 503 280 8832
E-mail: orders@isbs.com
Website: http://www.isbs.com

British Library Cataloguing in Publication Data
Data Available

ISBN: 978-1-84946-506-9

Typeset by Hope Services, Abingdon
Printed and bound in Great Britain by
TJ International, Padstow

FSC
www.fsc.org
MIX
Paper from
responsible sources
FSC® C013056

To Tana

ACKNOWLEDGEMENTS

This book was written during a magical period in which, perhaps due to an administrative blunder, I was not overburdened with teaching. I hope that at least some of the enthusiasm for the possibilities of academic life that I felt during that period have made their way onto these pages.

I would first like to give thanks to the other members of NIRG – Steven Churches, Jane Knowler and Charles Rickett – the reading group which laboured through an earlier draft of this material and challenged me to clarify and justify my views. I enjoyed it.

And a very grateful thank you to Richard Hart, Rachel Turner and all the others at Hart Publishing. Critics of *Rediscovering the Law of Negligence* have entirely failed to detect that book's greatest flaw: the absence, due to my forgetfulness, of an acknowledgement of the support that particularly Richard lent to that project. It is not at all difficult to see why Hart Publishing has made the enormous strides that it has. I feel privileged to be able to contribute to its stable once again.

And finally, a special thanks to my family for reasons that need not be mentioned. To Cathryn, Piri, Ineawa and especially here to the incandescent Tana.

ACKNOWLEDGEMENTS

CONTENTS

TABLE OF CASES

United States of America

TABLE OF LEGISLATION

TABLE OF CONVENTIONS, TREATIES ETC

1

Introduction

I. General

In an era of regulation, it is perhaps surprising that the law of private nuisance retains the vitality that it does. If my neighbour is annoying me, it is generally quicker and easier to have our dispute settled through other means. Why, then, has the law of nuisance not faded away? Why have the calls for the expansion of regulation not been sufficiently loud effectively to abolish this area of the law? What does the law offer us that regulation does not?

Moreover, though the social importance of the law of private nuisance has shrunk, this has not prevented important developments from occurring. On the contrary, especially in the United Kingdom, recent years have witnessed a number of important decisions from the courts, including *Hunter v Canary Wharf*,[1] one of the most significant cases of the last 100 years.

What is perhaps even more interesting is that, though the law of private nuisance continues to attract significant academic attention, the vast majority of this has been from law and economics scholars based in the United States. In the UK and elsewhere in the Commonwealth, the law of nuisance has been somewhat neglected. Thus, John Murphy begins his recent monograph on this area of the law by remarking that his was the first book-length examination of this law since 1996.[2]

I think it fair to say that, putting law and economics aside, this area of the law is under-theorised. As a result, the student of this law – whether scholar or practitioner – has little to guide her beyond the often conflicting, or at least apparently conflicting, case law. In particular, what is lacking is a sense of what this area of the law is about. We have no framework that seems to enable us to understand it. (This topic is pursued in detail in chapter two.)

This book is an attempt to provide such a framework. It is not a textbook on the law of private nuisance. Its analysis is by no means comprehensive. The book examines only those issues most important to our understanding of the law. And it aims to show that those issues, and by implication the others that are not canvassed, can be understood in a coherent and systematic fashion.

---

[1] *Hunter v Canary Wharf* [1997] AC 655 (HL).
[2] J Murphy, *The Law of Nuisance* (Oxford, Oxford University Press, 2010) vii.

No doubt, there is much more to be said about the law of nuisance. And I particularly wish to resist the suggestion that this book is intended to provide some kind of mechanical formula for determining the law in this area. The book is best understood as advancing a suggestion: that the law of nuisance is better understood by rejecting the contemporary understanding of it and beginning again with an approach that focuses on the prioritising of property rights. The book is only a beginning. But it is a beginning that I hope academics and practitioners will find useful in developing their understanding of the law.

II. Outlook

Like any area of the law, the law of nuisance can be difficult to understand. A major reason for this is that common law subjects of this kind are not formulated as wholes then neatly presented to us. Rather, we receive the law as an accumulation of a great many judicial decisions. It is largely because of this that this material must be interpreted by academics, whose primary function is not simply to learn the decided cases but to make sense out of what they find. In that way, the legal academy performs the same function – aiding understanding – as the rest of the university and appropriately serves the rest of the legal community.

There is no reason, in principle, why purely descriptive accounts of the law cannot be genuinely explanatory. If the law has been developed in the courts so that it presents an explanation adequate to it, then the academic has no interpretive role to play. She may, of course, question the justifications offered for the law by the courts and perhaps suggest alternative, prescriptive, theories. But in those circumstances, representing the law requires only a form of journalism: a reporting of what has been expounded elsewhere.

In saying this, I do not mean to deride journalism or the journalistic skill as it applies to law. It can take great skill to depict the decisions of courts in a way that permits the reader easily and efficiently to develop her understanding. Many of the greatest textbooks are journalistic in this sense (though they are never solely journalistic).

The problem is that law is seldom such that purely descriptive accounts are genuinely explanatory. Judges, of course, give explanations for their decisions. And it is always important to give due consideration to the explanations offered. They will only very occasionally be far wide of the mark.[3] But given that judges make decisions in response to particular problems that they are required to solve – cases, in other words – it is hardly surprising that the explanations they provide frequently conflict with other explanations provided by other courts looking to

---

[3] *cf* AC Danto, *The Philosophical Disenfranchisement of Art* (New York, Columbia University Press, 1986) 44–45.

solve different problems or indeed with the decisions that those courts reached. The problem, then, is that when one adds these explanations together, inconsistency results.

What is even less surprising is the fact that when the explanations offered by judges are brought together, they typically fail to provide a cohesive analysis of the law. Thus, even when we escape inconsistency, we are faced with incoherence. It is in these circumstances that interpretation is required. If we are to make sense of law of this kind, it will be necessary to go beyond the explanations offered by the courts.

This does not imply that the law will cease to operate without the academic's interpretations. As my car will function regardless of the state of my knowledge concerning the internal combustion engine, the law in the courts will continue to operate without the fuel of academic analysis. But on the other hand, I cannot claim to understand the functioning of my car simply on the basis that it is running well. The primary purpose of explanation is understanding.

That said, unlike cars, law is a social, norm-governed institution. Given that, developing a proper understanding of the law is likely to allow us to see previously invisible problems with it and to notice ways of improving it that were formerly opaque. Moreover, properly understanding the law is a prerequisite for properly evaluating it. It should be uncontroversial to say that law is not to be evaluated solely by what it does; it must also be judged according to why it does what it does. And the 'why' here is not solely or even most importantly a question about judges' subjective intentions. Rather, in order to know why the law does something, we must be able to explain the law. Evaluation requires interpretation.

How does the law of nuisance fit into this picture? It is an area of the law not presented to us coherently. This is most plainly revealed in the proclivity of commentators to describe the law as coming in separate parts – physical injury versus interference with comfort, for instance. We examine this tendency in the following chapter. We might describe this as a 'divide and explain' approach. The problem is that, by dividing, this approach cannot explain. No doubt distinctions must be made and areas of the law will receive different explanations, but those explanations must explain the differences or they entirely fail. It is no use saying that there are two parts of the law, explaining each part, but not why there are two parts or why they receive different explanations. That is a form of limited rationality.[4]

Accordingly, the law of nuisance cries out for interpretation, for an understanding that explains it adequately. This is an attempt to provide one.

---

[4] A Beever, *Rediscovering the Law of Negligence* (Oxford, Hart, 2007) 22–23.

III. Scope

This book is concerned only with the law of private nuisance. It does not attempt an analysis of public or statutory nuisances. I think it unlikely that there are explanatorily helpful connections between these concepts. These actions are called nuisances because they respond to troublesome events that share a similar character (noise, fumes, etc). And it is characteristic of the common law to think that its actions are to be understood in terms of the unwanted events (that is, losses) to which they respond. Thus, it can seem natural to think that the nuisances are all linked.

But it is surely quite unlikely that the key to understanding an action is the character of the undesirable event to which it responds. For instance, if I intentionally make smoke on my property in order that it spread to your neighbouring land and destroy your health, there is more than one moral basis upon which you are able to complain. You might accuse me of trying to injure you, of not caring enough for you, or of using my land in an inappropriate way, for instance. Legal actions that recognised those complaints would all respond to the same unwanted event, but they would possess importantly different structures.

I make no claim, therefore, that the analysis presented here has anything to teach us about public or statutory nuisance. Our focus is firmly on private nuisance.

IV. Use

This book places considerable emphasis on the concept of use. Because of this, and because some lawyers are inclined to adopt an ultra-literal interpretation of the concept, it is necessary to say something about the concept as employed here now.

To use something is to put that thing to one's purposes. This can be done physically or otherwise. Just as I use my fingers to type these characters, I might use my son to deliver a message. Likewise, use does not necessarily imply positive action; it is not inconsistent with omission. Thus, we can avoid the interminable and in the end pointless analysis as to whether a certain event was an act or an omission.[5] If I set up my back yard as a rock concert venue, then I am using it as such when rock bands play there, even if I am at the time fast asleep in a hotel on the other side of the world.

---

[5] It is pointless, because an omission can always be described as an act. For example, failing to turn up to the meeting can be described as staying at home and watching TV. Similarly, trying to sit still is clearly an action. I can succeed or fail to do it, though it could also be described from certain perspectives as an omission.

2

The Conventional View

I. A Debate: A Comment on Style

This book presents an analysis of the law of nuisance. I have found it useful to present this to some degree in the form of a debate. In other words, I depict the view that I advance as an attractive alternative to an opposing view. Because I think that this opposing view is at least in general outline the dominant contemporary understanding of the law of private nuisance, I label it the conventional view.

However, it is important to say that I do not mean to attribute the conventional view as such to any specific commentator or group of commentators. The view functions in this book as a heuristic device to further the argument, not as a label for particular targets at which I wish to shoot from under cover. Accordingly, it is not suggested that I am the only opponent of the conventional view. Nor is it denied that many commentators object to some aspects of that view. In fact, though I think that the overwhelming majority of lawyers adhere generally to the conventional view, very many object to one or more features of that theory. If the argument of this book is right, that is of course to be expected. The conventional view is a failure. To an extent at least, many recognise this. The problem is that, lacking something to put in its place, they have tried to redecorate the collapsing building rather than beginning with new foundations.

An important consequence of this is that some of the objections here raised against the conventional view have already been noticed by others, and indeed by others who otherwise adhere to the conventional view. That should not surprise us. The important point is that I take these difficulties to demonstrate, not that we must patch up our understanding of the law, but that we need a new beginning.

The argument of this book, then, does not imply a complete rejection of the past. To the contrary, it draws very heavily on the law's history. And it does not involve a blanket rejection even of contemporary scholarship. It rather attempts to use the insights found in this scholarship, as well as other notions, to suggest the need for and to begin to build a new understanding.

It is also necessary to say that we are looking for an explanation of the law that takes seriously the law's own demand that its decisions be justified and be justified in terms of the legal materials. The best way to explain these ideas is again to contrast them with alternatives.

Particularly when dealing with areas of law of some longevity, it is tempting to explain the law historically. And there is no doubt that historical explanations are enlightening. But they are not sufficient for our investigation. This is because they cannot provide justification – at least not on their own. As historical investigation explains attitudes such as anti-Semitism without defending them, it explains the existence of legal rules without supporting them. But this is never enough in law. You cannot justify a legal rule by elucidating how it came to be.

Moreover, though appeal to precedent is of course part of the bread and butter of lawyering, precedents bind courts, not understandings. The existence of a precedent alone never determines any legal issue, except to the extent that it is binding on a particular court. This is of course built into the system of the common law, where it is recognised that 'faulty' precedents can be altered in various ways by appropriate bodies, including the courts themselves. Given that the law insists that its decisions be justified, the appeal to history alone leaves that law in a state of arbitrariness from the standpoint of justification, a standpoint that the law itself insists must be taken.

Moreover, the justification must be in terms of the law itself, at least in the sense that the reasons that justify a decision ought to be found in the judgment itself. This is part of what it means for justice to be seen to be done. Now, of course, courts will sometimes make mistakes. Judges will see things differently from other judges and so on. We cannot expect perfection. But we are entitled to expect at the very least that the *kinds* of argument to which judges appeal can be used to provide a justificatory understanding of the law. This book argues that, generally speaking, this expectation can be met.

II. The View

What is the conventional view? In short, it is the view outlined in legal textbooks and assumed to be at least generally accurate by most commentators. It possesses four central features. First, it holds that the concept of reasonableness is the key to understanding the law. Thus, it holds to some variation of the idea that a defendant is liable in the law of nuisance if he acted unreasonably. As such, particular versions of the outlook take one or more of a series of possible stands on the proper place of fault within the law and thus on the relationship between the laws of nuisance, negligence and the cause of action based on *Rylands v Fletcher*.[1] Second, the outlook maintains that the point of the law is to achieve certain social goals, such as environmental protection and the efficient allocation of land use.[2]

---

[1] *Rylands v Fletcher* (1868) LR 3 HL 330.

[2] Against this understanding, JE Penner, 'Nuisance and the Character of the Neighbourhood' (1993) 5 *Journal of Environmental Law* 1, 11 argues that 'When there is no judicial recognition of the distinction between rights and mere interests judges may decide that the law of nuisance turns on balancing interests. At this point the law of nuisance changes from one in which tortfeasors are restrained from

Third, the outlook understands the law as coming in parts where different rules apply – that is, the law is understood to be disunified. So, for instance, it is often said that the rules are different depending on whether the complaint is that damage or discomfort has been caused. Fourth, the law must be understood to contain numerous exceptions to the general rules and principles that must be learnt independently, such as the location, sensitivity and duration rules examined in chapter four. Again, this suggests that the law is disunified.

I argue that these four notions are mistaken. The law is not usefully understood in terms of reasonableness. Instead, it must be understood as the law's mechanism for prioritising property rights in the sense to be explained below. Second, the law is not aimed at the realisation of social goals. Instead, it is focused on the parties' property rights. And in relation to the third and fourth aspects of the conventional view, the law is highly unified. It does not come in different parts or contain rules that are exceptions to its general principle. Instead, the law is the coherent working out of its general principle, so that its apparent parts reflect how that principle is to be applied in particular kinds of contexts and its apparently special rules are subsidiary principles, more concrete realisations of the general principle. Demonstrating this is the task of the material that follows.

III. An Account of the Law?

That elucidates my general points of disagreement. But why should the reader care? She is entitled to ask: What exactly is wrong with the conventional view that makes this new reading desirable?

The general answer is this: the conventional view is incapable of explaining the law of which it presents itself as an explanation. It achieves precision only by being wrong and correctness only by being vague. It is useless. Worse, it is obstructive; obstructive because it directs us to look for answers in the wrong places.

The book as a whole is intended to make good these claims. However, the problem can be noticed immediately. We encounter it as soon as we ask the most fundamental question about this area of the law: What is a nuisance? Naturally, the law's leading textbooks seek to answer this question. Here we examine one of the very best.

First, we are told that 'In modern parlance, nuisance is that branch of the law of tort most closely concerned with "protection of the environment"'.[3] As this is said

---

violating the rights of land occupiers to one where the law is called upon to resolve conflicting land uses by sanctioning some interests over others: on the economic view the resolution is made by determining which interests have the higher social value.' True. Unfortunately, however, in the eyes of many, this transformation has already occurred. I agree that these eyes have been blinded.

[3] WVH Rogers, *Winfield and Jolowicz on Tort*, 18th edn (London, Sweet & Maxwell, 2010) 705. See also C Gearty, 'The Place of Private Nuisance in a Modern Law of Torts' [1989] *CLJ* 214, 215–16.

by way of introduction, the natural implication is that the tort is fundamentally concerned with protecting the environment and that environmental protection is a key to understanding the tort's nature. That expectation is immediately thwarted, however, when we are told that many areas of the law of nuisance have no '"environmental" flavour' whatsoever and that environmental protection is in fact largely the province of statute.[4]

It is then alleged that a nuisance 'may be described as an unlawful interference with a person's use or enjoyment of land, or some right over, or in connection with it'.[5] We are not told how this is meant to relate to the protection of the environment. Later, it is maintained that the 'central issue of the whole law of nuisance is the question of reasonableness of the defendant's conduct'.[6] If that is right, then we can only wonder why this was not said at the beginning. We might also wonder why one person's right to use and enjoy his land should be determined in accordance with the reasonableness of the conduct of his neighbour.

In addition, it is said that the law must take into account the 'rule of give and take, live and let live', an idea that is meant to be taken into account when deciding whether the defendant acted reasonably;[7] that the location of the alleged nuisance must sometimes, but not always, be considered;[8] and that the duration of the event complained of may or may not be relevant.[9]

This introductory material also alleges that nuisances come in three forms: encroachment on the claimant's property, direct physical injury to the claimant's property and interference with the claimant's enjoyment of her property.[10] Later, however, we are told that nuisances come in two forms: one involving physical damage and the other containing interference with comfort.[11] Similarly, it is said that in nuisance cases 'the court is inevitably concerned to some extent with the utility or general benefit to the community of the defendant's activity'.[12] But it is also maintained that if the interference with the claimant's use and enjoyment of her land is significant, then those issues are irrelevant.[13] Likewise, it is said that the law ignores any special sensitivities of the claimant's, focusing instead on the ordinary reasonable person in the claimant's position;[14] but it is then asserted that the law refuses to impose liability in many cases involving complaints about states of affairs that the ordinary reasonable person would regard as nuisances.[15]

---

[4] WVH Rogers, *Winfield and Jolowicz on Tort*, 18th edn (London, Sweet & Maxwell, 2010) 706.
[5] ibid 712.
[6] ibid 714.
[7] ibid 715.
[8] ibid 716–18.
[9] ibid.
[10] ibid 712.
[11] ibid 716–17.
[12] ibid 718–19.
[13] ibid.
[14] ibid 719–20.
[15] ibid 720.

Furthermore, we are told that liability may turn on the defendant's malice on the basis of a decision of the Court of Appeal and High Court,[16] though the conclusion is directly contradicted by a decision of the House of Lords.[17]

Perhaps worst of all, it is admitted that it is entirely unclear what standard of liability operates in the law of nuisance. Sometimes the law seems to be strict. Sometimes is appears to be fault-based. And when it is fault-based, the operative notion of fault seems to be some free-floating standard, fluctuating somewhere in the space between strict liability and negligence.[18]

This is not presented as criticism of the textbook in question or of its author. The author's task is to depict the law as it is presented in the cases. The author succeeds. But what he succeeds in depicting is a failure. The problem is not that the law does the wrong thing. The problem is that it does not understand what it is doing. Consequently, even the best descriptive works fail to produce a proper understanding of the law.[19]

IV. Two Specific Difficulties with The Conventional View

As noted above, criticism of the conventional view is found throughout this book. However, two specific aspects of the conventional view must be examined now. Both are contained in the passage already quoted: 'The central issue of the whole law of nuisance is the question of reasonableness of the defendant's conduct'.[20] Though that definition is supported by the (recent) case law, it contains two critical errors: the law of nuisance does not respond to unreasonableness and its focus is not the defendant's conduct.

A. Reasonableness

In *St Helen's Smelting Co v Tipping*,[21] the defendant operated a smelting company on land neighbouring the claimant's property. Vapour caused by the defendant's operations damaged the claimant's trees and shrubs. The House of Lords upheld the finding that the defendant was committing a nuisance. In *Halsey v Esso*

---

[16] *Hollywood Silver Fox Farm Ltd v Emmett* [1936] 2 KB 468 (CA); *Christie v Davey* [1893] 1 Ch 316.
[17] *The Mayor of Bradford v Pickles* [1895] AC 587 (HL). WVH Rogers, *Winfield and Jolowicz on Tort*, 18th edn (London, Sweet & Maxwell, 2010) 724.
[18] WVH Rogers, *Winfield and Jolowicz on Tort*, 18th edn (London, Sweet & Maxwell, 2010) 726–31.
[19] I will not repeat here my analysis of the distinction between descriptive, interpretive and prescriptive legal theory. For that analysis, see A Beever and C Rickett, 'Interpretive Legal Theory and the Academic Lawyer' (2005) 68 *MLR* 320; A Beever, *Rediscovering the Law of Negligence* (Oxford, Hart, 2007) 21–25.
[20] WVH Rogers, *Winfield and Jolowicz on Tort*, 18th edn (London, Sweet & Maxwell, 2010) 714.
[21] *St Helen's Smelting Co v Tipping* (1865) 11 ER 1483 (HL).

Petroleum,[22] the claimant complained of the pollution, noise and smell produced by the defendant's oil depot. The Court of Queen's Bench held for the claimant. In *Bamford v Turnley*,[23] the defendant operated brick kilns neighbouring the claimant's land. The claimant complained of the fumes that the kilns created. Again, the Court of King's Bench held for the claimant. But there is nothing unreasonable about operating a smelting works, an oil depot or a brick-making business. On the contrary, these are useful and profitable activities.

But, it might be said, the issue is not the unreasonableness of the defendant's conduct considered alone, but of that conduct considering its impact on the claimant. Thus, we have the view that the 'gist of liability is unreasonable interference with the claimant's interest'.[24] On this view, for instance, the claimant succeeded in *Bamford v Turnley* because it was unreasonable for the defendant to make bricks in a way that produced fumes that so inconvenienced his neighbour.

This, the cornerstone of the conventional view, provides the most dramatic evidence of that view's failure. It is presented as an explanation of the operation of the law, but it does not, cannot, explain anything.

Let us take a simple case. Imagine that my son has misbehaved and I punish him by banning him from playing computer games for a week. After the inevitable furore has died down, we decide to talk about things calmly. He asks me why I chose the punishment that I did. I reply that I chose it because it was reasonable. Can you imagine him finding this answer satisfactory?

There are two problems. The first is that reasonableness in the abstract is too vague to provide a proper answer to my son's question. Saying that the punishment is reasonable is no better than saying that it is fair, just, good or right. The second problem is that, in the light of the first, the response is entirely redundant. Unless I am a tyrant with respect to my children, it can be taken as read that I chose the punishment because I believed it to be reasonable (and fair, just, good and right). When my son asks why I punish him as I do, he takes it for granted that I think the punishment reasonable. What he is asking me is why I think that punishment reasonable.

The situation in law is the same. The assertion that the defendant's interference with the claimant is unreasonable in the abstract is both too vague to be informative and redundant. It tells us nothing.

This position is usefully compared with the law of negligence. In negligence, too, the defendant cannot be liable unless she acted unreasonably. But leading cases in this area of the law have enunciated principles according to which the reasonableness of the defendant's behaviour is to be decided. So, for example, in *Bolton v Stone*[25] the House of Lords maintained that deciding whether a risk is

---

[22] *Halsey v Esso Petroleum* [1961] 1 WLR 683.
[23] *Bamford v Turnley* (1862) 3 B & S 66, 122 ER 27.
[24] S Deakin, A Johnston and B Markesinis, *Markesinis and Deakin's Tort Law*, 6th edn (Oxford, Clarendon Press, 2008) 509. See also J Murphy, *The Law of Nuisance* (Oxford, Oxford University Press, 2010) 44.
[25] *Bolton v Stone* [1951] AC 850 (HL).

unreasonable for the purposes of the law of negligence requires taking into account the likelihood of the risk materialising and the seriousness of the injury if the risk materialises. Furthermore, in *The Wagon Mound (No 2)*,[26] the Privy Council divided risks into three kinds: substantial, small, and fantastic or far-fetched. The Court maintained that the defendant acted unreasonably if she created a substantial risk, but not if she created a fantastic or far-fetched risk, and that if she created a small risk then she acted unreasonably unless the burden of eliminating the risk was high.

These principles are not rules or formulae for determining the outcomes of cases. They are nevertheless instructive. The principles capture the values that are to be taken into account. It is because of this that the claim that the law of negligence rests on the unreasonableness of the defendant's behaviour is informative. Here, 'unreasonableness' refers to concerns that guide the decisions of courts. In fact, it could be said that 'unreasonableness' in that context is a mere shorthand for the principles just examined.[27]

But that is not the case in the law of nuisance. Here, commentators are quick to stress that 'reasonableness' does not mean what it means in the law of negligence.[28] What does it mean then? We are not told. This is no mere oversight. It is the result of the fact that the law operates in accordance with no specific understanding of reasonableness whatsoever.[29]

Consequently, though the claim that 'The central issue of the whole law of nuisance is the question of reasonableness of the defendant's conduct'[30] accurately presents the conventional understanding of the law, it has no explanatory power. 'Reasonableness' in that sentence has no fixed meaning. To say that judges decide cases in terms of their perception of reasonableness is just to say that judges decide cases in terms of their perception of the right outcomes of the cases. But we knew that already.

Consider *Bamford v Turnley* again. According to the conventional view, the claimant succeeded in that case because it was unreasonable for the defendant to make bricks in a way that produced fumes that so inconvenienced his neighbour. But why? The answer can only be because it has already been decided that the claimant's interest in 'comfortable enjoyment' is more deserving of protection than the defendant's interest in making bricks. That may well be right, but whether

---

[26] *Overseas Tankship (UK) Ltd v Morts Dock & Engineering Co Ltd (The Wagon Mound, No 2)* [1967] AC 617 (PC).

[27] For analysis, see A Beever, *Rediscovering the Law of Negligence* (Oxford, Hart, 2007) ch 3.

[28] eg WVH Rogers, *Winfield and Jolowicz on Tort*, 18th edn (London, Sweet & Maxwell, 2010) 714.

[29] See also C Gearty, 'The Place of Private Nuisance' [1989] *CLJ* 214, 218, M Lee, 'What is Private Nuisance?' (2003) 119 *LQR* 298, 298. Thus, while a recent monograph on the law of nuisance points out that the interference with the claimant must be unreasonable, it can provide no account of what reasonableness means in this context. The analysis does consider factors that are said to bear on the question of reasonableness – such as the defendant's motive and the location of the premises in question – but they are not, and are not presented as, analyses of the meaning of reasonableness. J Murphy, *The Law of Nuisance* (Oxford, Oxford University Press, 2010) 44.

[30] WVH Rogers, *Winfield and Jolowicz on Tort*, 18th edn (London, Sweet & Maxwell, 2010) 714.

it is so is the real question here. The analysis under discussion simply assumes an answer to it.

Accordingly, the claim that the defendant's conduct was unreasonable means only that, in the circumstances, the defendant's activity must give way to the claimant's. Unreasonableness is not, as the conventional view pretends, a reason for liability. It is not a premise in an argument for or a precondition of liability. On the contrary, it is the obscured premature conclusion that, unless some defence can be raised, the defendant will be liable.[31] This is more or less admitted when we are told that '"Reasonableness" signifies what is legally right between the parties taking account of all the circumstances of the case',[32] a way of saying that 'reasonableness' is what the court mouths in order to pretend that its decision has a genuine rational basis.

The claim that the interference is unreasonable, then, simply means that it is an interference that, other things being equal, should not have happened or should not be allowed to continue. Thus, 'reasonable' and 'unreasonable' are merely labels for the intuitive response to the question 'Should the defendant be liable?' Reasonableness cannot be the key to understanding this area of the law.

Perhaps one might respond that what we need is a theory that explains what 'reasonableness' is 'getting at', what it means in this context. But that, I suggest, is mistaken. In negligence, 'reasonableness' is unpacked in such a way that it makes sense still to call it reasonableness. It is natural to say of someone who created a substantial risk of injury to another that she acted unreasonably, for example. But there is no reason to think that 'unreasonableness' will be unpacked in a similar way in the law of nuisance. The fact that we are not already in possession of such an account, as we are for the law of negligence, suggests that it will not be. Here, 'unreasonableness' is not even a signpost pointing us in the direction that we must travel. It is a signpost pointing to a dead end.

Because the conventional understanding of the law of nuisance begins with this unfortunate answer to the most fundamental question one can ask about that law, it is unsurprising that a genuine account of the law is never forthcoming.

B. The Defendant's Conduct

We turn now to the claim that liability in nuisance rests on the character of the defendant's conduct.

Recall the three cases examined at the beginning of this chapter. We have seen that there was nothing unreasonable about the defendants' conduct in any of them. What must also be clear is that this conduct was not wrongful in itself. There is nothing wrong with operating a smelting works, an oil depot or a brick-making business.

---

[31] And even then, things are woefully unclear. Does it make sense, for instance, to say of a defendant who created what would have been a nuisance but for the claimant's consent that the defendant acted unreasonably or that the interference was unreasonable?

[32] WVH Rogers, *Winfield and Jolowicz on Tort*, 18th edn (London, Sweet & Maxwell, 2010) 715.

These cases generated liability, not because of the defendant's conduct *per se*, but because of the impact of that conduct on the claimant. The defendant in *St Helen's Smelting Co v Tipping* was found liable, not because it is wrong to operate a smelter, but because it is wrong to operate a smelter in ways that cause damage to another's trees. The defendant in *Halsey v Esso Petroleum* committed a nuisance, not because it is wrong to operate an oil depot, but because it is wrong to operate a depot in ways that cause damage to another's property and make them suffer from the excessive noise and smell. The defendant in *Bamford v Turnley* was liable, not because it is wrong to manufacture bricks, but because it is wrong to manufacture bricks in ways that cause considerable noise that inconveniences one's neighbours. The wrongfulness cannot be found in the defendant's behaviour taken in isolation. The wrongfulness is found in the conflict between the defendant's and the claimant's use of land.

One consequence of this is that the nuisance action has the form of corrective or commutative justice[33] and not of distributive or retributive justice. It is an implementation of interpersonal, not societal, justice. Moreover, a finding that the defendant committed a nuisance does not import any personal wrongdoing to that person (though it is consistent with the defendant having committed such wrongdoing). The law of nuisance is unconcerned with personal responsibility. The law of nuisance is concerned with commutative justice. This is the first key to understanding this area of the law. It is about the relationship between the parties.

V. Conclusion

The conventional view of the law of nuisance is a failure. Its fundamental premises are false. For this reason, it is insufficient merely to revise the view. It is necessary to start again.

---

[33] For my reasons for preferring 'commutative' to 'corrective', though the point is entirely cosmetic, see A Beever, *Forgotten Justice: The Forms of Justice in the History of Legal and Political Theory* (Oxford, Oxford University Press, 2013) §2, ch 4.

3

The Grounds of Liability

I. Finding the Ground

We begin by asking: What is the basis of nuisance liability? This question is foundational, because it is a way of asking what the tort of nuisance is all about. Because of this, a proper answer to the question will guide the answers to the other questions we will need to ask about this area of the law. And a proper answer to those questions will result in a coherent understanding of the law of nuisance that flows from a conception of the tort's basic structure.

Let us return to two of the cases introduced in the previous chapter.[1] In *Halsey v Esso Petroleum*,[2] the claimant complained about the escape from the defendant's land of acid smuts and oily drops which damaged his property, and of noise and smell which caused no physical damage to him or his property but seriously interfered with his enjoyment of his land. Veale J dealt with these complaints in turn. With respect to the former, he said:

> liability for nuisance by harmful deposits could be established by proving damage by the deposits to the property in question, provided of course that the injury was not merely trivial. Negligence is not an ingredient of the cause of action, and the character of the neighbourhood is not a matter to be taken into consideration.[3]

In other words, following the decision of the House of Lords in *St Helen's Smelting Co v Tipping*,[4] Veale J held that the presence of any significant physical damage was sufficient to generate liability.

With respect to the noise and smell, again following *St Helen's Smelting Co v Tipping*, Veale J maintained:

> nuisance by smell or noise is something to which no absolute standard can be applied. It is always a question of degree whether the interference with comfort or convenience is sufficiently serious to constitute a nuisance. The character of the neighbourhood is very relevant and all the relevant circumstances have to be taken into account. What might be a nuisance in one area is by no means necessarily so in another.[5]

---

[1] Because of the way in which the issues in *St Helen's Smelting Co v Tipping* (1865) 11 ER 1483 (HL) were addressed, ie because they ignored the foundations of liability, that case is of no more use here.

[2] *Halsey v Esso Petroleum* [1961] 1 WLR 683.

[3] ibid 691.

[4] *St Helen's Smelting Co v Tipping* (1865) 11 ER 1483 (HL).

[5] *Halsey v Esso Petroleum* [1961] 1 WLR 683, 691–92.

The issue of the locale of the nuisance is something to which we will have to return. For now, our focus is on the other matters Veale J thought to be determinative of liability. He said:

> the law must strike a fair and reasonable balance between the right of the plaintiff on the one hand to the undisturbed enjoyment of his property, and the right of the defendant on the other hand to use his property for his own lawful enjoyment.[6]

This is a crucial point. The conventional view may incline us to misunderstand it.

Veale J did not claim that the issue was whether the defendant acted unreasonably. His claim was that the law must impose a solution that is fair and reasonable to both parties. That may appear little more than a truism, but it is in fact much more. Veale J tells us that the court's task is to realise commutative justice, fairness as between the parties: 'between the right of the plaintiff on the one hand . . . and the right of the defendant on the other'.

Second, the reference to balancing does not imply an enquiry into distributive or public policy concerns. Balancing must be done, but it is the rights of the parties that must be balanced, not the interests of all.

Finally, the rights in question are property rights: the 'right of the plaintiff . . . to the undisturbed enjoyment of his property' and of 'the defendant . . . to use his property for his own lawful enjoyment'. These are aspects of the parties' property rights.[7] Accordingly, the tort of nuisance is concerned with placing these aspects in some kind of hierarchy, so that conflicts between exercises of property rights can be resolved.

Consequently, though it deals with such action, the tort of nuisance is not *about* wrongful action. Rather, it is about providing a hierarchy of property rights. Thus, the way to understand the law of nuisance is not to investigate the kinds of action that it renders illegal. Rather, it is to explore the hierarchy that it recognises within property rights.

This is why at least much of what we know as the law of nuisance exists in other regimes as part of the law of property.[8] Though the commission of a nuisance is a form of wrongdoing, at its heart the tort is concerned with elucidating the consequences of property rights.

Turning now to the complaint about the noise, Veale J said:

> the operations of the defendants at night are particularly important. After all, one of the main objects of living in a house or flat is to have a room with a bed in it where one can sleep at night. Night is the time when the ordinary man takes his rest.[9]

---

[6] ibid 692.

[7] The idea that this tort is based on property is also a theme of D Nolan, '"A Tort Against Land": Private Nuisance as a Property Tort' in A Robertson and D Nolan (eds), *Rights and Private Law* (Oxford, Hart, 2011).

[8] eg BGB div 3, title 1.

[9] *Halsey v Esso Petroleum* [1961] 1 WLR 683, 696.

What is the significance of this?

Given what we have been told, the claim must be the following. The fact that the claimant is unable to sleep at night reveals that achieving the proper balance between the claimant's right to 'the undisturbed enjoyment of his property' and the defendant's right to 'use his property for his own lawful enjoyment' requires holding that the former trumps the latter. According to Veale J, then, the parties' property rights are to be prioritised – that is, placed in a hierarchy – so that the claimant's right to use his land in order to sleep takes precedence over the defendant's right to use his land as an oil depot. The wisdom of that conclusion is obvious, but the basis for it has not yet been made evident.

At this point, it is especially important to resist the contemporary reflex to appeal to public policy concerns; the suggestion being that public policy supports the claimant's position. This suggestion must be rejected for two main reasons. First, it is inconsistent with the idea that the issue is to be decided by balancing the rights of the parties. The suggestion is to ignore those rights – or at best treat them as mere interests to be considered along with the interests of others – and turn to the interests of the public. Second, the suggestion alone is without explanatory value. Why does public policy favour the claimant? No doubt some answer can be given, but that answer is sure to generate the problems outlined in the introduction to this book: the policy-based answers to this and to similar questions will result in an incoherent and often contradictory picture of the law.

Veale J was right to hold that the parties' rights must be balanced. He was also right to hold that, in this case, the balancing favours the claimant. It is not policy that is missing from Veale J's judgment, but an analysis of why the balancing comes out in favour of the claimant. We must turn to other cases for aid.

The claimant in *Bamford v Turnley* lived next to the defendant's brick manufacturing business. This business utilised brick kilns, which

> caused noxious and unwholesome vapours and smokes, fumes and smells to arise . . . and spread themselves over and about the said dwelling [ie the claimant's land] . . . whereby the air about the same became unhealthy and uncomfortable, and the claimant was annoyed and incommoded in his possession and enjoyment of his dwelling.[10]

The claimant sought an injunction to prevent the use of the kilns. The court obliged.

As we have seen, the modern view is that the court found for the claimant because it held that the defendant's conduct or the interference with the claimant was unreasonable. But that is not what Bramwell B said. His claim was that 'those acts necessary for the *common and ordinary* use and occupation of land and houses may be done, if conveniently done, without subjecting those who do them to an action'.[11] Similarly, in *Sedleigh-Denfield v O'Callaghan*, Lord Wright said that 'a useful test is perhaps what is reasonable according to the *ordinary* usages of

---

[10] *Bamford v Turnley* (1862) 3 B & S 66, 122 ER 27, 231.
[11] ibid 33 (emphasis added).

mankind living in society, or more correctly in a particular society'.[12] This is not the conventional view. While an appeal to reasonableness is made, the content of that concept is determined in accordance with 'the ordinary usages of mankind'. On this view, 'reasonableness' is a mere placeholder for 'the ordinary usages of mankind': a use is 'reasonable' if it corresponds to the ordinary uses of mankind, unreasonable if it does not.

According to this approach, ordinariness is the index by which property rights are to be prioritised.[13] Living comfortably in one's house and being able to sleep at night are more ordinary than operating a brick-making business or an oil depot. Hence, on this approach, the court must ask which party's use is the more ordinary and that party wins.

This is a promising suggestion, but it must ultimately be rejected. Fundamentally, this is because ordinariness is an inappropriate standard for determining liability. It would determine an individual's rights in accordance with the preferences and practices of others, an approach that would fail to take seriously the person as an individual worthy of moral consideration in her own right.[14] Our rights must not be determined by others' preferences and behaviours.

This principle receives recognition in the law, at least implicitly. This can be demonstrated by reference to three famous cases. The first is *Miller v Jackson*.[15]

The claimants purchased a newly built house neighbouring the defendants' cricket club in Burnopfield, County Durham, where cricket had been played for over 70 years. Despite the efforts of the cricket club, cricket balls were hit onto the claimants' land, frightening them, exposing them to physical danger and occasionally damaging their house. Though the Court of Appeal controversially refused to award an injunction against the defendant, a point to which we will also return, the majority of the court, in accordance with the orthodox understanding of the law, accepted that the defendant was guilty of a nuisance.

In the circumstances, however, it is arguable that the defendant's activities were the most ordinary. After all, cricket had been played at that location for 70 years and the houses had only recently been constructed. Moreover, surely building a house is less common than playing cricket, at least in a country such as England. What is telling is that this argument played no role in the case, even for Lord Denning MR, who held in favour of the defendant.

A second example is the famous American case, *Fontainebleau Hotel Corp v Forty-Five Twenty-Five Inc*.[16] The parties owned neighbouring hotels on the Miami Beach strip. The defendant intended to construct extensions that would cast a shadow over the cabana, swimming pool and sunbathing area of the claimant's hotel during the height of the Florida tourist season. Because this would

---

[12] *Sedleigh-Denfield v O'Callaghan* [1940] AC 880 (HL), 903 (emphasis added).

[13] See also EJ Weinrib, *The Idea of Private Law* (Cambridge, Mass, Harvard University Press, 1995) 192–93.

[14] *cf* Kant, *Metaphysics of Morals* (Cambridge, Cambridge University Press, 1996) 6: 237–38, 314.

[15] *Miller v Jackson* [1977] QB 966 (CA).

[16] *Fontainebleau Hotel Corp v Forty-Five Twenty-Five Inc* 114 So 2d 357 (FL Dist CA 1959).

make the claimant's hotel significantly less attractive to potential patrons, the claimant sought an injunction preventing the defendant from building, alleging that the construction would cause significant harm. The claim, however, was rejected by the Florida District Court of Appeal.

The explanation for this cannot be that the claimant's activity was less ordinary than the defendant's. It was not. The relevant activity was sunbathing, relaxing, etc.[17] On the Miami Beach strip at any rate, that is more ordinary than building.

The third case is the decision of the House of Lords in *Hunter v Canary Wharf*.[18] One of the issues in that case was that, as a result of the defendant's construction of a tower block in London's Docklands, the claimants' television reception was impaired. The claim that this constituted a nuisance was rejected by the House of Lords. Nevertheless, it seems clear that watching television is more ordinary than building a tower block, or than building at all.

The suggestion will not do. The law does not prioritise property rights in terms of ordinariness. It is right not to do so. Can some alternative be found?

One extremely helpful proposal can be found in the decision of the New York Court of Appeal in *Hay v Cohoes*.[19] Delivering the judgment of the court, Gardner J laid down the following principle.

> It is an elementary principle in reference to private rights, that every individual is enti-tled to the undisturbed possession and lawful enjoyment of his own property. The mode of enjoyment is necessarily limited by the rights of others – otherwise it might be made destructive of their rights altogether. . . . If these rights conflict, [one] must yield to the [other], as the more important of the two, since, upon grounds of public policy, it is better that one man should surrender a particular use of his land, than that another should be deprived of the beneficial use of his property altogether.[20]

The defendant in *Hay v Cohoes* had blasted rocks with gunpowder in the pro-cess of digging a canal. As the result of the explosions, material had been depos-ited on the claimant's land, damaging it. According to Gardner J, 'The defendants had the right to dig the canal. The plaintiff the right to the undisturbed possession of his property'.[21] These rights conflicted. And, 'the former must yield to the lat-ter', because the alternative would have the potential of depriving the claimant of all beneficial uses of his property.

> [I]f the defendants in excavating their canal, in itself a lawful use of their land, could . . . demolish the stoop of the plaintiff with impunity, they might, for the same purpose . . . demolish his house, and thus deprive him of all use of his property.[22]

---

[17] In the following chapter, I argue that these descriptions of the activity are inappropriate. But that follows only after the approach suggested below has been adopted. Hence, it is appropriate to ignore this point now.

[18] *Hunter v Canary Wharf* [1997] AC 655 (HL).

[19] *Hay v Cohoes* 2 NY 159 (NY CA 1849).

[20] ibid 161.

[21] ibid.

[22] ibid.

Here, then, we see an alternative test for determining the existence of a nuisance: particular uses of land must give way to those upon which all beneficial use ultimately rests.

Again, the wisdom of this view is clear. Naturally, a party cannot be allowed to perform an activity that robs the other of all of the benefit of his land. But there are two problems. The most obvious is that this principle cannot be used to account for more than a small minority of cases. The second is that, though it is evident that the principle makes good sense, we do not yet know why it makes good sense. We examine the second difficulty first.

As we have seen, Gardner J maintained that the principle rests 'upon grounds of public policy'.[23] What exactly does that mean? There is no particular reason for thinking that Gardner J used the term in the modern sense, to refer to considerations that extend beyond examination of the rights of the parties: distributive justice, social policy and the like. On the contrary, the fact that Gardner J considered no such concerns, determining the case by reference only to the parties' rights, indicates otherwise. In this context, the claim that the proffered approach accords with 'public policy' appears to mean only that the approach is appropriate. However, there are two main reasons to doubt that this is so.

The first problem stems from the fact that the approach conjoins two concepts that are of different kinds. The particular use of land is a relative concept. No use is particular *per se*. Uses are only more or less particular than others. Conversely, the concept of being deprived of all beneficial uses of one's land is absolute. One either is or is not deprived of such use. Consequently, Gardner J's approach combines two terms, one a sliding scale, the other a fixed point. Because of this, courts may face cases in which one of the parties' uses falls between the concepts.

Regarding *Bamford v Turnley*, for instance, while one might be happy with the idea that manufacturing bricks is a particular use of land, allowing the defendant to continue would not have divested the claimant of all of the beneficial use of his land. Nor would this have been the case in *Halsey v Esso Petroleum*. There, too, allowing the defendant to continue would not deprive the claimant of all of the beneficial use of his land. The approach set out in *Hay v Cohoes* can tell us nothing about these cases.

In that light, we can see that the fundamental problem with Gardner J's approach is that it incorporates an absolute standard. Because the law must favour one or other of the parties, no absolute standard is applicable. Both parties may fall on the same side of an absolute standard. The approach must consist only of relative standards. What is more, the approach must contain only one standard. If it contained two standards, then the activities of one or of both parties could fall in between them.

This suggests that Gardner J's approach can be improved by jettisoning the idea that liability materialises only if one of the parties would be deprived of all of the beneficial uses of his land and retaining only the focus on the particularity of the

[23] ibid.

parties' activities. On this approach, then, the court's task is to compare the parties' activities, judge which is the most particular, and decide for the opposing
party. This can be expressed equivalently by saying that relatively general uses of
land trump relatively particular uses.[24]

These suggestions are helpful, but they are not sufficient to answer the questions with which this chapter began. This is because two crucial problems remain.

First, we do not know why general uses of land should trump particular uses, no
matter how immediately intuitive the idea. Second, it is not entirely clear what it
means to say that a use is more or less particular than another, especially if, for the
reasons examined above, we do not take 'particular' to mean ordinary. Thankfully,
however, answers to these difficulties can be discovered by re-examining Gardner
J's judgment.

Gardner J was surely right to hold that one person's use of his land must not be
allowed to prevent another altogether from enjoying the use of his land. But why
exactly? No doubt, policy-based answers can be supplied. Perhaps, for instance,
the alternative would be economically inefficient. But there is a different answer
closer to hand; closer, that is, to the parties whose rights we are meant to be inves-
tigating. The answer is that the alternative cannot respect the moral equality of the
parties. The point is perhaps best revealed in this way.

One cannot assert that *A* has an entitlement to use his land in a way that
destroys *B*'s use of his land because, given the moral equality of persons, the claim
that *A* is entitled to use his land entails that *B* is likewise entitled, and that implication is inconsistent with the assertion (*A*'s use, remember, will destroy *B*'s).[25]

Note that the inconsistency is not itself the problem. The point is that the
inconsistency reveals that *A*'s action cannot respect the moral equality of *B*.
Allowing *A* to proceed would be inconsistent with recognising the equivalent
entitlement in *B*. Accordingly, *A*'s action is unfair as between the parties.[26]

Note also that this view imputes no personal wrongdoing to *A* (though such
wrongdoing might be present). The idea is not that *A* *is asserting* a claim inconsistent with the moral equality of *B*, in which case *A* would be making an exception
for himself and being unfair. Rather, the idea is that *it is not possible for anyone to
assert* the relevant claim consistent with the moral equality of *B*.[27] This is an
approach that focuses on the action rather than the agent. The notion is that the
defendant's action is impermissible because permitting it would be unfair as
between the parties. Again, the claim is not that the defendant was being unfair as
between the parties.

Can this approach be extended to apply to the revised version of Gardner J's
view detailed above? Can we say the following? One cannot assert that *A* is entitled
to use his land in a particular way that prevents *B* using his land in a more general

---

[24] Note that these are not two different standards. 'General' here is simply the converse of 'particular'.
[25] See also EJ Weinrib, *The Idea of Private Law* (Cambridge, Mass, Harvard University Press, 1995)
191.
[26] Naturally, this analysis was inspired by Kant's moral philosophy.
[27] And this is part of the reason why, in Kantian terms, the issue is juridical and not ethical.

way, because that assertion entails that *B* is entitled to use his land in that particular way, an implication inconsistent with the assertion. The answer is No.

Sometimes this approach will work. It works when *A*'s use can be described as belonging to a subset of *B*'s. So, for instance, if the assertion is that *A* is able to build on his land in a way that destroys the buildings on *B*'s, then the claim entails that *B* is entitled to have buildings on his land, an entailment inconsistent with the assertion. But the approach will not work when *A*'s use is not a subset of *B*'s. Imagine that *A* mows his lawn with a machine that causes *B*'s buildings to be destroyed. Here, it seems right to say that *A*'s use is more particular, *B*'s use more general. But the assertion that *A* is entitled so to mow his lawn at the expense of *B* does not generate any notion inconsistent with the idea that *B* has no right to retain his buildings.[28] This of course is not to say that the assertion is fair. It clearly is not. We demand that *B* has such a right. But the point is that the unfairness of *A*'s action cannot be demonstrated in this way.

With this issue left unresolved, we now turn to the second. What does it mean to say that one use of land is more particular than another if 'particular' does not mean ordinary? Many suggestions could be made. But only one seems satisfactory: a use is relatively general (non-particular) to the extent that it is fundamental to our understanding of property, particular to the extent that it is peripheral to that understanding. Crucially, on this approach, the argument just examined succeeds.

One cannot assert that *A* is entitled to use his land in a way that interferes with *B*'s more fundamental use because, given the moral equality of persons, the assertion entails that *B* is entitled to use his land in as fundamental a manner as *A*, an implication inconsistent with the assertion. That, I submit, is the key to understanding the law of nuisance.

We require a law that prioritises property rights so that more fundamental rights trump the less fundamental. The moral equality of persons demands that if we did not have such a law, we would have to invent it. But we do not have to invent it. We must only properly understand the law of nuisance.

II. Examining the Ground

It is important to stress that I do not advance this theory in the spirit of rejecting the approaches found in the cases examined above. The argument is not that those views are wrong and so are to be replaced by this one. I am instead trying to build on those approaches. The claim is that the view advanced here is the best theoretical reconstruction of them.

It is also true that, to an extent, this analysis also captures the use of 'reasonable' and 'unreasonable' in this area of the law. It is natural to suggest that a use of land

---

[28] This is a version of the familiar problem with the golden rule.

that interferes with a more fundamental use is unreasonable. Moreover, as we will see, this analysis fits most of the cases. But one ought not to hide the fact that 'unreasonable' is often intended to mean something different. As we see particularly in chapters seven and eight, 'unreasonable' is often taken to indicate, or at least be connected to, fault. Though it would make my task easier, it would be fraudulent to pretend that this was not so. I must instead argue that this tendency is mistaken. I do so in those chapters.

Four additional points need to be stressed. First, the issue is how fundamental to the conception of property the parties' uses are, not how socially valuable they are. Second, the conception of property in question is not necessarily the one found in the heads of laymen, political philosophers, economists or the like,[29] but that held by those experienced in law, in particular, of course, in the laws of tort and property. Third, it is not suggested that property rights are presented to us in some pre-ordained or entirely *a priori* hierarchy. On the contrary, our conception of property takes into account, and needs to take into account, how human beings actually utilise property and the role that property plays in their lives. I have more to say about this in following chapters. Fourth, the claim is not that a clearly defined hierarchy of property rights can be produced that can then 'mechanically' be applied to solve disputes. On the contrary, the concept of a more or less fundamental right is one that requires judgement in order to be applied. Occasionally, reasonable people will disagree in their judgements.[30] Nevertheless, this approach provides an understanding of the basis of nuisance liability that is more than sufficiently perspicuous. It is important now to elucidate the structure of this kind of thought.

III. The Structure of Analysis

This analysis of the law of nuisance rests on three broad levels. At the most abstract is the relevant form of justice. It has been argued that this form is corrective or commutative justice. Next is the principle that relates to this particular area of the law. The position advanced here is that this principle is that more fundamental uses of land must trump less fundamental. Then come the specific doctrines of the law, such as the so-called 'rule of give and take, live and let live' examined in chapter four. The question is: What is the relationship between these levels?

---

[29] I say not necessarily because, of course, these people may share the lawyer's understanding.
[30] Historical matters are also relevant here. For instance, though I personally find the claim implausible, it is perhaps not impossible to understand how having a brothel operate in one's neighbourhood might be said to 'constitute a sensible interference with the comfortable and convenient enjoyment of his residence, where live with him his wife, his son and his servants' (*Thompson-Schwab v Costaki* [1956] 1 WLR 335, 339) in the 1950s. But it would surely be beyond the pale to make that claim today. I submit, for example, that it is difficult to read the judgment in *Laws v Florinplace Ltd* [1981] 1 All ER 659 (pornography store) without thinking the case against the defendant, as expressed by the plaintiff and the judge, to be more than a little hysterical.

On the view advanced here, the relationship is intimate. However, it is important to clarify immediately that there is no suggestion that the relationship is deductive. The principled ground of liability cannot be deduced from commutative justice and the specific doctrines of the law cannot be deduced from the principled ground of liability. Rather, each level is connected by judgement and each level relies on the other in the following sense. Commutative justice demands fairness as between the parties. But that principle is not in itself sufficiently perspicuous to determine the resolution of the issues that arise in the law of nuisance. If the issue is how conflicts in land use should be resolved, the injunction 'Treat the parties fairly' cannot itself resolve it. But that does not mean that commutative justice is empty and unhelpful. On the contrary, it provides a frame of reference for deciding the issue.[31]

Thus, what I will call the principled ground of liability in the law of nuisance – the notion that more fundamental uses trump the less fundamental – is intended as the principle that best enunciates the demands of commutative justice as they relate to the circumstances of nuisance. In other words, the principle is advanced as a guide as to how fairness as between the parties can be achieved when their uses of land conflict. So, then, the principle is commutative justice as applied to a specific area of human concern.

This is not to say that the principle is derived from commutative justice or that the principle is analytic to or contained in commutative justice. On the contrary, the principle serves to realise commutative justice. It does so by giving commutative justice more perspicuous content in the limited sphere to which the principle applies.

The same analysis applies to the relationship between the second and third levels (and to that between the first and third). In many circumstances, the injunction 'Ensure that the most fundamental use of land trumps' will be insufficiently perspicuous to enable a decision to be made. For that reason, a functioning system of morality requires doctrines of positive law that serve as guidelines or directives as to how relevant principles should be applied in practice.[32] Most significantly, it is for the courts to lay down rules – whether they be precedents or not – that can be used to decide whether a use is more fundamental than another. That is the role of case law.

On this view, it is important to see that purported doctrines of the law can be mistaken. This occurs when the doctrine does not well reflect the principled ground of liability and commutative justice. A court that enunciates such a doctrine makes a moral and legal mistake. The removal of the doctrine is what used to be called the law working itself pure.

It is therefore not a consequence of the position advanced in this book that it is always apparent which party's use of land is the most fundamental. Not

---

[31] Note that reasonableness does not do this. Fairness *as between the parties* does not give us all our answers, but it tells us where to look for the answers. Reasonableness does not direct us at all.

[32] This formulation and discussion is heavily influenced by the work of Martin Stone. See especially M Stone, 'Legal Positivism as an Idea About Morality' (2011) 61 *University of Toronto Law Journal* 313.

infrequently, this issue can be determined only by reference to the case law. There is no sense, then, in which the theory advanced here is to be understood as a replacement for the positive law.

It is also important to say more about the role of the positive law in this theory. One reviewer of an earlier draft of the book asked why I do not at this point engage with theories of property law and the like in order to develop my points. This is an important question. There are three general answers.

The first is that there is no particular reason to expect that the theory of property law will be of any direct relevance to the issues that confront us here. This is because we are dealing with issues that relate to what we know as the law of nuisance rather than the law of property *per se*. It is not normal for a theorist of property to consider our fundamental question: How should conflicts in the use of land be resolved?

Second, the theory of property is at least as riven with dispute as the theory of anything else. As such, no appeal to that body of work could settle any of the issues that we are examining, because the same disagreements with which we are engaged here arise in that context also. Thus, all I can do is draw attention to the kinds of property analysis that fit the account here, rejecting the alternatives.[33] Of course, this book cannot expand to become also an examination of theory of property.

Third, of even more importance is that, on the analysis presented here, this looking away from the law to theory is mistaken. Let me explain.

In 1972, Richard Posner claimed that the basic problem with the law of negligence is that we lack a theory of negligence liability.[34] Accordingly, he set about providing one. But this, I suggest, was a mistake. We already have a theory of negligence liability. We call it the law of negligence.[35]

If, for instance, we want to understand why that law imposes a duty of care on some people rather than others, the first place to turn is not to economics, political theory or the like. It is to examine the reasons offered by judges in cases in which the duty of care has been considered. And if we read cases such as *Donoghue v Stevenson*[36] and *Palsgraf v Long Island Railroad Co*,[37] we are presented with answers.[38] In other words, when we ask 'Why?', answers are found in the legal materials. Now, for reasons discussed in the introduction to this book, those

---

[33] I would, for example, wish to refer the reader to the relevant material in A Beever, *Forgotten Justice: A History of Political and Legal Theory* (Oxford, Oxford University Press, 2013); as well as J Gordley, *Foundations of Private Law: Property, Tort, Contract, Unjust Enrichment* (Oxford, Oxford University Press, 2006); EJ Weinrib, 'Poverty and Property in Kant's System of Rights' (2003) 78 *Notre Dame Law Review* 79; BS Byrd and J Hruschka, *Kant's Doctrine of Right: A Commentary* (New York, Cambridge University Press, 2010).

[34] RA Posner, 'A Theory of Negligence' (1972) 1 *JLS* 29, 29.

[35] See also M Stone, 'Legal Positivism as an Idea About Morality' (2011) 61 *University of Toronto Law Journal* 313, 333–34.

[36] *M'Alister (or Donoghue) (Pauper) v Stevenson* [1932] AC 562 (HL Sc).

[37] *Palsgraf v Long Island Railroad Co* 162 NE 99 (NY CA 1928).

[38] Not, incidentally, the ones given by most academic lawyers. These cases do not speak of the duty of care as a control mechanism, for instance.

answers are unlikely to be entirely adequate. But that does not mean that we are to turn from the law to other subjects. On the contrary, the first task of the legal theorist is to subject the legal materials to rigorous analysis in order to shape them so as to provide a coherent understanding.[39] This book is an attempt to provide such an analysis of the law of nuisance.

The claim is that the law of nuisance is the common law's method for prioritising property rights so that conflicts between the uses of land can be settled and that the law does so by allowing more fundamental uses of land to trump the less fundamental. If that theory is correct, then the first place to look for an account of what it means for a use to be more fundamental than another is to the law of nuisance itself. That law is the practical way in which our societies have attempted to determine which uses of land are more fundamental than others.

It may help to put the matter this way. Imagine that we find ourselves shipwrecked on an uninhabited island and have to begin a new society from scratch. Imagine also that we decide to do so by laying down principles that will govern our way of life and that, recognising that conflicts in the use of land may arise, we decide that more fundamental uses of land will trump the less fundamental. Now, of course, what we need is a way of determining which uses of land are the more fundamental. In this situation, we might ask a collection of theoretically minded individuals to come up with some abstract analysis of this issue. On the other hand, we might instead appoint a body of people to adjudicate on disputes concerning conflict in the use of land, instructing them to apply the principle on a case-by-case basis and hope to end up, in time, with a developed understanding of fundamentality in this context. What I am saying is that there is some analogy between this second strategy and what actually happened.

With that in mind, it is time to return to the case law.

IV. The Case Law

The remainder of this chapter explores a selection of famous cases, some already introduced. The suggestion is that, in each case, as the facts are presented, it is *clear* that the successful party was using his land in a manner more fundamental to the concept of property than the party who lost. We see, therefore, that the approach advanced here is perspicuous and that the law reflects it. It is important to say immediately that one may question the way in which the facts are presented, but that is a matter that must be left until chapter five.

In *St Helen's Smelting Co v Tipping*, the House of Lords ruled that vapour from the defendant's smelter that damaged the claimant's trees and shrubs constituted a nuisance. Retaining property (that is, undamaged) on one's land is more fundamental than running a business of any kind.

---

[39] eg A Beever, *Rediscovering the Law of Negligence* (Oxford, Hart, 2007).

In *Halsey v Esso Petroleum*, the Court of Queen's Bench held that the pollution, noise and smell emanating from the defendant's oil depot that damaged the claimant's property and interfered with his comfort was a nuisance. Again, retaining property on one's land is more fundamental than running a business. Moreover, being able to live on one's land – and in particular being able to sleep at night on it – is more fundamental than running an oil depot.

In *Bamford v Turnley*, the Court of King's Bench maintained that the defendant committed a nuisance when his brick kilns expelled vapour onto the claimant's land that seriously interfered with his comfort. The argument is the same.

In *Fontainebleau Hotel Corp v Forty-Five Twenty-Five Inc*, the Florida District Court of Appeal held that it would not be a nuisance for the defendant to build up on his land causing a shadow to be cast over the land of the claimant, resulting in business losses. Being able to build on one's land is more fundamental than being able to sunbathe, swim etc around the pool and cabana area of one's hotel. After all, those things could be done only if building had already occurred.

Likewise, in *Hunter v Canary Wharf*, the House of Lords ruled that it was not a nuisance to build up and cause interference with the claimants' television reception. Being able to build on one's land is more fundamental than being able to watch television (in an already built apartment).

In *Bryant v Lefever*,[40] the Court of Appeal ruled that the defendants committed no nuisance when they extended their house and stored timber on their roof, though it resulted in wind patterns that caused the claimant's fire to smoke. Being able to build and store chattels on one's land is more fundamental than being able to light a fire – after all, if one could not build and store chattels, then one would have no fireplace or firewood.

In *Sturges v Bridgman*,[41] the Court of Appeal this time ruled that the defendant who operated machinery neighbouring the claimant's property that created vibration resulting in considerable noise in one of the claimant's rooms was guilty of committing a nuisance. Operating machinery is less fundamental than being able to occupy and use a room for activities such as reading, talking and the like.

Similarly, in *Miller v Jackson*, the Court of Appeal found a defendant liable who occupied land upon which cricket was played when cricket balls were struck out of that property and onto the claimants', damaging their property and significantly inconveniencing them. Retaining one's property and being able to occupy it in safety and comfort is more fundamental than playing cricket on it.

And in *Kennaway v Thompson*,[42] the same court held that the claimant did not have to put up with the considerable noise caused by motor boat races, for which the defendant was responsible. Being able to live in comfort on one's land is more fundamental than racing motor boats.

This is the key to understanding the law of nuisance. That law is the common law's way of prioritising property rights so that conflicts in the use of property can

---

[40] *Bryant v Lefever* (1879) 4 CPD 172 (CA).
[41] *Sturges v Bridgman* (1879) 11 Ch D 852 (CA).
[42] *Kennaway v Thompson* [1981] QB 88 (CA).

be resolved. Unsurprisingly, on reflection at least, it holds that more fundamental uses of property have priority over less fundamental uses. This involves no appeal to policy considerations or the like. On the contrary, the law utilises its own standards to resolve the disputes that come before it.

Not only does this approach tell us how to decide cases, it tells us why they should be decided in that way. Fundamental uses of land are given priority because they are fundamental. As we have seen, an alternative approach would be unfair as between the parties. The principle provides both explanation and justification.

But this is only the beginning. I have not proved that the principle under examination provides the best understanding of the law of nuisance. I have shown only that it is plausible to think that it might. The test is whether this principle provides a utile framework for understanding all the other issues that we must examine in this book. Nor have I demonstrated how the principle is applied. That again comes later when we examine more specific issues. The argument for the principle, then, has only just begun.

4

Illustrations of the General Principle

This chapter examines five issues often thought to relate to exceptions to, or at least additional considerations that operate on, the general principle of the law of nuisance. In each case, it is argued that in fact the law's treatment of the issue merely reflects a proper understanding of that principle.

I. The Rule of Give and Take, Live and Let Live

As we have seen, the defendant in *Bamford v Turnley*[1] operated brick kilns neighbouring the claimant's land. The claimant complained of the fumes the kilns created. Our focus begins with the defendant's reply. He first referred to cases in which actions such as 'burning weeds, emptying cess-pools, making noises during repairs, and other instances which would be [illegal] if done wantonly or maliciously, nevertheless may be lawfully done'.[2] He then argued that these cases were not actionable, because the actions complained of were in the public interest. Therefore, he concluded, because his actions were in the public interest, he should not be liable either.

The Court rejected this argument. This made it necessary to provide an alternative explanation for why the listed cases were not actionable. It was in that context that Bramwell B introduced the rule of give and take, live and let live.

He said:

> There must be . . . some principle on which such cases must be excepted. It seems to me that that principle may be deduced from the character of these cases, and is this, viz., that those acts necessary for the common and ordinary use and occupation of land and houses may be done, if conveniently done, without subjecting those who do them to an action. . . . There is an obvious necessity for such a principle as I have mentioned. It is as much for the advantage of one owner as of another; for the very nuisance the one complains of, as the result of the ordinary use of his neighbour's land, he himself will create in the ordinary use of his own, and the reciprocal nuisances are of a comparatively trifling character. The convenience of such a rule may be indicated by calling it a rule of give and take, live and let live.[3]

[1] *Bamford v Turnley* (1862) 3 B & S 66, 122 ER 27.
[2] ibid 33.
[3] ibid.

The reference to convenience, advantage and the like has led many to the conclusion that Bramwell B was thinking of utilitarian concerns. Perhaps he was. But, in fact, Bramwell B's appeal is to fairness between the parties. His claim is that one person cannot rightly complain about an activity of a kind that he himself will need to perform. For example, when my neighbour conducts repairs on her house, that disturbs my peace; but I cannot legitimately complain about that as I will have to conduct repairs on my house and disturb her peace. Likewise, in the England of the day, though burning weeds and emptying cesspools no doubt disturbed neighbours, those activities were ones that all needed to carry out. (Note here, then, the impact of the way in which property is used, as well as historical considerations, on the decision.)

As Goddard LJ said in *Metropolitan Properties v Jones*:

> If my neighbour is going to put up some bookcases in his house, or put in a new fireplace, for a day or two I shall be exposed, no doubt, to a considerable disturbance . . . but the law does not regard that as a nuisance. A man may be doing that which is necessary for his house, or his own comfort, just as I may do the same thing in my own house the following month. It is one of those things which one has to put up with.[4]

This 'rule', therefore, is not rightly understood as an exception or addition to the general approach of the law. It does not involve appeal to policy. On the contrary, it is an illustration of the law's general principle. One must give and take, live and let live, because fairness between the parties requires it.

II. The Location

In *St Helen's Smelting Co v Tipping*, Lord Westbury said:

> it is a very desirable thing to mark the difference between an action brought for a nuisance upon the ground that the alleged nuisance produces material injury to the property, and an action brought for a nuisance on the ground that the thing alleged to be a nuisance is productive of sensible personal discomfort. With regard to the latter, namely, the personal inconvenience and interference with one's enjoyment, one's quiet, one's personal freedom, anything that discomposes or injuriously affects the senses or the nerves, whether that may or may not be denominated a nuisance, must undoubtedly depend greatly on the circumstances of the place where the thing complained of actually occurs. If a man lives in a town, it is necessary that he should subject himself to the consequences of those operations of trade which may be carried on in his immediate locality, which are actually necessary for trade and commerce, and also for the enjoyment of property, and for the benefit of the inhabitants of the town and of the public at large. If a man lives in a street where there are numerous shops, and a shop is opened next door to him, which is carried on in a fair and reasonable way, he has no

---

[4] *Metropolitan Properties v Jones* [1939] 2 All ER 202, 205.

ground for complaint, because to himself individually there may arise much discomfort from the trade carried on in that shop.[5]

Similarly, in *Sturges v Bridgman* Thesiger LJ said:

> whether anything is a nuisance or not is a question to be determined, not merely by an abstract consideration of the thing itself, but in reference to its circumstances; what would be a nuisance in *Belgrave Square* would not necessarily be so in *Bermondsey*; and where a locality is devoted to a particular trade or manufacture carried on by the traders or manufacturers in a particular and established manner not constituting a public nuisance, Judges and juries would be justified in finding, and may be trusted to find, that the trade or manufacture so carried on in that locality is not a private or actionable wrong.[6]

We begin by examining the arguments in favour of the rule found in the passages above. According to Lord Westbury:

> If a man lives in a town, it is necessary that he should subject himself to the consequences of those operations of trade which may be carried on in his immediate locality, which are actually necessary for trade and commerce, and also for the enjoyment of property, and for the benefit of the inhabitants of the town and of the public at large.[7]

Notice the mixing up of, on the one hand, the claimant's and defendant's interests and, on the other, the public welfare. Naturally, the claimant must accept the defendant's uses of land that 'are actually necessary for . . . the enjoyment of property'. That follows from what has already been said. But it is quite another thing to maintain that the claimant's rights must be curtailed in order to favour the public interest. On such an approach, it is not clear that we would have any rights at all.[8]

Note also the claim that:

> If a man lives in a street where there are numerous shops, and a shop is opened next door to him, which is carried on in a fair and reasonable way, he has no ground for complaint, because to himself individually there may arise much discomfort from the trade carried on in that shop.[9]

If this is the view that a defendant who has acted reasonably cannot be liable then, as we have seen, it is false. If it is the view that liability would not be imposed when it is fair and reasonable to allow the defendant to continue, then of course it is right; but the problem then is that the position is vacuous and redundant and leaves unanswered the central question: whether it is fair and reasonable to permit a shop owner to produce 'much discomfort' for his neighbours.

Moreover, both passages claim that if a locale is given over to a certain industry, then a claimant who lives in that locale cannot complain about an activity that

---

[5] *St Helen's Smelting Co v Tipping* (1865) 11 ER 1483 (HL), 1486.
[6] *Sturges v Bridgman* (1879) 11 Ch D 852 (CA), 865.
[7] *St Helen's Smelting Co v Tipping* (1865) 11 ER 1483 (HL), 1486.
[8] I take it that, as Ronald Dworkin has argued, one of the points of a right is to trump the public interest. R Dworkin, *Taking Rights Seriously* (Cambridge, Mass, Harvard University Press, 1977) ch 7.
[9] *St Helen's Smelting Co v Tipping* (1865) 11 ER 1483 (HL), 1486.

belongs to that industry. But that is false. No *ratio* supports this view and it is surely inconsistent with the thrust of the law of nuisance which, as is stressed in chapter six, does not take account of who arrived in the locale first. Interestingly, this was a point that Thesiger LJ seemed to acknowledge immediately.[10]

What is more, the extant case law appears to show that if the doctrine exists at all, it comes to little in practice. Perhaps most significantly, though the Court of Appeal in *Rushmer v Polsue & Alfieri Ltd*[11] insisted that they were respecting the doctrine under examination, it nevertheless ruled that a defendant who operated a printing press at night in a way that disturbed the claimant and his family was guilty of a nuisance, even though the parties occupied premises in Fleet Street.[12]

Let us now turn to Thesiger LJ's claim that 'what would be a nuisance in *Belgrave Square* [a well-to-do area of London] would not necessarily be so in *Bermondsey* [then a slum]'. No doubt, the claim possesses considerable intuitive force. We feel that it must be right. But why, exactly?

What might constitute a nuisance in Belgrave Square that would not in Bermondsey? There are two kinds of suggestion. One kind is of the following form. The inhabitants of Belgrave Square will have to put up with their neighbours playing Rachmaninoff but not Rap, while the inhabitants of Bermondsey must bear with Rap but not Rachmaninoff. I have chosen this example deliberately, as it seems that the view under examination is a result, at least in part, of a form of snobbery inconsistent with the moral equality of persons. The idea is that the well-to-do have more rights, or higher quality rights, than the less well off. To the extent that this thought lies behind the notion that courts must take the location of the nuisance into account, that notion is entirely objectionable. It may be found in some cases, but it is so inconsistent with accepted legal principle that we cannot describe it as representing the law.

On the other hand, the idea might be more along the following lines. Because of the placement and the construction of houses in these areas – the proximity of the dwellings, the quality of the materials from which they are constructed, the thickness of the walls, etc – as well as related issues, occupants of houses in Bermondsey have to put up with more noise from their neighbours than those in Belgrave Square. That is true, but it makes a different point. This difference between Belgrave Square and Bermondsey is not normative but merely factual.

For the sake of convenience, let us say that a decibel level of 50 would be sufficient to constitute a nuisance in Bermondsey where one of 40 would be enough in Belgrave Square. But to produce such noise in their neighbour's houses, the inhabitants of Bermondsey have to produce a noise of 60 decibels while, because of their thicker walls etc, those in Belgrave Square must produce one of 100. As this thought

---

[10] *Sturges v Bridgman* (1879) 11 Ch D 852 (CA), 865–66.

[11] *Rushmer v Polsue & Alfieri Ltd* [1906] 1 Ch 234 (CA). Affirmed by *Polsue & Alfieri Ltd v Rushmer* [1907] AC 121 (HL).

[12] Incidentally, this decision has been criticised on the ground that it is economically inefficient (AI Ogus and GM Richardson, 'Economics and the Environment: A Study of Private Nuisance' [1977] *CLJ* 284, 298), but what this criticism in fact shows is that the law of nuisance is not concerned with economic efficiency.

experiment helps to reveal, the reason for the difference is that, due to the conditions, fairness as between the parties calls for different approaches. That is, the same principle must be applied differently in each case because of the circumstances. Requiring defendants in Bermondsey to keep their noise low so that it produces no more than 40 decibels in their neighbours' houses would be unfair due to the large impact that such an approach would have on them. Conversely, allowing defendants in Belgrave Square to create noise in their neighbours' houses of 50 decibels would be unfair, as that would allow them to impose significant discomfort in circumstances in which avoiding it would pose little inconvenience.

Accordingly, cases which suggest that the location of the nuisance can augment or remove either party's rights are on that matter wrongly decided. It is a violation of a fundamental legal principle to hold that the lower classes, for instance, have lower class rights.[13] But the location can nevertheless be relevant as it can affect what constitutes fairness as between the parties; where the balance between the competing rights lies.

Moreover, the claim that there are two approaches depending on the nature of the interference – specifically, that the location is ignored when the claimant complains of property damage or personal injury, but the location is considered when the complaint concerns interference with comfort – is incorrect. It is true that the location needs to be considered only when the claimant complains of discomfort, but that is not because the law of nuisance is divided into two parts. The location need not be considered when the interference is property damage, because in those cases the location cannot establish that fairness between the parties will allow the damage. But the location must be considered when the interference is discomfort, because there the location might show that fairness between parties will allow the discomfort. Again, the crucial point is that these conclusions flow from a unified understanding of the law. The different treatment here is not evidence of a law of two parts. It is the unfolding of a coherent approach applied to different circumstances.

A claim that falls between the two categories just outlined is the following, from Lord Halsbury's judgment in *Colls v Home and Colonial Stores Ltd.*

> A dweller in towns cannot expect to have as pure air, as free from smoke, [and] smell . . . as if he lived in the country, and distant from other dwellings, and yet an excess of smoke, [and] smell . . . may give a cause of action, but in each of such cases it becomes a question of degree, and the question is in each case whether it amounts to a nuisance which will give a right of action.[14]

If the claim is that inhabitants of the city have less of a right to be free of smoke and smell than those in the country, then the claim is a violation of the moral equality of persons. That may reflect the reality of some decisions, but it is not possible to accept that it represents the law. That is because it is inconsistent with

---

[13] Of course, this is not to deny that courts may have decided cases in a way that, in fact, provided for lower class rights. The point is not that this cannot have happened. It is that this cannot be accepted.

[14] *Colls v Home and Colonial Stores Ltd* [1904] AC 179 (HL), 185.

The Sensitivity of the Claimant   33

the principle just mentioned. But the claim need not be understood in this way. It could mean only that those who live in the city have no right to be as free of smoke and smell as those who live in the country *are in fact*. To that claim there is no objection. That claim is only uninteresting.

The location of the nuisance, then, is relevant, but not in the way frequently supposed. What is more, its relevance is explained by the understanding of liability advanced here.

III. The Sensitivity of the Claimant[15]

In *Rogers v Elliott*,[16] the claimant maintained that he was sent into convulsions when the bells of the neighbouring church were rung. He sought an injunction to prevent the ringing. The Supreme Judicial Court of Massachusetts refused. Knowlton J said:

> The right to make a noise for a proper purpose must be measured in reference to the degree of annoyance which others may reasonably be required to submit to. In connection with the importance of the business from which it proceeds, that must be determined by the effect of noise upon people generally, and not upon those, on the one hand, who are peculiarly susceptible to it, or those on the other, who, by long experience, have learned to endure it without inconvenience; not upon those whose strong nerves and robust health enable them to endure the greatest disturbances without suffering, nor upon those whose mental or physical condition makes them painfully sensitive to everything about them.[17]

In other words, the standard to be applied in this context is an objective, not a subjective one. The question is not the degree to which the particular claimant is affected by the defendant's activity, but the degree to which an ordinary reasonable person in the claimant's position would be affected.

Clearly, then, the effect on the claimant – if one believes his story – was significant. That suggests that an injunction should have been awarded. But an ordinary reasonable person would not have been sent into convulsions. In fact, it was 'not contended that the ringing of the bell for church services in the manner shown by the evidence materially affected the health or comfort of ordinary people in the vicinity'.[18] Accordingly, as an ordinary reasonable person in the claimant's position would not have been adversely affected by the ringing, the Court ruled that the defendant was not committing a nuisance. What is the justification for this approach?

---

[15] In *Network Rail Infrastructure Ltd v Morris* [2004] EWCA Civ 172, [2004] Env LR 41 (CA), the Court attempted to deal with this issue in terms of foreseeability and negligence. As ch 7 and ch 8 make clear, I regard that as an error.

[16] *Rogers v Elliott* 15 NE 768 (MA SJC 1888). See also *Heath v Mayor of Brighton* (1908) 98 LT 718.

[17] *Rogers v Elliott* 15 NE 768 (MA 1888) 771.

[18] ibid 772.

In *Rogers v Elliott*, Knowlton J maintained:

> Upon a question whether one can lawfully ring his factory bell, or run his noisy machinery, or whether the noise will be a private nuisance to the occupant of a house near by, it is necessary to ascertain the natural and probable effect of the sound upon ordinary persons in that house, not how it will effect a particular person who happens to be there to-day, or who may chance to come to-morrow.[19]

According to this view, a subjective approach cannot be adopted, because it would entail that one's liberty varied according to who one's neighbours were. This is a highly plausible claim, but it is important to pursue its justification. Exactly what would be wrong with allowing individuals' liberty to vary according to the idiosyncrasies of their neighbours?

According to Knowlton J:

> If one's right to use his property was to depend upon the effect of the use upon a person of peculiar temperament or disposition, or upon one suffering from an uncommon disease, the standard for measuring it would be so uncertain and fluctuating as to paralyze industrial enterprises. The owner of a factory containing noisy machinery, with dwelling-houses all about it, might find his business lawful as to all but one of the tenants of the houses, and as to that one, who dwelt no nearer than the others, it might be a nuisance. The character of his business might change from legal to illegal, or illegal to legal, with every change of tenants of an adjacent estate, or with an arrival or departure of a guest or boarder at a house near by; or even with the wakefulness or the tranquil repose of an invalid neighbor on a particular night. Legal rights to the use of property cannot be left to such uncertainty.[20]

This is the familiar type of policy argument. The claim is that a subjective approach would render one's liberty uncertain and, apparently, that is unacceptable because it would paralyse industry.

That claim is more than a little melodramatic. Perhaps a subjective approach would damage industry – though it would create opportunities as well – but the claim that industry would be paralysed is hyperbole. And in any case, why is that concern thought to be relevant in a case such as this one? What is more, there is an alternative account available, an account that Knowlton J's argument even suggests.

Why should one's liberty not vary depending on the idiosyncrasies of one's neighbours? To put the question the other way around, why should it be impossible for one's neighbour's idiosyncrasies to impose obligations on one? The answer is that such would be unfair as between the parties.

If the claimant had succeeded in *Rogers v Elliott*, then his peculiar susceptibility to noise would have placed an obligation on the defendant that the defendant would not otherwise have had. That susceptibility was no doubt a misfortune for the claimant, but that does not justify transferring the consequences of that

---

[19] ibid 771.
[20] ibid 772.

misfortune to the defendant.[21] As the Privy Council said in *Eastern and South African Telegraph Co Ltd v Cape Town Tramway Cos Ltd*, applying the principle to a specific type of circumstance, 'A man cannot increase the liabilities of his neighbour by applying his own property to special uses, whether for business or pleasure'.[22]

In *Robinson v Kilvert*,[23] the claimant occupied a floor of a building above the floor occupied by the defendants. In order to carry out their trade, the defendants heated the air on their floor. This heat escaped into the claimant's premises. The heat was said to be entirely acceptable for ordinary purposes. It did not, for instance, 'incommode the workpeople on the Plaintiff's premises'.[24] However, the claimant used the premises to store a special type of paper that was dried out by the heat, causing loss.

The Court of Appeal ruled that the defendants were not committing a nuisance. According to Lopes LJ, 'A man who carries on an exceptionally delicate trade cannot complain because it is injured by his neighbour doing something lawful on his property, if it is something which would not injure anything but an exceptionally delicate trade'.[25]

This aspect of the law of nuisance is the equivalent of the objective approach to the standard of care in the law of negligence. In that regard, *Rogers v Elliott* and *Vaughan v Menlove*[26] are mirror images of each other.

The defendant in *Vaughan v Menlove* built a haystack next to the claimant's barn. The haystack caught fire, which spread to and destroyed the barn. The defendant argued that he had not been negligent because, though an ordinary reasonable person would have known of the risk of fire, he was too stupid to have done so. The Court of Common Pleas rejected the relevance of this reply. According to Tindal CJ, the question was not 'What could have been expected of the defendant?' but 'What could have been expected of "a man of ordinary prudence"?'[27] Accordingly, negligence's standard of care is not determined with regard to the peculiarities of the defendant but by reference to a creation of the law: the ordinary reasonable person.

If *Rogers v Elliott* stands for the principle that the claimant's peculiarities cannot impose obligations on the defendant, *Vaughan v Menlove* stands for the notion that the defendant's idiosyncrasies cannot remove rights from the claimant. These cases circle around the barycentre of commutative justice.

Against this line of reasoning, one might reject the notion that fairness between the parties calls for an objective approach. It might rather seem that this moral

---

[21] Whether the claimant should be compensated for this misfortune by the more fortunate, in accordance with distributive justice, is another matter entirely. No stand is taken on that issue here.

[22] *Eastern and South African Telegraph Co Ltd v Cape Town Tramway Cos Ltd* [1902] AC 381 (PC), 393.

[23] *Robinson v Kilvert* (1889) LR 41 Ch D 88 (CA).

[24] ibid 94.

[25] ibid 96.

[26] *Vaughan v Menlove* (1837) 3 Hodges 51, 132 ER 490.

[27] ibid 493.

concern demands that the parties' idiosyncrasies be taken into account fairly. Let us return to *Rogers v Elliott*.

One might agree that fairness between the parties in *Rogers v Elliott* meant that the claimant was not entitled to demand that the defendant refrain from all noise injurious to him. But one might nevertheless maintain that fairness required the defendant to take some account of the claimant's peculiar susceptibility to noise. The idea here is that fairness between the parties calls for some kind of compromise: perhaps the defendant should be permitted to make noise that is, as it were, half way between that acceptable to an ordinary reasonable person and that acceptable to the claimant with his idiosyncrasies.

There are occasions on which an approach of that kind might be justified. But *Rogers v Elliott* was not one of them. Two points are especially pertinent.

First, one might think that special obligations were owed to the claimant, not merely because he possessed a peculiarity, but because he had a disadvantage. That, however, is not relevant to the relationship between the parties. The possession of the disability by the claimant cannot itself constitute a wrong as between the claimant and the defendant. Hence, that disability cannot generate obligation in the defendant specifically. But one might argue that the claimant's disability generates an obligation to him in all those who are advantaged vis-à-vis him. If so, that is a matter of distributive justice. It includes the defendant in its scope, and it might even be right to argue that failure to compensate the claimant for his disability is wrongful, but even if so that wrong is not committed specifically by the defendant. The wrong consists of failing to provide the claimant with the social response necessary to ensure that he has a fair go in life. As such, it cannot ground an obligation that specifically the defendant owes to the claimant. In short, then, that argument can ground an entitlement in the claimant to demand social assistance in the form of social welfare or the like, but it cannot ground a special obligation owed to the claimant by the defendant in tort.

The second important point is that the parties in *Rogers v Elliott* were strangers or at least were not engaged in a common activity that related to the ringing of the bells. Had they been, things may have been different. Had the parties been involved in setting up a community together, for instance, and had the defendant known of the claimant's condition, then fairness between the parties may have called for a different result. This is because, as the activity complained of belonged to a wider activity in which the parties were together engaged, and because the defendant engaged with the claimant knowing of the claimant's condition, fairness as between the parties would normally require taking that condition into account.

In practice, the law normally deals with this issue through contract. This can be demonstrated by considering *Robinson v Kilvert* once more.

The defendants in *Robinson v Kilvert* were the claimant's landlords. They had leased the floor above their premises to the claimant so that the claimant could use it as a warehouse. At the time that the lease was entered into, the defendants were not aware that the claimant intended to store paper that would be damaged by the heat.

Here, then, though the parties were engaged in a common endeavour of one kind, the activity of which the claimant complained was not an aspect of that endeavour. The endeavour was to lease premises to be used as a warehouse. The defendants did not prevent that happening. They prevented the premises being used as a warehouse to store the particular type of paper the claimant wished to store, but they did not enter into a common endeavour in that regard. Hence, fairness between the parties demanded that the particular use to which the plaintiff put the premises be ignored. The Court dealt with this issue by saying that the lease contained no warranty that the premises would be suitable to store the particular kind of paper.[28]

However, had the claimant made his intentions clear to the defendant before the lease was formed and had the lease been entered into on that basis, then the parties would have entered into a common endeavour, an aspect of which would have been storing the paper in question. In those circumstances, fairness between the parties would have demanded that attention be paid to the particular use to which the claimant intended to put the premises. The Court would have taken this into account by finding that the lease contained a relevant warranty.[29]

Again, we see that the law's approach to the sensitivity of the claimant is not to be understood as some policy-based exception to a general approach. On the contrary, it is mandated by a proper understanding of that approach.

IV. The Duration of the Interference

Two caveats must be recorded before this discussion can begin. First, we are not here interested in the relevance of this issue with respect to the issuing of an injunction. The issue now is the impact of the interference's duration on liability. Second, we are not here exploring the relationship between nuisance and the cause of action based on *Rylands v Fletcher*. Specifically, no stand is taken on whether an isolated event can constitute a nuisance. That issue is examined in the following section.

In *Harrison v Southwark and Vauxhall Water Co*,[30] in the exercise of its statutory powers, the defendants sank a shaft in land neighbouring the claimant's house in order to run lift pumps. The noise of this activity seriously inconvenienced the claimant. In response to the claimant's allegations, Vaughan-Williams J said:

> In the first place, it seems to me that if the Defendants had without statutory authority sunk this shaft and done this pumping for any lawful and ordinary purpose in the exercise of their powers as private owners of the land they would not have been responsible

---

[28] *Robinson v Kilvert* (1889) LR 41 Ch D 88 (CA), 94.
[29] ibid 95.
[30] *Harrison v Southwark and Vauxhall Water Co* [1891] 2 Ch 409.

as for a nuisance. It frequently happens that the owners or occupiers of land cause, in the execution of lawful works in the ordinary user of land, a considerable amount of temporary annoyance to their neighbours; but they are not necessarily on that account held to be guilty of causing an unlawful nuisance. The business of life could not be carried on if it were so. For instance, a man who pulls down his house for the purpose of building a new one no doubt causes considerable inconvenience to his next door neighbours during the process of demolition; but he is not responsible as for a nuisance if he uses all reasonable skill and care to avoid annoyance to his neighbour by the works of demolition. Nor is he liable to an action, even though the noise and dust and the consequent annoyance be such as would constitute a nuisance if the same, instead of being created for the purpose of the demolition of the house, had been created in sheer wantonness, or in the execution of works for a purpose involving a permanent continuance of the noise and dust. For the law, in judging what constitutes a nuisance, does take into consideration both the object and duration of that which is said to constitute the nuisance.[31]

Strictly, of course, all this was *obiter dicta*. There was no possibility of liability, as the defendant was acting within his statutory authority, an issue examined in chapter eleven. Unfortunately, this has not prevented this passage having an influence that it does not deserve.

In an attempt to justify his position, Vaughan-Williams J appealed to the notion that individuals must be permitted to create the inconveniences concomitant with demolishing their houses. That argument can succeed only if the reason for that permission also generates an entitlement to run the defendant's pumps. What is the evidence for that?

Indeed, people must be permitted to demolish their houses. This is because demolishing structures on one's land is a fundamental aspect of the right to property. Specifically as envisaged by Vaughan-Williams J, it is an aspect of the ability to build on one's land. That right is not absolute. It must give way to the more fundamental property rights of others. Hence, it is a nuisance to demolish one's house in a way that destroys one's neighbours' quality of life, by preventing them from being able to live in their houses or from sleeping, etc. But while this might justify the noise created by the sinking of the pumps, it does not justify the noise from the lift pumps. In particular, if *Harrison v Southwark and Vauxhall Water Co* asserts that an occasional event cannot be nuisance, then the case was in that regard wrongly decided.

However, if the claim is only that the duration of the event is one of the things that must be taken into account when determining the presence of a nuisance, then the claim ought to be endorsed. This is simply because the duration can affect the nature of the interference. Being annoyed by noise for a few days is not the same as being annoyed for months, for instance. Only the latter will make living in my property wearisome and hence only it can be described as a fundamental violation of my right to my land. Similarly, the timing of the nuisance can be

---

[31] ibid 413–14.

significant. For instance, in *Munro v Southern Dairies*[32] it was rightly said that noise at night is more likely to constitute a nuisance than noise during the day. This is because the former has more impact, particularly on one's ability to sleep, and thus constitutes a more fundamental interference.

There is, accordingly, no rule according to which a nuisance must last for a substantial duration, though it may well be true that most nuisances do.[33]

It is sometimes said that the distinction between interferences that cause physical damage and those that interfere with discomfort is relevant here also, in that the rule that the duration of the interference can be relevant applies only in the latter case.[34] There is truth in this view, but it must again not be understood as implying that the law of nuisance comes in two parts, only one of which is concerned with duration. The relevant features of the law are ordinary products of the law's general principle.

As a right to the integrity of one's property must be the most fundamental aspect of one's general right to it, no physical damage to that property can be justified on the ground that the event that causes it is of short duration.[35] But when dealing with discomfort, the duration of the event can affect the nature of the interference itself, as has been shown. Again, then, this aspect of the law, properly understood, is an illustration of its general principle.

V. Isolated Events

It is now well established that isolated, that is, single events can constitute nuisances.[36] Nevertheless, it has been suggested that this position is odd, an exception to the general approach, or even mistaken. Is this so?

In his recent analysis of the relationship between nuisance and the rule in *Rylands v Fletcher*, Donal Nolan maintains:

> extending private nuisance to isolated escapes undermines the essential nature of the cause of action. This becomes clear if we go back to the tort's origins in the assize of nuisance, for the object of the assize was abatement, a remedy which depended on the continuation of the interference down to the time of the action: hence [Francis] Bohlen's definition of a nuisance as a 'condition capable of abatement after it is known to be injurious.' Indeed, even in the modern law, the 'nuisance' is defined as the state of affairs that causes the interference, rather than the interference itself, which presupposes an element

---

[32] *Munro v Southern Dairies* [1955] VLR 332.

[33] *cf Cunard v Antifyre Ltd* [1933] 1 KB 551, 557: 'Private nuisances, at least in the vast majority of cases, are interferences for a substantial length of time by owners or occupiers of property with the use or enjoyment of neighbouring property'.

[34] S Deakin, A Johnston and B Markesinis, *Markesinis and Deakin's Tort Law*, 6th edn (Oxford, Clarendon Press, 2008) 522–23.

[35] See also M Lee, 'What is Private Nuisance?' (2003) 119 *LQR* 298, 308. Against: C Gearty, 'The Place of Private Nuisance' [1989] *CLJ* 214.

[36] See the cases examined below and also *Cambridge Water Co v Eastern Counties Leather plc* [1994] 2 AC 264 (HL).

of continuity. Moreover, because a nuisance is a wrongful state of affairs, it can be enjoined by a *quia timet* injunction before any harm has occurred.[37]

The claim that, historically, a nuisance had to be continuous is well made. But the conclusion that continuation belongs to the 'essential nature' of the tort does not follow from it. This argument commits a genetic fallacy. I was an infant, but I hope it can be agreed that infantilism is not an essential part of my nature. Legal history is of great importance, but the nature of our modern actions is not chained to it.

Second, we must be careful with the claim that a nuisance is 'the state of affairs that causes the interference, rather than the interference itself'. In this regard, Nolan refers to the work of Warren Seavey, who has this to say.

> *The Meaning of the Term.* – Nuisance has been treated as if the term were so amorphous and protean as to make impossible a description of the area which it covers. However, as in the case of other words which have been used by the courts in various senses, it is worthwhile to attempt a terse description of the conduct and the results which are included in the judicial use of nuisance. As commonly used, it connotes a condition or activity which unduly interferes with the use of land or of a public place.[38]

The claim here is ambiguous. This is because it is not clear how the 'which' in the final sentence of the passage is meant to function. The sentence could mean that 'nuisance' refers to a condition or activity, and it just so happens that this activity interferes. But the sentence could just as easily mean that 'nuisance' refers to a condition or activity that interferes.

It may be that the first reading captures Seavey's intention. But again we must be careful. The passage clearly sets out Seavey's belief that a proper analysis of 'the judicial use of nuisance' is required. But the final sentence of the passage is not an attempt to provide it. That analysis is provided by the article as a whole. Thus, the sentence in question is not intended as an answer to the question 'What is a legal nuisance?' but as an answer to the question 'How do people commonly use the word "nuisance"?' In that regard, Seavey is surely right. People do use the term to refer, not to the interference, but to the state of affairs that caused the interference. But that is not relevant to the issues under examination here.

Legal nuisances require interference. That remains the case, though we frequently refer to the state of affairs that causes the nuisance as 'the nuisance'. Thus, even if a state of affairs that causes a legal nuisance must be continuous, it would not follow that the interference, and thus the legal nuisance itself, must be continuous. Moreover, it does not follow from the fact that a state of affairs must cause a nuisance that the cause of a nuisance must be continuous. A state of affairs need not be continuous (at least not in the sense required). A one-off, isolated event constitutes a state of affairs.

---

[37] D Nolan, 'The Distinctiveness of *Rylands v Fletcher*' (2005) 121 *LQR* 421, 437 (citations omitted). Quoting FH Bohlen, 'The Rule in *Rylands v Fletcher*' (1911) 59 *University of Pennsylvania Law Review* 298, 312.

[38] WS Seavey, 'Nuisance, Contributory Negligence and Other Mysteries' (1952) 65 *Harvard Law Review* 984, 984.

Further, it is true that *quia timet* injunctions can be awarded, but as these are awarded to prevent legal wrongs occurring, that does not support the position for which these injunctions are called as evidence. The existence of the injunction shows only that a nuisance in the legal sense *may* result from a continuing state of affairs.

An alternative tack is to attempt to undermine the cases that permit nuisance recovery for isolated events. This strategy is adopted by John Murphy. We must, therefore, examine the cases that he explores.

The first is *Midwood & Co Ltd v Manchester Corp.*[39] An explosion occurred on the defendant's property that was caused by inadequate insulation of the defendant's electricity mains. The explosion damaged the claimant's property, for which the claimant successfully recovered in nuisance.

Murphy maintains that the Court in *Midwood & Co Ltd v Manchester Corp* was 'seduced'[40] to this view by the nature of the parties' pleadings. But as he points out, Collins MR stated:

> There was a gradual accumulation of explosive gas brought about by the fusion of the bitumen by the operation of the overheated electric wires, which process went on for some three hours, and ultimately resulted in an explosion. If that was not a nuisance I do not know what would be one.[41]

It may have been that Collins MR was led to this view by the pleadings, but this cannot obscure the fact that this is an emphatic statement of the view that an isolated event can constitute a nuisance.

The second case is *Spicer v Smee.*[42] Again due to defective wiring, a fire started on the defendant's property and spread to the claimant's. In finding for the claimant, Atkinson J said:

> Nuisance and negligence are different in their nature, and a private nuisance arises out of a state of things on one man's property whereby his neighbour's property is exposed to danger. . . . I am satisfied that the state of the defendant's bungalow around that plug, with a bare wire in contact with wet wood, did constitute a nuisance on the defendant's property and that it exposed the neighbouring property to danger and, in the end, caused the escape of a dangerous thing, to wit, fire.[43]

The third case is *British Celanese Ltd v A H Hunt (Capacitors) Ltd.*[44] Metal foil from the defendant's premises was blown onto the claimant's, causing the claimant's power supply to be interrupted resulting in significant loss. The defendant was held liable on the basis of *Midwood & Co Ltd v Manchester Corp.*

Murphy objects to these cases on the following grounds.

> [T]he only way in which these cases can be understood as involving private nuisance is if the prior (ongoing) dangerous state of affairs is considered to be the nuisance. Yet in

---

[39] *Midwood & Co Ltd v Manchester Corp* [1905] 2 KB 597.
[40] J Murphy, *The Law of Nuisance* (Oxford, Oxford University Press, 2010) 13.
[41] *Midwood & Co Ltd v Manchester Corp* [1905] 2 KB 597, 605.
[42] *Spicer v Smee* [1946] 1 All ER 489.
[43] ibid 493.
[44] *British Celanese Ltd v A H Hunt (Capacitors) Ltd* [1969] 1 WLR 959.

Midwood, where this line of authority began, Mathew LJ was adamant – and for good reason – that the defendant's defective wiring was not itself a nuisance.[45]

The claim that a legal nuisance cannot be the event that causes the interference is correct. But these cases are not explicable on this basis only. Certainly, Atkinson J in *Spicer v Smee* seemed to propound that view – the view enunciated by Seavey – but that is understandable in the light of what has been said above. More carefully expressed, the claimant in that case succeeded because the fire constituted a legal nuisance when it spread to the claimant's property. The claim that these cases require the view that Murphy rightly rejects is wrong. They are supported by the view advanced here.

Murphy goes on to say that:

> leaving aside the juridical niceties of the matter, it seems impossible to reconcile the approach in these cases with various other important *dicta*. First, quite apart from the fact that liability for fire and nuisance enjoyed a long history of being treated quite separately from one another, it is difficult to square the decision in *Spicer v Smee* with Lord Goddard CJ's negligence-laden *dictum* in *Balfour v Barty-King* where he said: 'a person in whose house a fire is caused by negligence is liable if it spreads to that of his neighbour, and this is true whether the negligence is his own or that of his servant or his guest'. Similarly problematic is the job of reconciling all three of the 'one-off' cases with Lord Denning's more general pronouncement in *Att-Gen v PYA Quarries* that:
>
>> [A] private nuisance always involves some degree of repetition and continuance. An isolated act which is over and done with, once and for all, may give rise to an action in negligence or an action under the rule in *Rylands v Fletcher*, but not an action for nuisance.[46]

It is odd to think that principled arguments, rather than judicial disagreements, should be described as juridical niceties. What is more, it is not easy to see what to make of these judicial claims or why these two remarks should be given preference over the other cases with which we have been presented. And in any case, Lord Goddard's comment is perfectly consistent with the finding of nuisance in *Spicer v Smee* as well as in the other cases. Finally, as Lord Denning presents no argument for his view, and given that we are not here merely listing authorities but attempting to decide between them on the basis of argument, giving Lord Denning's claim the attention it deserves means ignoring it.

Isolated events can be nuisances. Though the development of this view is historically interesting, there is nothing odd about it. On the contrary, the attempt to preserve the alternative view seems to amount to little more than an unprincipled and largely unmotivated conservativism. The actionability of isolated events flows from the ordinary principles of the law.

---

[45] J Murphy, *The Law of Nuisance* (Oxford, Oxford University Press, 2010) 14.

[46] ibid 15 (citations omitted). Quoting from *Balfour v Barty-King* [1957] 1 QB 496, 504 and *Attorney-General v PYA Quarries* [1957] 2 QB 169, 192.

5

The Activity

This chapter deals primarily with the issue of describing the conflict between the parties. This is no simple matter and it cannot be approached formulaically, but guidelines are provided. It is suggested that the appropriate descriptions are ones that capture the nature of the parties' dispute in a way that, if possible, reflects their rights. In the second section of the chapter, this analysis is applied to cases in which the defendant is actuated by malice.

I. The Description of the Parties' Activities

On the view advanced in the previous chapter – and indeed on any view – it is necessary to begin with a description of the parties' activities. In *Bamford v Turnley*,[1] for instance, the defendant was described as operating a brick-making business that produced an objectionable vapour and the claimant was portrayed as suffering from that vapour during his occupation of his land. Those were not the only descriptions available. The defendant's activity could have been described in minute detail, the court going into the precise constitution of the bricks, the kilning process, the transportation of the bricks to market, the defendant's business relations with his customers and so on. Alternatively, the defendant could have been described simply as making a smell. Likewise, details of the claimant's life could have been recorded or he could have been described only as coughing. All of these descriptions are accurate. Why, then, were they not examined in *Bamford v Turnley*?

The answer is that a court's task is to adopt descriptions of the parties' activities that are both accurate and appropriate. This raises the question: What makes a particular description appropriate? We answer this question now.

A. The Nature of the Dispute

The first point to be made in this regard is that the description of the parties' activities must capture the nature of their dispute. It is useful again to examine *Sturges v Bridgman* in this regard.

---

[1] *Bamford v Turnley* (1862) 3 B & S 66, 122 ER 27.

The defendant was a confectioner who had installed two mechanical mortars and pestles against the party wall that he shared with the claimant. The claimant physician constructed extensions to his house, building a consulting room along that party wall. His complaint was described as follows.

> The Plaintiff alleged that when the Defendant's pestles and mortars were being used the noise and vibration thereby caused were very great, and were heard and felt in the Plaintiff's consulting-room, and such noise and vibration seriously annoyed and disturbed the Plaintiff, and materially interfered with him in the practice of his profession. In particular the Plaintiff stated that the noise prevented him from examining his patients by auscultation for diseases of the chest. He also found it impossible to engage with effect in any occupation which required thought and attention.[2]

There is enough in this passage to suggest that the Court could have described both parties' activities as operating a business. Given such a description, of course, neither party's use of land could be said to have been more fundamental than the other's. That seems to suggest that the Court's decision was based on the notion that medical care is more important than confectionary.

In fact, however, though the description in question is accurate, it must be clear that it is inappropriate. For one thing, the claimant's complaint was not that the defendant was running a business. It was that the defendant was making a great deal of noise and vibration. Of course, the defendant made the noise and vibration in order to operate his business, but the claimant's complaint was not about that but about the noise and vibration itself. For another thing, the complaint was not merely that the noise and vibration prevented the claimant from operating his business, it was that it prevented him from operating his business because it was of so high a degree that he was annoyed, disturbed and unable to hear or think properly. Importantly, that would have been so had he used the room, not as a consulting room, but as a kitchen, living room, bedroom or the like.

Hence, the appropriate description of the parties' activities is not one of competing business interests. It is one that compares the use of the machinery with the normal occupation of a room. It must be clear that the latter is more fundamental to property than the former.

Incidentally, this case can also be used to reveal the nature of the judgement being made. Were human beings or their environment different, the result in *Sturges v Bridgman* may also have been different. For instance, if human beings were unable to live in houses without having mechanical mortars and pestles operating along party walls, then the opposite result to the one reached in *Sturges v Bridgman* would have been appropriate; similarly were human beings insusceptible to noise and vibration. The required judgment is made on the basis of *a priori* principles, but it is not itself *a priori*.

Likewise in *Bryant v Lefever*,[3] in which the claimant complained that the defendant's building up caused his fireplace to smoke. The Court found for the

---

[2] *Sturges v Bridgman* (1879) 11 Ch D 852 (CA), 853.
[3] *Bryant v Lefever* (1879) 4 CPD 172 (CA).

defendant, but it is possible to imagine circumstances being different. If, for instance, human beings were highly susceptible to smoke and cold and if the fireplace could not be relocated so that having a fire was a matter of life and death for the claimant, then the case may have been decided the other way.

Consider also *Fontainebleau Hotel Corp v Forty-Five Twenty-Five Inc.*[4] In chapter three, I argued that the absence of liability in this case turns on the fact that the defendant's intended activity (building) was more fundamental than the claimants' (sunbathing around the pool and the like). But why interpret the facts in that way? Why not understand the defendant to be building *extensions* to his hotel, an activity that might at first appear less fundamental than the claimant's?[5] The answer is that this interpretation is not relevant to the claimant's complaint. Now, this is quite consistent with the fact that the claimant actually complained about the fact that the defendant was building extensions. The issue here is the real complaint, not the words that the claimant used. Let me explain.

The problem for the claimant was that the defendant's plans would result in a shadow being cast over its property. It made absolutely no difference to the claimant – whatever the claimant said – that this shadow would be the result specifically of an extension. It would have made no difference had the shadow been the result of an original building. The claimant's actual complaint, then, was that the defendant was intending to build in a way that cast a shadow; it was incidental that the building was of an extension.

In fact, it is likely that claimants in these circumstances will refer to extensions and the like because of the distorting effect created by the conventional view's focus on reasonableness. In *Fontainebleau*, it enables the claimant to suggest that it should win because it is unreasonable to permit the defendant's hotel to get *even bigger* when that would cause loss to the claimant, inviting the court to entertain some distributive considerations. For the reasons that I have argued, this is a distraction.

B. Judgement

i. Judgement and the Law of Nuisance

We have seen that the appropriate description of the parties' activities is the one that most accurately captures their dispute. This is not to pretend that this matter can be solved in any mechanical or deductive fashion. It is possible only to make a judgement on the basis of the principle just enunciated taking into account the facts of the case. Because of this, reasonable people may sometimes disagree as to the most appropriate descriptions. That is inescapable.

Though the approach advanced here provides no mechanistic test for determining the appropriate description of the parties' activities or the existence of a

---

[4] *Fontainebleau Hotel Corp v Forty-Five Twenty-Five Inc* 114 So 2d 357 (FL 1959).
[5] In fact, I think that this is doubtful. Is it possible to operate a hotel in the long term without constructing extensions and the like?

nuisance, it offers a set of principles that can be used to guide the judgement of judges, and of the parties themselves, in these and in like matters.

Moreover, even if we wanted a deterministic alternative, none is available. And none is needed. What is needed is an approach that allows courts to map the appropriate moral concerns onto the world when faced with the cases that come before them. Given the abstract and often somewhat imperspicuous nature of the principles of justice, while a deterministic approach may make the judges' task easier, it can do so only by separating the law from the justice that it is meant to be implementing.[6] Because of this, judgement is inescapable. The attempt to eliminate it can only generate it in other places.[7]

ii. Judgement in General

At this point, it is important to discuss two related and widespread errors concerning the nature of judgement.

The first is the notion that judgement necessarily, or even frequently, hides policy concerns. With respect to the theory presented here, the argument has the following structure.

(1)   It is said that courts must use the principles enunciated above to direct their judgement concerning the appropriate description of the parties' activities.
(2)   But those principles cannot determine the result that the courts must reach.
(3)   Therefore, the courts must utilise policy arguments in order to reach their conclusions.

Alternatively, a weaker conclusion might be:

(3*)   Therefore, the courts are able to utilise policy arguments to reach their conclusions.

Neither conclusion follows from (1) and (2); neither is consistent with the nature of judgement.

First, the form of the argument is clearly invalid. My concept of a drinking glass does not determine which objects in the world are drinking glasses. I must always apply judgement to distinguish drinking glasses from other objects. But that does not mean that I use policy to do so. I do not. In the moral context, I recognise a duty to be loyal to my friends, but when I need to decide whether this duty requires me to buy my round of drinks or call a taxi, I make a judgement without considering policy goals.

In that light, it can be seen that the argument (1)–(3) is guilty of denying the possibility of judgement. The reason for thinking that a policy concern must be present is merely that the principles do not determine the result. The assumption

---

[6] For discussion of the basic idea in operation here, see M Stone, 'Legal Positivism as an Idea About Morality' (2011) 61 *University of Toronto Law Journal* 313.

[7] See also K Oliphant, 'Against Certainty in Tort Law', in S Pitel, J Neyers and E Chamberlain (eds), *Tort Law: Challenging Orthodoxy* (Oxford, Hart, forthcoming 2013).

here is that reasoning proceeds on a mechanistic basis – a somewhat ironic fact given that those who make the assumption generally regard 'mechanistic' as a term of utmost disapprobation. The existence of this assumption is why, given the supposition that a line of reasoning that generates a result is rational, the absence of an explicit mechanism is taken to be evidence for an implicit one: covertly appealing to policy concerns. This involves a fundamental misunderstanding of the nature of human rationality, indeed of human life. Human reasoning is not mechanistic. This idea is nowhere better expressed than in the following (though it has perhaps been more clearly expressed and is more commonly thought to have been discovered by Ludwig Wittgenstein).

> General logic contains no precepts at all for the power of judgment, and moreover cannot contain them. For **since it** [ie general logic] **abstracts from all content of cognition** [ie logic is the form of thought, not the content of thought], nothing remains to it but the business of analytically dividing the mere form of cognition into concepts, judgments, and inferences, and thereby achieving formal rules for all use of the understanding. Now if it wanted to show generally how one ought to subsume under these rules, i.e., distinguish whether something stands under them or not, this could not happen except once again through a rule. But just because this is a rule, it would demand another instruction for the power of judgment, and so it becomes clear that although the understanding is certainly capable of being instructed and equipped through rules, the power of judgment is a special talent that cannot be taught but only practiced.[8]

Concepts are not applied to the world via rules, and they cannot be so applied as any rule is itself a concept and so must be applied to the world. Concepts are applied to the world via judgements.

The second conclusion (3*) is little better than the first. Take again the example of a drinking glass. Certainly, my concept of a drinking glass does not determine which objects in the world are drinking glasses. And when I am deciding whether a particular object is a drinking glass, there is nothing to prevent me considering policy concerns such as the public interest. But the moment I do so I am no longer trying to decide whether a particular object is a drinking glass. Likewise, if I am trying to decide whether loyalty requires me to buy my friend a drink or call him a taxi, I could turn to examine the public interest. But when I do so, I am not any more trying to determine the demands of my duty of loyalty.

It is pertinent to stress this feature of policy. The conventional view is wrong to hold that attention to policy is the mark of a legal analysis engaged with its subject matter. On the contrary, that attention is the mark of an analysis that has turned away from the law to consider something else. Policy is, quite literally, a distraction.

The second error is found in the idea that reliance on judgement necessarily introduces a problematic level of subjectivity. In this context, the notion is that if judges are required to make judgements of the kind I have outlined, then their judgments are bound to be inappropriately subjective.

---

[8] I Kant, *Critique of Pure Reason*, P Guyer and A Wood (trs) (Cambridge, Cambridge University Press, 1998) A132–133/B171–172.

This claim requires more discussion than can be provided here. However, the general point to make is that it is wrong to think that judgement is essentially subjective. On the contrary, given the ubiquity of judgement in human life, unless the vast majority of our judgements were at least intersubjective, and in that sense objective, we would be unable to communicate with each other.[9]

With respect to the law in particular, it is first necessary to admit that it is impossible entirely to eliminate the judge's subjectivity from her judgments. As has been said, reasonable people may disagree in their judgements. But in this context the best protection against this is the law itself, specifically the history of its case law. Although findings of fact have no precedential value in the sense that they are not binding,[10] past cases are a record of the judgements made by judges over the law's history. Individual judges are to make their judgements in the light of this material. As far as it is humanly possible, then, the judgment is to emanate from this body of law, though of course it can do so only through the vehicle of the individual judge's mind. This is imperfect, but the imperfection is an inescapable consequence of the human condition.

C. Rights

We have said that the appropriate description of the parties' activities is the one that most accurately captures their dispute. Also of significance is that, if it can be, this dispute must be understood in terms of the parties' rights. This is because a party who cannot demonstrate that her rights are in question cannot succeed.

As discussed in the previous chapters, the defendant in *Fontainebleau Hotel Corp v Forty-Five Twenty-Five Inc*[11] intended to build up on his land in a way that would cause a shadow to be cast over the claimant's hotel at the height of the Florida tourist season. It was claimed that 'the construction would interfere with the light and air on the beach in front of [the claimant's hotel] and cast a shadow of such size as to render the beach wholly unfitted for the use and enjoyment of its guests, to the irreparable injury of the plaintiff'.[12]

The trial judge had ruled in favour of the claimant, arguing that:

> The ruling is not based on any alleged presumptive title nor prescriptive right of the plaintiff to light and air nor is it based on any deed restrictions nor recorded plats in the title of the plaintiff nor of the defendant nor of any plat of record. It is not based on any zoning ordinance nor on any provision of the building code of the City of Miami Beach nor on the decision of any court, nisi prius or appellate. It is based solely on the propo-

---

[9] By intersubjective, I mean communicable. For the most important discussion of judgement, see I Kant, *Critique of the Power of Judgment*, P Guyer and E Matthews (trs) (Cambridge, Cambridge University Press, 2000).

[10] *Qualcast (Wolverhampton) Ltd v Haynes* [1959] AC 743 (HL).

[11] *Fontainebleau Hotel Corp v Forty-Five Twenty-Five Inc* 114 So 2d 357 (FL 1959). See also *Dalton v Angus* (1881) 6 App Cas 740 (HL); *Newcastle CC v Shortland Management Services* [2003] NSWCA 156.

[12] *Fontainebleau Hotel Corp v Forty-Five Twenty-Five Inc* 114 So 2d 357 (FL 1959) 358.

sition that no one has a right to use his property to the injury of another. In this case it is clear from the evidence that the proposed use by the Fontainebleau will materially damage the Eden Roc.[13]

This was because the presence of the shadow would make the Eden Roc much less attractive to patrons, thus causing the claimant significant economic loss.

That argument was emphatically rejected by the Florida District Court of Appeal.

> This is indeed a novel application of the maxim *sic utere tuo ut alienum non laedas.* This maxim does not mean that one must never use his own property in such a way as to do any injury to his neighbor. . . . It means only that one must use his property so as not to injure the lawful *rights* of another. . . . In *Reaver v. Martin Theatres* . . . under this maxim, it was stated that 'it is well settled that a property owner may put his own property to any reasonable and lawful use, so long as he does not thereby deprive the adjoining landowner of any right of enjoyment of his property *which is recognized and protected by law, and so long as his use is not such a one as the law will pronounce a nuisance.*'[14]

This is a reflection of what was noticed in the previous chapter: the law of nuisance is concerned with the parties' property rights. Hence, to succeed, the claimant must point to an activity with which the defendant will interfere that is covered by a right. This means that many of the parties' activities are irrelevant.

Take the issue of sunbathing, for instance. As we have seen, the claimant maintained that the shadow would 'render the beach wholly unfitted for the use and enjoyment of its guests',[15] meaning, inter alia, that the guests would not be able to use it for sunbathing. But does one have a right to sunbathe? The answer is 'Yes and no', depending on what is meant by sunbathing. Yes, one has a right to lie exposed before the elements on loungers on one's property. Likewise, one has a right that one's guests so use one's land. Would the shadow have prevented this, then the claimant would have succeeded. But the shadow did not prevent this. Shadows do not stop people lying out in the open. What stops them in that context is the fact that they want to lie in the open in order to expose themselves to the sun and the shadow prevents them lying in the open in order to satisfy that desire. Now, the point is that the desire is itself irrelevant as the claimant had no right that it be fulfilled.

In that light, the only chance the claimant had of succeeding was to argue that it had a right to sunlight. Naturally, if such existed and if it were held against the defendant, then the defendant's building up would violate that right. That does not mean that in such circumstances there would be a nuisance. It would still be necessary to ask whether the claimant's right was more fundamental than the defendant's. But that question did not need to be asked in *Fontainebleau.* As the Court said, 'No American decision has been cited, and independent research has revealed

---

[13] ibid 359.
[14] ibid (emphasis added in *Fontainebleau*).
[15] ibid 358.

none, in which it has been held that – in the absence of some contractual or statutory obligation – a landowner has a legal right to the free flow of light and air across the adjoining land of his neighbour'.[16] There is, in other words, no such right.[17]

Similarly, though the claimant correctly maintained that the defendant's extension would cause it significant business losses, those losses would not be the result of any violation of the claimant's rights. There is no right that one's business be profitable and the claimant held no right as against the defendant that anyone patronise its establishment.[18]

In the end, then, the claimant in *Fontainebleau* failed because it could not point to any activity with which the defendant's extension would interfere to which the claimant had any right. Because of this, the Court did not need to balance the rights of the parties: no right of the claimant's was in question.

Victoria Park Racing v Taylor[19] is another case of this kind. The first defendant erected a platform on his land in order to view the neighbouring claimant's racecourse. The second defendant broadcast from the platform radio commentary on the claimant's races. As a result, many of the claimant's potential patrons stayed away, causing the claimant to suffer economic loss. The claimant alleged that the defendants were guilty of committing a nuisance. By a majority, the High Court of Australia disagreed and rightly so. The claimant had a right to use its land, but that right was not violated by the defendants. The claimant had no right to the patronage of its potential customers. Absent breach of copyright or privacy, then, no tort can have been committed.

Likewise, if a defendant (negligently or otherwise) cuts a power cable on someone else's land that interrupts the supply of electricity to my property,[20] that cannot be a nuisance. This is because my (paucital) right to the electricity, if I have one at all, is held only as a result of the supply agreement with the utility company.[21]

We have been examining the importance of rights from the perspective of the claimant. Naturally, the issue also arises with respect to the defendant. Of course, the claim here is not that the description of the defendant's activity must refer to the defendant's rights. A claimant has no case unless her rights are in question, but it does not defeat a claimant's argument that the defendant's activity related to no right in the defendant; on the contrary, that strengthens the claimant's position. If the claimant's activity relates to a right that she possesses and the defendant's relates to no right held by him, then the claimant must succeed.

A good illustration of this principle is found in *Matheson v Northcote College*.[22] The claimant occupied land adjacent to the defendant's school. Pupils of the

---

[16] ibid 359.

[17] See also the court's discussion of the doctrine of ancient lights, ibid.

[18] This point has been analysed in more detail in A Beever, *Rediscovering the Law of Negligence* (Oxford, Hart, 2007) 239–50.

[19] *Victoria Park Racing v Taylor* (1937) 58 CLR 479 (HCA).

[20] This, of course, is based on *Spartan Steel & Alloys Ltd v Martin & Co (Contractors) Ltd* [1973] QB 27 (CA).

[21] *Anglian Water Services Ltd v Crawshaw Robbins Ltd* [2001] BLR 173.

[22] *Matheson v Northcote College* [1975] 2 NZLR 106 (SC).

school, inter alia, threw objects on to the claimant's land and took fruit from the claimant's trees. These were not activities over which the defendant had any right. The right to land does not give any entitlement to place objects on another's land or take another's property. Accordingly, with respect to this aspect of the claim, no balancing was required. The defendant's activity was one that interfered with a right in the claimant but was not covered by a right in the defendant. There could therefore be no question as to whose right was the most fundamental.

For this reason, the issue actually litigated in *Matheson v Northcote College* was not whether a nuisance existed. It was solely who committed it: the defendant or only the pupils. We return to this question in chapter ten.

II. The Malice Doctrine

A. Malice

The preceding discussion allows us to deal with a difficult issue concerning the state of the defendant's mind. The issue here centres on what lawyers know as malice. The question is this: Is an otherwise legal activity converted into a nuisance if the defendant performed the activity in order to damage the claimant? Some cases indicate that the answer to this question is 'No'.[23] Others, however, are frequently thought to support the opposite response. This, as we will see, is an error generated by the fundamental problem with the conventional view.

In *Bradford v Pickles*,[24] the claimant owned land beneath which were water springs that were used for more than 40 years to supply Bradford with water. The defendant owned land on a higher level than the claimant. Under the defendant's land was a natural reservoir and water flowed from this reservoir down to the claimant's springs. The defendant sank a shaft into his land in order to alter the flow of the water, seriously reducing the amount of water that flowed into the claimant's springs. He did so, not in order to provide any direct benefit to himself, but simply to deprive the claimant of water so as to come to a beneficial financial arrangement with the town. The claimant insisted that this was malicious and hence that it was entitled to an injunction.

The House of Lords disagreed. After deciding that the claimant had no case absent the allegation of malice, Lord Halsbury LC said:

> The only remaining point is the question of fact alleged by the plaintiffs, that the acts done by the defendant are done, not with any view which deals with the use of his own land or the percolating water through it, but is done, in the language of the pleader, 'maliciously.' I am not certain that I can understand or give any intelligible construction to the word so used. Upon the supposition on which I am now arguing, it comes to

---

[23] See also C Gearty, 'The Place of Private Nuisance' [1989] *CLJ* 214, 228.
[24] *Bradford v Pickles* [1895] AC 587 (HL).

an allegation that the defendant did maliciously something that he had a right to do. If this question were to have been tried in old times as an injury to the right in an action on the case, the plaintiffs would have had to allege, and to prove, if traversed, that they were entitled to the flow of the water, which, as I have already said, was an allegation they would have failed to establish.

This is not a case in which the state of mind of the person doing the act can affect the right to do it. If it was a lawful act, however ill the motive might be, he had a right to do it. If it was an unlawful act, however good his motive might be, he would have no right to do it. Motives and intentions in such a question as is now before your Lordships seem to me to be absolutely irrelevant.[25]

Likewise, Lord Watson said, 'No use of property, which would be legal if due to a proper motive, can become illegal because it is prompted by a motive which is improper or even malicious'.[26] This view was also echoed in *Allen v Flood*.[27]

This position follows from the approach advanced here. The issue is which party's use of land is most fundamental to the concept of property. The malice of the defendant *per se* (or of the claimant in bringing the action) is entirely irrelevant. But against this must be set two decisions that appear to run the other way: *Christie v Davey*[28] and *Hollywood Silver Fox Farm Ltd v Emmett*.[29]

The parties in *Christie v Davey* occupied neighbouring properties in a semi-detached dwelling, separated by only an (apparently thin) party wall. The female claimant taught music, and she, her children and some others played musical instruments in the property an estimated 17 hours per week.[30] This infuriated the defendant, who responded by producing 'a series of noises in his house whenever the playing of music was going on in the Plaintiffs' house – such as knocking on the party-wall, beating on trays, whistling, shrieking, and imitating what was being played in the Plaintiffs' house'.[31] The claimants sought an injunction to prevent this behaviour. The Court obliged.

The received understanding of this case has been heavily influenced by the way in which the defendant presented his arguments. For instance, he maintained that 'I have a perfect right to amuse myself on any musical instrument I may choose . . . What I do is simply for recreation's sake, and to perfect myself in my musical studies'.[32] In other words, the defendant was saying 'My use of my land is the same as the claimants' use of their land'.

Likewise, the defendant insisted, 'you say that I interfere with your clients' professional pursuits. Just so; this is simply reversing my complaint, and what is sauce for the goose is sauce for the gander'.[33] On this understanding, the activities of the

---

[25] ibid 594.
[26] ibid 598.
[27] *Allen v Flood* [1898] AC 1 (HL).
[28] *Christie v Davey* [1893] 1 Ch 316.
[29] *Hollywood Silver Fox Farm Ltd v Emmett* [1936] 2 KB 468 (CA).
[30] *Christie v Davey* [1893] 1 Ch 316, 322.
[31] ibid 318.
[32] ibid 319.
[33] ibid 320.

parties were of the same order. How, then, can one party's activity be legal and the other's illegal? The answer must be that the latter was motivated by malice. It is malice that turns an otherwise legal activity into an illegal one.

The key passage in North J's judgment is the following.

> In my opinion the noises which were made in the Defendant's house were not of a legitimate kind. They were what, to use the language of Lord Selborne in *Gaunt v. Fynney*, 'ought to be regarded as excessive and unreasonable.' I am satisfied that they were made deliberately and maliciously for the purpose of annoying the Plaintiffs. If what has taken place had occurred between two sets of persons both perfectly innocent, I should have taken an entirely different view of the case. But I am persuaded that what was done by the Defendant was done only for the purpose of annoyance, and in my opinion it was not a legitimate use of the Defendant's house to use it for the purpose of vexing and annoying his neighbours. . . . This being so, I am bound to give the Plaintiffs the relief which they ask.[34]

It is inevitable that a reader in the grip of the conventional view will interpret the passage in a way that fits the analysis above. According to this view, the parties' activities were of the same kind. However, because the defendant was motivated by malice, his activity was illegal. It was illegal because, as it was so motivated, it could not have been reasonable. Hence, we have the view that 'The law of private nuisance gives to each party a qualified privilege of causing harm to the other. When the activity of one party is motivated principally by malice, his privilege is at an end and he is liable for the damage he has caused'.[35]

Though it is an impeccable presentation of the conventional view, this account suffers from the fact that it is inconsistent with the decisions of the House of Lords in *Bradford v Pickles* and *Allen v Flood*. It is also committed to the mistaken view that the law of nuisance is focused on the reasonableness of the defendant's conduct. What is more, this reading of North J's judgment is inevitable only if we accept the conventional view. If we reject that view, then a quite different interpretation becomes available.

There is something very odd about the conventional reading of *Christie v Davey*. As we have seen, it holds that the parties were engaged in the same activity, though the defendant's malice meant that he became liable. But this is an extraordinary way of understanding the case. Before we became swamped in the legal doctrines, who but the shrewd defendant would have thought of claiming that the parties' activities were of the same kind? Recall what they were doing. The claimants and their guests were playing music. The defendant was 'knocking on the party-wall, beating on trays, whistling, shrieking, and imitating what was being played in the Plaintiffs' house'.[36] Same activities?

Now, in accordance with a point made in the first section of this chapter, it is possible to describe these activities in the same terms. They can both be described

---

[34] ibid 326–27 (citation omitted).
[35] WVH Rogers, *Winfield and Jolowicz on Tort*, 18th edn (London, Sweet & Maxwell, 2010) 725. See also J Murphy, *The Law of Nuisance* (Oxford, Oxford University Press, 2010) 45–47.
[36] *Christie v Davey* [1893] 1 Ch 316, 318.

as making noise, for instance. But while that description is accurate, the notion that it is appropriate, that it captures the nature of the dispute between the parties is, well, silly.

No better is the idea that it was the intention of the defendant that turned his action from a legal into an illegal one. This view can make sense only on the assumption that the defendant's actions can strongly be separated from his intentions. But that is impossible. To focus on the claimants for a moment, the reason that they were *playing* or *practising* music was not because of the movements of their bodies alone, but also because of their intentions. A person who falls on a keyboard and produces a noise that sounds like Beethoven's *Moonlight Sonata* is not playing the sonata. The content of an action is determined in part by the intention that produces it.[37]

In *Christie v Davey*, the defendant's malice was decisive. But it was decisive not because it turned a legal activity into an illegal one but because it revealed the nature of the activity that the defendant performed. The claimants' activity was playing music. The defendant's activity was banging on the walls etc in order to disrupt the claimants' playing music. It must be clear that the former is more fundamental than the latter.[38]

Reading North J's judgment again with these points in mind reveals that he espoused this, and not the conventional, view. He said that 'the noises which were made in the Defendant's house were not of a legitimate kind'.[39] Likewise, he claimed that they 'were what, to use the language of Lord Selborne in *Gaunt v Fynney*, "ought to be regarded as excessive and unreasonable"'.[40] The focus here is on the nature of the defendant's activity. The claim is that this activity is wrongful *per se*. The claim is not that an activity innocent *per se* is transformed into an illegal one because of the way in which it was motivated. The reason that the activity was wrongful was because the noises 'were made deliberately and maliciously for the purpose of annoying the Plaintiffs',[41] but that is because that intention partly constitutes the activity itself.

North J went on to say that 'If what has taken place had occurred between two sets of persons both perfectly innocent, I should have taken an entirely different view of the case',[42] but that does not support the conventional reading. His claim is not that absent malice the defendant would have escaped liability because his action innocent *per se* would then not have been rendered illegal by his malice. His claim is rather that absent malice the defendant's action would have been different. It would not have been banging on the walls etc in order to disrupt the

---

[37] It is the defendant's intentions-in-action that are in question here, not his prior intentions. Strictly, the intention-in-action does not produce the action, it is part of the action. For discussion, see JR Searle, *Intentionality: An Essay in the Philosophy of Mind* (Cambridge, Cambridge University Press, 1983).

[38] Though, strictly, it was not this that had to be balanced.

[39] *Christie v Davey* [1893] 1 Ch 316, 326.

[40] ibid (citation omitted).

[41] ibid.

[42] ibid 326–27.

claimants' playing music. There is no inconsistency, or even tension, between *Christie v Davey* and *Bradford v Pickles*.

The claimant in *Hollywood Silver Fox Farm Ltd v Emmett* operated a fox farm on his property and placed a sign advertising the farm. The defendant neighbour worried that this sign would suppress interest in his development and asked the claimant to remove it. The claimant refused. The defendant then threatened to fire guns on his property close to the claimant's breeding pens during the breeding season, guaranteeing the claimant that 'you will not raise a single cub',[43] reflecting the fact that 'Such noises may put a vixen off mating for [a] season, or, if the vixen has mated, may bring about a miscarriage of the litter, or, where she has whelped, may cause her to kill and devour her own young'.[44] This threat was carried out by the defendant's son, resulting in considerable loss to the claimant. The Court found that the defendant had committed a nuisance.

In an effort to defend himself, the defendant claimed that he had instructed his son to shoot at rabbits on his property as it was overrun.[45] This testimony was rejected by the judge, but it set up a certain, unfortunate pattern of thought according to which the correct description of the activity for which the defendant was responsible was, simply, shooting. The issue was whether the shooting was motivated by a desire to rid the defendant's property of pests or to damage the claimant. If it were the former, then the defendant would not be liable. If the latter, then liability followed. Given this line of thought, the move to the ideas that the defendant's liability turns on malice and that the fundamental issue is the reasonableness of the defendant's conduct is inexorable.

Unfortunately, for our purposes, the judgment in *Hollywood Silver Fox Farm Ltd v Emmett* is unhelpful. Though Macnaghten J considered the view that malice may turn a legal activity into an illegal one, he did not endorse or reject it or base his decision on the endorsement or rejection of it. The judge simply considered some of the relevant case law and concluded:

> In my opinion the decision of the House of Lords in *Bradford Corporation v. Pickles* has no bearing on such cases as this. I therefore think that the plaintiff is entitled to maintain this action. I think also that in the circumstances an injunction should be granted restraining the defendant from committing a nuisance by the discharge of firearms or the making of other loud noises in the vicinity of the Hollywood Silver Fox Farm during the breeding season . . . so as to alarm or disturb the foxes kept by the plaintiffs at the said farm, or otherwise to injure the plaintiff company.[46]

This is a conclusion without an argument. It supports neither the conventional view nor the one advanced here. Nevertheless, the judgment is quite consistent with the latter.

---

[43] *Hollywood Silver Fox Farm Ltd v Emmett* [1936] 2 KB 468 (CA), 470.
[44] ibid.
[45] ibid 470–71.
[46] ibid 476–77 (citation omitted).

Had the defendant's son been shooting at rabbits, then his action would have been perfectly legal. Why? Because shooting or otherwise removing rabbits was, in the circumstances, necessary in order to maintain one's land. If the defendant's son shot rabbits for this purpose and the claimant complained about that activity, then the appropriate description of that activity would have been, not simply shooting, but shooting in order to maintain the integrity of the land. In that case, the defendant's use would have been more fundamental than the claimant's. But as it was, the defendant's son was shooting in order to cause injury to the claimant. Given that this was what the claimant complained of, the appropriate description was not merely shooting, but shooting in order to damage the claimant. Here, it is clear that this use was less fundamental than the claimant's.

Again, before we became swamped in the legal doctrines, who would have thought of describing the defendant's activity simply as shooting a gun? Had you asked me 'Why was the claimant angry at the defendant?' and had I answered 'Because the defendant had fired a gun', you would have thought that I had misled you. This is not because my answer is inaccurate. It is not. It is because the answer is inappropriate.

Malice is significant. But its significance does not lie in turning a legal activity into an illegal one. Rather, malice can affect the nature of the activity in question. In this regard, there is nothing special about malice. It is simply one kind of intention that contributes to determining the nature of the defendant's activity. It is mistaken, then, to draw any special attention to the issue of malice. *Christie v Davey* and *Hollywood Silver Fox Farm Ltd v Emmett* were rightly decided, but that flows from the ordinary principles of the law of nuisance. It does not require any special doctrine related to malice.

B. The Decision in *Bradford v Pickles*

The apparent inconsistency between *Bradford v Pickles* on the one hand and *Christie v Davey* and *Hollywood Silver Fox Farm Ltd v Emmett* on the other has led to several previous attempts at reconciliation. Because it is useful for our understanding of this issue and of the law in general, I examine two of these now. Both attempt to retain the conventional understanding of the role of malice. For that reason, neither succeeds.

The first attempt argues as follows.

> It can be argued . . . that *Bradford v Pickles* can be distinguished from *Christie* and *Hollywood Silver Fox*, because the *Bradford* case involved interference by *obstruction* of a benefit, whilst *Christie* and *Hollywood Silver Fox* involved interference by the *emanation* of noise. It is important to remember that in an *obstruction* case a claimant can only sue if she can show that she has a right to receive the benefit that has been obstructed. Now – the claimants in *Bradford v Pickles* could not establish that they had a right to the water which the defendant obstructed. Thus it did not matter that the defendant had acted maliciously in obstructing the water. If the claimants had no right to receive the

water, they had no claim in private nuisance. So the House of Lords' broad statements about malice in *Bradford v Pickles* could be seen as being limited to situations where A unreasonably prevented something going onto B's land which B had no right to receive.[47]

The second attempt begins by rejecting the first. It argues that:

this argument, turning as it does on the claimant's alleged absolute right to extract water, is unconvincing. There is a no less absolute right to use one's land for lawful purposes even where a substantial interference is thereby caused to one's neighbour. What this attempt at reconciliation seems to miss is the fact that [the] focus [of the decision in *Bradford v Pickles*] was not so much on the *reasonableness* of the interference, but upon its *gravity*.[48]

This response misunderstands the position it criticises. The argument is that the claimant in *Bradford v Pickles* could not recover as its complaint related to something over which it had no right. The complaint, remember, was that the defendant prevented water from reaching its reservoir. But the claimant had no right that any water reached its reservoir. Therefore, the claimant had to fail. That analysis is correct. It has nothing to do with the extent to which rights are absolute. And it has nothing to do with reasonableness. The claim is not that the defendant escaped liability because, as he did not violate a right in the claimant, he acted reasonably. The claim is that the defendant escaped liability because he did not violate a right in the claimant, full stop.

Moreover, the focus in *Bradford v Pickles* was not on the gravity of the defendant's interference with the claimant. The claim is that the concern expressed in *Bradford v Pickles*:

was primarily with whether the act complained of has occasioned a substantial interference, since the notions of *factual* and *legal* interference are by no means coextensive . . . [The] point, then, was that, in the absence of substantial harm, any action in nuisance based on the malicious conduct of the defendant must fail. This accords with the principle *de minimis non tutor lex*, long since deemed to be applicable to nuisance cases, as we have already seen.[49]

This explanation of the decision in *Bradford v Pickles* is implausible. Certainly, the concepts of factual and legal interference are not coextensive. A legal interference is a violation of a right. There was no violation of a right and hence no legal interference in *Bradford v Pickles*. That was not because there was an interference that was *de minimis*. It was because there was, in this sense, no interference at all.

Alternatively, if one insists on a different understanding of legal interference, an understanding that focuses on the significance or 'gravity' of the impact on the claimant, then it is plain that the interference was not *de minimis*. The inability to secure the town's water supply was of utmost seriousness for a town as important

---

[47] NJ McBride and R Bagshaw, *Tort Law*, 2nd edn (Harlow, Pearson Education Ltd, 2005) 370–71 (citation omitted).
[48] J Murphy, *The Law of Nuisance* (Oxford, Oxford University Press, 2010) 46–47 (citation omitted).
[49] ibid 47 (citation omitted).

as the Bradford of the day.[50] Moreover, the suggestion is not reflected in any of their Lordships' judgments.

But this defence of the first view does not extend to its analysis of the treatment of malice in *Bradford v Pickles*. The claim that 'the House of Lords' broad statements about malice in *Bradford v Pickles* could be seen as being limited to situations where A unreasonably prevented something going onto B's land which B had no right to receive' cannot be accepted.[51] The statements are too broad.

It is not *Bradford v Pickles* that must be limited so as to fit with *Christie v Davey* and *Hollywood Silver Fox Farm Ltd v Emmett*. It is our understanding of the last two cases that must be revised.

An important consequence of this discussion is that it shows that *Langford Properties Ltd v Surrey CC*[52] is wrongly decided.[53] The defendants caused a subsidence on the claimant's land as a result of pumping away underground water. The Court held that the decision in *Bradford v Pickles* entailed that there could be no liability. That is not so. In *Bradford v Pickles*, the claimant's complaint was that the defendant deprived him of water to which it had no right. In *Langford Properties*, on the other hand, the complaint is that the claimant's land is being damaged. Naturally, that implicates the claimant's rights.

---

[50] D Campbell, 'Gathering the Water: Abuse of Rights After the Recognition of Government Failure' (2010) 6 *Journal of Jurisprudence* 487.

[51] NJ McBride and R Bagshaw, *Tort Law*, 2nd edn (Harlow, Pearson Education Ltd, 2005) 370–71 (citation omitted).

[52] *Langford Properties Ltd v Surrey CC* [1970] 1 WLR 161.

[53] See also *Stevens v Anglia Water Authority* [1987] 1 WLR 1381, in which, perhaps as a result of *Langford Properties*, nuisance was not pleaded.

6

Coming to a Nuisance

This chapter examines the issue of coming to a nuisance. The basic idea is that it is, as it were, no defence to a claim in nuisance that the defendant was performing the activity complained of before the claimant arrived, even if the claimant knew about the defendant's activity before arriving.

This principle has attracted a fair amount of criticism. For instance, it has been alleged that it is inconsistent with the principle behind the defence of *volenti non fit injuria* that operates in the law of negligence.[1] Imagine, for instance, that the claimant chooses to purchase a house next to a restaurant that has been operating for many years and then complains about the smell of the cooking. As the claimant knew about the presence of the restaurant and the smell before purchasing the house, it may seem unfair to permit the claimant to succeed in a nuisance claim against the defendant. One also frequently hears complaints of this kind from non-lawyers.

Against these criticisms, this chapter demonstrates that the law has good reasons for adopting the approach that it takes. These reasons are largely enunciated in the leading cases themselves, though they are now unfortunately often ignored.

I begin, then, by examining some of these cases. Not all of the judgments in them are consistent with the view advanced here. Nevertheless, they have much to teach us about the nature of this issue.

I. *Bliss v Hall*[2]

The defendant in *Bliss v Hall* operated a candle-making business on land neighbouring the claimant's. The defendant, who was the first occupier in the district,[3] had been in business three years before the claimant occupied his land. The claimant successfully complained of the smell the defendant created. In response to the argument that the claimant should fail because he came to the nuisance, Tindal CJ replied, 'That is no answer to the complaint in the declaration; for the Plaintiff

---

[1] T Weir, *An Introduction to Tort Law*, 2nd edn (Oxford, Oxford University Press, 2006) 163.
[2] *Bliss v Hall* (1838) 4 Bing (NC) 183, 132 ER 758.
[3] ibid 759.

came to the house he occupies with all the rights which the common law affords, and one of them is, a right to wholesome air'.[4]

This puts paid to the argument that a claimant who comes to a nuisance has impliedly consented to the continuance of that nuisance. That argument is no more persuasive than the claim that, knowing that people frequently drive carelessly, one consents to careless driving when one chooses to go out on the street.[5]

In the course of their judgments, Tindal CJ, Park and Vaughan JJ implied that the argument under examination – that the claimant came to the nuisance – is a mistaken way of putting a related and genuinely relevant argument: that the defendant possessed a 'prescriptive right' to conduct his business.[6] This is the idea that, had the defendant been conducting his activity for a sufficient length of time, he might have acquired an easement by prescription that would have permitted him to continue. We must pause for a moment to examine this notion.

An easement is a right to the use of another's property. The most common example is a right of way: a right of access over another's land. An easement of this kind confers an entitlement to perform an act that would otherwise constitute a trespass. Similarly, easements can generate entitlements to act in ways that would otherwise be nuisances. Easements are property rights and, in the language of the law, they run with the land. So, if I have a right of way over someone's land, that right of way belongs to my land so that if I sell my land to you, you gain the right of way.

Easements can be acquired by prescription. The general principle is that if a party acquiesces for a certain length of time in the commission of a legal wrong by another, the right held by the party becomes an entitlement in the other. So, for instance, if I trespass on your property for the relevant length of time and you acquiesce in my doing so, your right to prevent me can be transformed into an entitlement in me to enter your land. That entitlement would be an easement. The relevant period for prescription in the cases we discuss is 20 years.

Hence, had the defendant in *Bliss v Hall* been operating for 20 years before the claimant complained, it might have been possible for him to have argued that he had obtained an easement to create the smell by prescription. But as he had been operating for only three years, that was not a possibility.

II. *Sturges v Bridgman*[7]

The plaintiff physician in *Sturges v Bridgman* first occupied his property, which he used as a surgery, in 1865. The defendant was a confectioner who had installed

---

[4] ibid.
[5] For analysis in relation to the *volenti* defence, see A Beever, *Rediscovering the Law of Negligence* (Oxford, Hart, 2007) 345–72.
[6] *Bliss v Hall* (1838) 4 Bing (NC) 183, 132 ER 758, 759 (Tindal CJ).
[7] *Sturges v Bridgman* (1879) 11 Ch D 852 (CA).

two mechanical mortars and pestles along the party wall between his and the claimant's property. For more than 60 years, this caused no inconvenience. In particular, the claimant and those who occupied his property were not disturbed by the operation of the mortar and pestles because the party wall did not connect with the claimant's buildings. However, in 1873 the claimant constructed a new consulting room in what was formerly his garden, so that only the party wall stood between the room and the defendant's mortars and pestles. Given the new construction, the vibrations from the machinery passed into the claimant's property and caused the noise of which he complained. So convinced was the Court that it was irrelevant that the claimant had come to the nuisance that it did not consider the issue for even a moment.

As in *Bliss v Hall*, however, the Court also examined whether the length of the defendant's activity created an easement. As the defendant in *Sturges v Bridgman* had been operating his equipment for over 60 years, it seemed that he could easily satisfy the period of prescription. But the idea that the defendant had acquired an easement was emphatically rejected by the Court.

> Consent or acquiescence of the owner of the servient tenement lies at the root of prescription, and of the fiction of a lost grant, and hence the acts or user, which go to the proof of either the one or the other, must be, in the language of the civil law, *nec vi nec clam nec precario*; for a man cannot, as a general rule, be said to consent to or acquiesce in the acquisition by his neighbour of an easement through an enjoyment of which he has no knowledge, actual or constructive, or which he contests and endeavours to interrupt, or which he temporarily licenses. It is a mere extension of the same notion, or rather it is a principle into which by strict analysis it may be resolved, to hold, that an enjoyment which a man cannot prevent raises no presumption of consent or acquiescence.[8]

One acquiesces in a legal wrong only if a wrong is being committed. As the operation of the defendant's machinery caused no nuisance until the claimant built his consulting room, there was no legal wrong committed until that point, nothing of which the claimant could complain and so no acquiescence. When the consulting room was built, a nuisance came into existence, but soon after that point, and well before the prescription period in relation to the noise had passed, the claimant complained. There was never any acquiescence. Accordingly, there could be no easement.

III. *Miller v Jackson*[9]

The defendants ran a cricket club with a ground on which cricket had been played for over 70 years. The land surrounding the ground had until recently been farmland. Though balls were sometimes struck onto this land and players entered the

---

[8] ibid 963.
[9] *Miller v Jackson* [1977] QB 966 (CA).

land to regain the balls, no one complained. As Lord Denning MR put it, 'The animals did not mind the cricket'.[10] However, the land had been developed and a parcel of it was sold to the claimants. They did mind the cricket. Balls were hit onto their land, frightening them, exposing them to physical danger and occasionally damaging their house. They sued, seeking an injunction to prevent cricket being played.

We are not here interested in what is perhaps the most interesting aspect of the case: the decision as to whether or not to award an injunction. That is examined in chapter twelve. We are focused now only on the existence of a nuisance.

In that regard, the Court of Appeal, by a majority, decided in line with *Bliss v Hall* and *Sturges v Bridgman* that the defendant was committing a nuisance even though the claimant had come to it. Lord Denning, however, dissented on this issue. It is his judgment that we examine here.

First, Lord Denning distinguished *Sturges v Bridgman* by arguing that this case 'turned on the old law about easements and prescriptions, and so forth'.[11] That claim is misleading. The suggestion that *Sturges v Bridgman* supports the position of the claimants in *Miller v Jackson* only because of the earlier Court's treatment of easements and prescriptions is wrong. The Court in *Sturges v Bridgman* ruled that no easement was present in that case, exactly the conclusion reached by Lord Denning in *Miller v Jackson*.[12] *Contra* Lord Denning, the cases are parallel.

Having fended off the challenge posed by precedent, Lord Denning then turned to the facts of the case. Applying the view that the existence of a nuisance is determined in accordance with the reasonableness of the defendant's behaviour,[13] his Lordship asked:

> Is the use by the cricket club of this ground for playing cricket a reasonable use of it? To my mind it is a most reasonable use. Just consider the circumstances. For over 70 years the game of cricket has been played on this ground to the great benefit of the community as a whole, and to the injury of none. No one could suggest that it was a nuisance to the neighbouring owners simply because an enthusiastic batsman occasionally hit a ball out of the ground for six to the approval of the admiring onlookers. Then I would ask: does it suddenly become a nuisance because one of the neighbours chooses to build a house on the very edge of the ground – in such a position that it may well be struck by the ball on the rare occasion when there is a hit for six? To my mind the answer is plainly No. The building of the house does not convert the playing of cricket into a nuisance when it was not so before. If and in so far as any damage is caused to the house or anyone in it, it is because of the position in which it was built. Suppose that the house had not been built by a developer, but by a private owner. He would be in much the same position as the farmer who previously put his cows in the field. He could not complain if a batsman hit a six out of the ground, and by a million to one chance it struck a cow or even the farmer himself. He would be in no better position than a spectator at Lord's or the Oval or at a motor rally.[14]

[10] ibid 976.
[11] *Sturges v Bridgman* (1879) 11 Ch D 852 (CA), 981.
[12] *Miller v Jackson* [1977] QB 966 (CA), 978–79.
[13] ibid 980.
[14] ibid 980–81.

This crucial passage makes for good rhetoric, but as an argument it is desperately flawed. None of its important claims can be accepted.

The argument is built on the idea that no nuisance was being committed before the houses were built and hence no nuisance can have been committed when they were built. This argument needs to be examined in depth.

First, though we cannot be sure, the way the facts are presented suggests that the farmer, expressly or impliedly, permitted the activities in question. If so, then it is true that the defendant was not committing a legal wrong before the houses were built. But that is because the defendant had a licence to perform the activities. Unlike easements, licences do not run with the land. Thus, if this is why the defendant was not originally committing a nuisance, it gives no reason to hold that no nuisance occurred after the houses were built. If I permit my neighbour to cross my land, that does not mean that you must also when I sell my land to you. When the land is mine, the neighbour can cross because I have given permission. When the land is yours, she can cross only if you give yours.

This point is elementary. It is impossible to believe that Lord Denning did not understand it. Accordingly, his position must rather have been that the defendant was committing no nuisance before the houses were built for reasons other than the farmer's consent.

The problem now is that, if we put aside the possibility that the farmer consented, then we have no reason to think that there was no nuisance before the houses were built. Balls were being hit into the farmer's land and fielders were entering the land to retrieve them. That looks for all the world to constitute a nuisance on the part of the defendant.[15] Certainly, we are told, no one complained about this. But that does not prove (on its own, see VI) that the club had not been committing a nuisance for the whole 70 years it had been in existence. That 'The animals [and the farmer] did not mind the cricket' shows only that the animals and the farmer did not mind the nuisance that was being committed.[16] It is no more than rhetoric to maintain that 'No one could suggest that it was a nuisance to the neighbouring owners simply because an enthusiastic batsman occasionally hit a ball out of the ground for six to the approval of the admiring onlookers'.

Moreover, if we again ignore the possibility that the farmer consented to the defendant's activities, there is no reason to think that the farmer would have had no cause of action had he or his cows been injured by a ball.

In this regard, Lord Denning suggested that had the farmer or his cows been damaged, it would have been 'by a million to one chance'. This recalls the decision of the House of Lords in *Bolton v Stone*,[17] a case that must be outlined now.

---

[15] cf *Matheson v Northcote College* [1975] 2 NZLR 106 (SC).

[16] Here, I think, we hear an echo of the modern law's unfortunate obsession with loss. The idea is that a farmer who does not mind the activities in question cannot have suffered a loss and so cannot have been wronged. This is a mistake. A trespass is a wrong, even if it causes no loss. It is a wrong even if the landowner is not bothered. Consent generates a licence. But not being bothered is not the same as giving consent.

[17] *Bolton v Stone* [1951] AC 850 (HL).

The claimant was struck by a cricket ball while walking on a little-used road adjacent to the defendant's cricket ground. The House of Lords ruled that, given the 'infinitesimal'[18] risk created by the defendant, he was not liable in negligence for the claimant's injuries as he did not fall below the standard of care.[19] In speaking of the 'million to one chance' of the farmer or his cows being struck, Lord Denning sought to link the decision of the House of Lords in *Bolton v Stone* to the facts in *Miller v Jackson*, the argument being: if the claimant in *Bolton v Stone* failed to recover for the materialisation of a million to one chance, then the farmer in this hypothetical must also.

Again, this is misleading. First, the House of Lords decided in *Bolton v Stone* that, as the risk created by the defendant was only 'infinitesimal', the defendant could not have been *negligent* for creating it. It follows that, if the risk in our hypothetical would have been similarly small, then the defendant also could not have been negligent vis-à-vis the farmer. That means that the defendant could not be liable in the tort of negligence. But it does not follow from this that the defendant could not be liable in the tort of private nuisance. Though Lord Denning suggested that nuisance is not distinguishable from negligence,[20] that is surely wrong.

In reply, one might argue as follows: the claimant in *Bolton v Stone* was unable to recover in the law of negligence for the reasons stated. But she was also unable to recover in the law of private nuisance. Given that, it follows that the farmer in our hypothetical must have no cause of action. This, perhaps, is the point of the appeal to 'a spectator at Lord's or the Oval or at a motor rally'. But the reason these individuals cannot sue in private nuisance is because their use and enjoyment of their land has not been invaded. The claimant in *Bolton v Stone* was in the same position. She was not on her land when she was struck by the ball. Thus, the only possible nuisance in her case was public, not private, nuisance. The farmer in our hypothetical is in an entirely different position.

In conclusion, the premise of Lord Denning's argument – that the farmer would have had no cause of action – seems false.

What is more, even if no nuisance were committed before the houses were built, it would not follow that there could be none after the houses were constructed. It is perfectly legal for me to shoot a gun at a target in a shooting range, but if someone steps in front of me I am not permitted to continue. Similarly, if a parcel of land is unowned, I commit no wrong by walking on it; but if it then becomes owned, walking on the land is 'suddenly' 'converted' into a trespass. Likewise if an owner who consented to my being on the land sold the property to a person who had not consented, I now commit a trespass. Lord Denning's argument has no force.

---

[18] *Overseas Tankship (UK) Ltd v Morts Dock & Engineering Co Ltd (The Wagon Mound, No 2)* [1967] AC 617 (PC), 666.

[19] The House of Lords also refused to find the defendant liable in public nuisance. That issue is examined in ch 8.

[20] *Miller v Jackson* [1977] QB 966 (CA), 979.

Finally, the suggestion that it is obvious that there would have been no nuisance had the claimant's house been built by a private owner is false. Frankly, it makes no difference who built the house.

We are left, then, with only one claim: that the fact that the club had been in operation for 70 years meant that the defendant's behaviour was reasonable and therefore could not constitute a nuisance. Enough has been said about the reliance on reasonableness already. The length of time is examined in VI below.

IV. *Kennaway v Thompson*[21]

The claimant in *Kennaway v Thompson* built a house on land neighbouring a lake on which a motor-boat racing club had been racing for about 10 years. She complained of the noise created by the boats. The Court of Appeal found for the claimant without expressing any temptation to follow Lord Denning's approach in *Miller v Jackson*. The discussion in *Kennaway v Thompson* focused almost entirely on the issue of the remedy; it was all but taken for granted that it made no difference to liability that the claimant came to the nuisance. As far as this issue is concerned, then, Lord Denning's judgment in *Miller v Jackson* must be regarded as a dead letter. The question now is Why?

V. Why 'Who Got There First?' Does Not Matter

Another way of expressing the idea that coming to a nuisance is not a defence is to say that, as far as the law of nuisance is concerned, it does not matter who got there first. Sometimes, however, it does matter who got there first. What we need to know, then, is why it matters when it does and why it does not when it does not.

'Who got there first?' matters when the issue concerns a claim to previously unowned property. This is captured most prominently by the doctrine of original or first possession, according to which the first possessor of a piece of property holds rights in it because she possessed it before anyone else. In these circumstances, then, 'Who got there first?' matters because, in getting there first, the first possessor acquired rights that are no longer available to latecomers.

But the law of nuisance is not concerned with situations of that kind. It deals with cases in which all the relevant property is owned. In *Miller v Jackson*, for instance, the properties in question were owned by the parties, an ownership that was not in question. The fact that the defendant got to his property before the claimant got to hers, then, is irrelevant.

[21] *Kennaway v Thompson* [1981] QB 88 (CA).

The 'defence' in question has intuitive appeal because we are inclined to confuse these two situations. When the issue concerns unowned land, the 'defence' can be appropriate. In raising the 'defence', the defendant says, as it were, 'I was here first and so I acquired rights in land to which no one before had rights.' That 'defence' is recognised by the law of property. But in the cases we are examining, the 'defence' cannot be appropriate. To hold otherwise would be to allow the defendant to assert, 'I was here first and so I acquired rights in land to which you or another already had rights, such that my acquisition was at the expense of your or another's rights'. Such acquisition cannot occur without the consent of the other party.

In *Sturges v Bridgman*, Thesiger LJ considered the following hypothetical.

> The case also is put of a blacksmith's forge built away from all habitations, but to which, in course of time, habitations approach . . . It would be on the one hand in a very high degree unreasonable and undesirable that there should be a right of action for acts which are not in the present condition of the adjoining land, and possibly never will be any annoyance or inconvenience to either its owner or occupier; and it would be on the other hand in an equally degree unjust, and, from a public point of view, inexpedient that the use and value of the adjoining land should, for all time and under all circumstances, be restricted and diminished by reason of the continuance of acts incapable of physical interruption, and which the law gives no power to prevent. The smith in the case supposed might protect himself by taking a sufficient curtilage to ensure what he does from being at any time an annoyance to his neighbour, but the neighbour himself would be powerless in the matter.[22]

If we put aside the apparent appeal to public policy – likely to be misconstrued when viewed through modern eyes in any case – we can see that this argument hits the nail right on the head. If coming to a nuisance was a defence, then the defence would give the defendant control over land that is owned by another. But that control must be gained through the law of property and contract. Let me explain.

First, take the case of the blacksmith where we assume that the surrounding land is at first owned by the future occupants, though they have yet to move in. Here, if the fact that the defendant blacksmith made noise before the claimants moved in entailed that the defendant was able to continue, then the result would be that the blacksmith gained control over the claimants' land. That control would be the entitlement to make noise affecting the land that would otherwise constitute a nuisance. But from where did this entitlement come? It did not come from the consent of the claimants. The result would be a unilateral confiscation of the claimants' rights.

The situation is identical if the land surrounding the claimants was originally owned by a third party. Here again, recognition of the defence would permit the defendant to acquire a right in the land of the third party, and subsequently of the claimants', to which neither the third party nor the claimants had consented. It would amount to unilateral confiscation.

---

[22] *Sturges v Bridgman* (1879) 11 Ch D 852 (CA), 865–66.

This hypothetical fits the facts in *Miller v Jackson*.[23] And if there could be any doubt about the accuracy of what is being claimed here, it ought to be noted that Lord Denning all but celebrated the fact that his decision had just these consequences.

> If he finds that he does not like [cricket being played, the claimant] ought, when cricket is played, to sit on the other side of the house or in the front garden, or go out: or take advantage of the offers the club have made to him of fitting unbreakable glass, and so forth. Or, if he does not like that, he ought to sell his house and move elsewhere.[24]

The reasoning holds even in circumstances in which the land in question is originally unowned. Take now the case of the blacksmith but assume that the surrounding land is at first unowned and is acquired by the claimants only after the defendant has begun his work. Here, it is possible for the defendant to acquire rights over the surrounding land without the consent of the claimants, but only *before* they come to own the land. Moreover, if that were to happen, the acquisition would be affected by the law of property and not by the back door via a defence to the law of nuisance. That must be the case, as the law of nuisance can have no application before the surrounding land is owned, there being no possible nuisance in such circumstances.

Accordingly, though it may seem 'reasonable', it would in fact be most unjust to allow a defence of coming to a nuisance. It would allow the defendant unilaterally to gain control over land that is not his property. That would violate commutative justice.

VI. *Miller v Jackson* Revisited

In *Miller v Jackson*, Lord Denning argued that it followed from the fact that cricket had been played at the defendant's ground for over 70 years that the defendant ought to be allowed to continue. Despite what has been said above, this claim can be defended.

Though the relevant facts are unclear, the following again assumes that the farmer had not given the cricketers a licence to hit balls into or to enter his land. In fact, though we know that he did not complain about these activities, we do not know whether he expressly permitted them or simply chose not to exercise his right to have them prevented. For the sake of our discussion, as we have seen, we must assume the latter.

As we saw, Lord Denning insisted that no nuisance was committed before the surrounding houses were built and that this showed that no nuisance could have

---

[23] Though not perfectly as the land in question in that case was, in fact, originally owned by the same third party. This raised the issue of derogation from grant, but that is not relevant here.

[24] *Miller v Jackson* [1977] QB 966 (CA), 981.

occurred when the houses were built. We saw that this argument is unsound, both because it begins with a false premise and is invalid. With special relevance here, it was suggested that the defendant was guilty of a nuisance for all of the 70 years of its existence, though that nuisance did not bother the farmer or his animals. What is more, on the assumption we are making, it is quite clear that the cricketers committed repeated acts of trespass when they hit balls into and entered the farmer's land to retrieve the balls without the farmer's consent. The fact that the farmer did not complain about this activity does not in any way alter this fact.

But these considerations support the contention that, on the assumption outlined above, the cricket club had obtained an easement by prescription to hit balls onto the land in question and also to retrieve them. In other words, although Lord Denning's argument was 'There was no nuisance originally and so there can be no nuisance now', it ought to have been 'There was a nuisance originally and so there can be none now'.

Unfortunately, however, Lord Denning had closed off that possibility when he insisted that the defendant 'could not claim an easement because there is no such easement known to the law as a right to hit cricket balls into your neighbour's land'.[25] But that is surely an overly narrow description of the club's activities. For 70 years, balls had been hit onto the land in question and cricketers had entered that land to retrieve the balls. These were constant acts of nuisance and trespass in which the farmer acquiesced. It was surely possible, therefore, to argue that the cricket club had acquired what is sometimes called an ingress/egress easement. It is worth noting that recognising such an easement would certainly have caused less, if any, upheaval to the law of property than Lord Denning's suggested reforms would have caused the law of nuisance.

It is also important to note that the creation of an easement by prescription is entirely consistent with the argument above. I have insisted that the defendant can obtain control over the claimant's land only through the law of property and contract (that is, through consent). That is the case here too. As Thesiger LJ said in *Sturges v Bridgman*, 'Consent or acquiescence of the owner of the servient tenement lies at the root of prescription'.[26] When an easement is obtained through prescription, it arises via the operation of the law of property acting on the implicit consent of the servient tenement holder. Hence, the ability to obtain an easement through prescription in no way constitutes an exception to the principle that underlies the rule that coming to a nuisance constitutes no defence.

---

[25] ibid 978.
[26] *Sturges v Bridgman* (1879) 11 Ch D 852 (CA), 863.

7

A Nuisance Coming to You

The previous chapter examined the law's response to a claimant who occupies property already subject to the nuisance of which she complains. This chapter explores the law's response to the opposing set of circumstances: to when the nuisance complained of enters or is created on the defendant's land by something or someone for whom the defendant is not responsible. The law has experienced great difficulty dealing with situations of this kind, in no small part because the basis of liability in the tort in general has been so misunderstood. Accordingly, we must begin by examining the conventional understanding of this area of the law.

I. Three Views

Views about this area of the law can be divided into three categories that we may label traditional, intermediate and modern.

The traditional view held that, in general, one could not be liable for a nuisance that came to one. However, if a nuisance came to one and one understood the risk posed to one's neighbour, one acquired an obligation to inform one's neighbour of the risk and – should one not wish to eliminate the risk oneself – to permit the neighbour to access one's land to abate the nuisance.[1]

The intermediate view, witnessed in cases such as *Goldman v Hargrave*,[2] holds that when a nuisance comes to one, one is under a duty to act reasonably in eliminating the attached risk. Thus, according to this approach, if one fails to act reasonably in eliminating the risk, one can be liable. This suggests that the tort of nuisance has at least two parts, one strict and one fault-based: the strict form applying when the defendant created the event or activity complained of and the fault-based pertaining when the event or activity was created by another.[3]

More recently, the idea has arisen that, to a degree still under debate, the entire law of nuisance is fault-based, though the extent of fault required for liability

---

[1] For a clear statement, though not endorsement, see *Leakey v National Trust* [1980] 1 QB 485 (CA), 528.

[2] *Goldman v Hargrave* [1967] 1 AC 645 (PC).

[3] S Deakin, A Johnston and B Markesinis, *Markesinis and Deakin's Tort Law*, 6th edn (Oxford, Clarendon Press, 2008) 526.

depends on the circumstances of the case.[4] Here, it is thought, the law places more emphasis on fault when the nuisance came to the defendant than when the nuisance was created by the defendant. We may describe this as the modern view.

The following chapter examines the role of fault in the law of nuisance. Accordingly, the distinction between the intermediate and modern approaches is relevant there. This chapter examines fault only with respect to the issue of a nuisance coming to you. It argues that there should be no special approach adopted when the nuisance comes to a defendant; that the law of nuisance should be no more or less strict here than it is elsewhere. Hence, it argues against the idea that the law should be understood to come in the two forms discussed above.

The strategy adopted is the following. First, we examine cases that emanate from the traditional approach. Second, we explore the move to the intermediate and modern approaches in more recent case law. For convenience, we can refer to this as constituting the contemporary view. Third, criticisms of the contemporary view are examined. Fourth, an alternative approach is presented that reconciles the results of the contemporary approach with the ratios of the traditional. In other words, though it is slightly inaccurate to put it this way, we see that the traditional approach generated the wrong results for the right reasons while the contemporary approach generates the right results for the wrong reasons.

II. The Traditional Law

This section examines some of the cases that constitute the traditional view. By no means all the cases are examined, nor necessarily what are considered to be the leading ones. But these cases are important because, as we see in VI.A, they help to provide us with the key to understanding this area of the law.[5]

The defendant in *Giles v Walker*[6] cultivated land that had originally been forest. After the land had been cultivated, thistles grew up on it. Because the defendant did not control the thistles, they seeded and spread to the claimant's land. The claimant sued but failed. Lord Coleridge CJ maintained, 'I never heard of such an action as this. There can be no duty as between adjoining occupiers to cut the thistles, which are the natural growth of the soil.'[7]

The defendant in *Sparke v Osborne*[8] failed to control the noxious weed prickly pear, which spread to the claimant's property. Though the weed is exotic to Australia, the High Court treated it as a natural growth as it had long existed

---

[4] See, eg, ibid 526–28. Support for this view is said to be found in, eg, *Cambridge Water Co v Eastern Counties Leather plc* [1994] 2 AC 264 (HL), 300.

[5] Not coincidentally, all of these cases were examined in *French v Auckland City Corp* [1974] 1 NZLR 340 (SC).

[6] *Giles v Walker* (1890) 24 QBD 656.

[7] ibid 657.

[8] *Sparke v Osborne* (1908) 7 CLR 51 (HCA).

there. Again, the claimant failed. Griffith CJ said, 'I can find no trace in the law of any doctrine that would authorize the Court to say that the owner of land afflicted by nature with a curse of this sort is under any liability to his neighbour because he is unable to keep it down'.[9] Similarly, Higgins J maintained:

> I know of no duty imposed by the British common law apart from such statutory duty as Parliament may impose – on a landowner to do anything with his land, or with what naturally grows on his land, in the interest of either his neighbour or himself. If he use the land, he must so use it as not thereby to injure his neighbours: *sic utere tuo ut alienum non laedas*. But if he leave it unused, and if thereby his neighbours suffer, he is not responsible. So long as he does nothing with it, he is safe. It is not he who injures the neighbour – it is Nature; and he is not responsible for Nature's doings.[10]

In *Molloy v Drummond*,[11] nuts, leaves and twigs from a gum tree growing on the defendant's land blew onto the claimant's roof, making a noise and blocking his downpipes. The claimant failed because the tree appeared to have been 'naturally upon the land' and 'There is no obligation upon an owner to prevent damage arising from the effect of natural agencies operating upon his land in its ordinary or natural state'.[12]

The defendant in *Seligman v Docker*[13] attracted a large number of pheasants onto his land, which ate the claimant's crops. Romer J ruled that the defendant was not liable, relying on the fact that the birds were 'feræ naturæ' and the principle in *Giles v Walker*.[14]

In *Neath Rural District Council v Williams*,[15] water from a stream that passed over the defendant's land flooded the claimants' properties because of an obstruction. Lord Goddard CJ maintained that 'the common law of England has never imposed liabilities upon landowners for anything which happens to their land in the natural course of affairs if the land is used naturally'.[16]

These cases form a clear line of authority. As indicated above, however, they have been overtaken by contemporary developments. We turn to those now.

III. The Slide to Negligence

The claimants in *Job Edwards Ltd v The Company of Proprietors of the Birmingham Navigations*[17] purchased land for mining but found it to be worthless for that

---

[9] ibid 59–60.
[10] ibid 75.
[11] *Molloy v Drummond* [1939] NZLR 499 (SC).
[12] ibid 503.
[13] *Seligman v Docker* [1949] Ch 53.
[14] ibid 66.
[15] *Neath Rural District Council v Williams* [1951] 1 KB 115.
[16] ibid 122.
[17] *Job Edwards Ltd v Birmingham Navigations Proprietors* [1924] 1 KB 341 (CA).

purpose. They left it unused and unoccupied. After some time, a third person dumped refuse on the land without the claimant's permission. This continued for some years. In 1920, the refuse caught fire and, as the fire was in danger of spreading to the defendant's land and causing significant damage, the parties agreed that the defendant would enter the claimant's land in order to extinguish the fire and that the cost of doing so would be split equally without prejudice to either party's legal position. The claimants attempted to recover their expense by gaining a declaration that they would not have been liable to pay for the costs of extinguishing the fire or of the fire had it spread to the defendant's land. The Court of Appeal decided 2-1 in favour of the claimants. However, the case is now best known for Scrutton LJ's influential dissent. That is examined now.

First, Scrutton LJ maintained that if a nuisance comes to a defendant, then the defendant can be liable only if she continued the nuisance. He further held that a defendant continues a nuisance if she knows about the attached risk to her neighbour and fails to take reasonable care in abating that risk.[18] In this case, Scrutton LJ maintained that, as the defendant may have known of the presence of refuse on his land and hence have been aware of the risk of fire, the defendant may have continued the risk. Accordingly, Scrutton LJ would have ordered a new trial.

This reflects the contemporary view outlined above. The references to risk and reasonable care call to mind concerns at the heart of the law of negligence. Moreover, Scrutton LJ specifically linked his position to that area of the law.

> I appreciate that to get negligence you must have a duty to be careful, but I think on principle that a landowner has a duty to take reasonable care not to allow his land to remain a receptacle for a thing which may, if not rendered harmless, cause damage to his neighbours.[19]

Though Scrutton LJ's view did not win the day in *Job Edwards*, the House of Lords adopted his conclusions in *Sedleigh-Denfield v O'Callaghan*.[20]

A trespasser laid a pipe for carrying away rainwater on the defendant's land and placed a grating over the pipe in a place that left the pipe prone to blocking. This posed a risk of flooding to the claimant's property. Although the defendant was in no way responsible for the laying of the pipe or the placement of the grating, he subsequently learnt of their existence. He did not replace the grating and hence did not eradicate the risk. During a heavy rainstorm, the pipe became blocked and the claimant's property was flooded and damaged as a result. He sued the defendant in nuisance.

The House of Lords allowed the claim. The reasoning of the Court must be examined in detail later, but suffice it to say that the Court ruled that because the defendant knew of the pipe and grating and of the risk to the claimant, the defendant had continued and adopted the nuisance. Because of this, the defendant was obliged to eliminate the risk. As he had not done so, he was liable.

---

[18] ibid 357.
[19] ibid 358.
[20] *Sedleigh-Denfield v O'Callaghan* [1940] AC 880 (HL).

In *Goldman v Hargrave*,[21] a tree on the defendant's land was struck by lightning and caught fire. As it was impossible to extinguish the fire while the tree was standing, the defendant informed the authorities and, while waiting for the arrival of a tree feller, cleared a space around the tree and doused it with water. The tree was cut down the next day, but the defendant did not do anything more to stop the fire spreading, believing that the fire would burn itself out. A few days later, the weather changed and the fire spread, damaging the claimants' property. The trial judge ruled that the fire could have been extinguished after the tree had been cut down if water had been sprayed onto it and that it was negligent for the defendant not to have done so.

The judgment of the Privy Council was given by Lord Wilberforce. Importantly, he said that 'Their Lordships propose to deal with these issues . . . without attempting to answer the disputable question whether if responsibility is established it should be brought under the heading of nuisance or placed in a separate category' such as the law of negligence.[22] Because of this, it is difficult to know what the intentions of the judges in *Goldman v Hargrave* were regarding the law of nuisance, if they had any clear intentions at all. Nevertheless, *Goldman v Hargrave* is now widely understood to be a nuisance case, or at least to have affected that area of the law.[23] In particular, the courts in the nuisance cases examined below took their cue in part from *Goldman v Hargrave*. Given that, it is appropriate to treat the case at least as if it were decided in the law of nuisance.

In that light, the following claim is highly significant. 'The issue is . . . whether in such a case [that is, when the nuisance comes to the defendant's land] the occupier is guilty of legal negligence, which involves the issue whether he is under a duty of care, and, if so, what is the scope of that duty.'[24] This clearly aligns this element of the law of nuisance with the law of negligence. Not only are we talking about negligence, ie the failure to observe the standard of care, we are also exploring the duty of care and the scope of that duty, concerns at the heart of the law of negligence.[25]

In *Goldman v Hargrave*, the Privy Council held that in cutting down the tree, the defendant created a 'fresh risk' of injury to the claimant that he negligently failed to eliminate,[26] that the risk materialised and hence that the defendant was liable.

Lord Wilberforce also argued that we require:

some definition of the scope of [the defendant's] duty. How far does it go? What is the standard of the effort required? What is the position as regards expenditure? It is not enough to say merely that these must be 'reasonable,' since what is reasonable to one man may be very unreasonable, and indeed ruinous, to another: the law must take

---

[21] *Goldman v Hargrave* [1967] 1 AC 645 (PC).

[22] ibid 656.

[23] Compare J Murphy, *The Law of Nuisance* (Oxford, Oxford University Press, 2010) 17.

[24] *Goldman v Hargrave* [1967] 1 AC 645 (PC), 656.

[25] See also ibid 662.

[26] ibid 656.

account of the fact that the occupier on whom the duty is cast has, *ex hypothesi*, had this hazard thrust upon him through no seeking or fault of his own. His interest, and his resources, whether physical or material, may be of a very modest character either in relation to the magnitude of the hazard, or as compared with those of his threatened neighbour. A rule which required of him in such unsought circumstances in his neighbour's interest a physical effort of which he is not capable, or an excessive expenditure of money, would be unenforceable or unjust. One may say in general terms that the existence of a duty must be based upon knowledge of the hazard, ability to foresee the consequences of not checking or removing it, and the ability to abate it.[27]

This understanding of the standard of care is sometimes referred to, inaccurately, as a 'measured duty of care'.[28] There is an important sleight of hand here, as we see below.

This position appears to be inconsistent with the normal approach to the standard of care in the law of negligence. There, the law imposes an objective test that except in special circumstances ignores concerns of the kind listed above. The point of drawing attention to this feature is not to criticise the 'measured duty of care'. I have argued in support of it elsewhere.[29] The point is so that we have it in mind when we turn to examine its influence on the following two cases.

Burrow Mump is a hill and historic site in Somerset. It contains some Roman archaeological remains, three medieval pits, masonry from a twelfth-century building and the ruins of the fifteenth-century St Michael's Church. In 1946, ownership of Burrow Mump was gifted to the National Trust who then became the occupiers of the land.

The hill was prone to slipping. This, as was stressed, was entirely the result of nature:

> there has been no human activity . . . which has in any way affected or increased the labile condition of the land. Its instability, its propensity to slip, which admittedly exists, is caused by nature: the contours, the geological structure and material, and the effect thereon of sun, rain, wind, frost and other natural agencies.[30]

In 1976, soil slipped from the hill onto the claimants' land. They sued the defendant, inter alia, for the damage this caused. In *Leakey v National Trust*, the Court of Appeal held in favour of the claimants.

Taking his cue from *Goldman v Hargrave*, Megaw LJ leant heavily on the law of negligence, drawing explicitly on that law's leading case, *Donoghue v Stevenson*,[31] and linking it with *Sedleigh-Denfield v O'Callaghan*:

> That change in the law [ie that worked by *Goldman v Hargrave*], in its essence and in its timing, corresponds with, and may be viewed as being a part of, the change in the law of tort which achieved its decisive victory in *Donoghue v Stevenson* [1932] A.C. 562:

---

[27] ibid 663.

[28] eg *Holbeck Hall Hotel Ltd v Scarborough BC* [2000] QB 836 (CA), 860.

[29] A Beever, *Rediscovering the Law of Negligence* (Oxford, Hart, 2007) 326–33.

[30] *Leakey v National Trust* [1980] 1 QB 485 (CA), 510. In fact, there was an exception to this, though the Court was prepared to ignore it. It is not entirely clear why.

[31] *M'Alister (or Donoghue) (Pauper) v Stevenson* [1932] AC 562 (HL Sc).

though it was not until eight years later, in the House of Lords decision in *Sedleigh-Denfield v. O'Callaghan* [1940] A.C. 880, that the change as affecting the area with which we are concerned was expressed or recognised in a decision binding on all English courts.[32]

Given this starting point, it is no surprise to find Megaw LJ claiming that the defendant's liability in *Leakey v National Trust* was the result of 'an obligation to use reasonable care'[33] and a failure to act reasonably.[34] According to Megaw LJ, this failure occurred because the defendant knew of the risk, could have taken steps to eliminate or at least mitigate it, but failed to do so.

Megaw LJ also adopted Lord Wilberforce's 'measured duty of care' approach, maintaining:

> The defendant's duty is to do that which it is reasonable for him to do. The criteria of reasonableness include, in respect of a duty of this nature, the factor of what the particular man – not the average man – can be expected to do, having regard, amongst other things, where a serious expenditure of money is required to eliminate or reduce the danger, to his means. Just as, where physical effort is required to avert an immediate danger, the defendant's age and physical condition may be relevant in deciding what is reasonable, so also logic and good sense require that, where the expenditure of money is required, the defendant's capacity to find the money is relevant. But this can only be in the way of a broad, and not a detailed, assessment; and, in arriving at a judgment on reasonableness, a similar broad assessment may be relevant in some cases as to the neighbour's capacity to protect himself from damage, whether by way of some form of barrier on his own land or by way of providing funds for expenditure on agreed works on the land of the defendant.[35]

Cumming-Bruce LJ agreed with Megaw LJ. So did Shaw LJ. But Shaw LJ's judgment must be one of the most reluctant concurring judgments of all time. The reasons for this reluctance are examined below. For the moment it suffices to say that Shaw LJ felt it clear that, however regrettably, the law as it stood was as it was represented in Megaw LJ's judgment.

Our final case is *Holbeck Hall Hotel Ltd v Scarborough BC*. The claimants owned a hotel and leased the land on which the hotel stood, which lay at the top of a cliff overlooking the North Sea. The defendant, Scarborough Borough Council, owned the undercliff between the claimants' land and the sea. The cliff was highly susceptible to marine erosion and in consequence was inherently unstable.

A slip below the claimants' hotel occurred in 1982. Because of this, the defendant commissioned an investigation by engineers, who recommended enhancing the stability of the cliff by improving drainage. The engineers also suggested attempting to locate the slip plane and carrying out a stability analysis. Some, but not all, of this work was done. A massive landslip occurred in 1993, causing loss of support to the hotel and its grounds. The hotel had to be demolished.

---

[32] *Leakey v National Trust* [1980] 1 QB 485 (CA), 515.
[33] ibid 517.
[34] ibid 524.
[35] *Holbeck Hall Hotel Ltd v Scarborough BC* [2000] QB 836 (CA), 526.

The Court of Appeal ruled that the defendant was liable as it knew of the risk of a landslip.[36] Again, these ideas were explicitly linked to the law of negligence, its duty of care and the concept of reasonable foreseeability.[37] Also in line with these ideas, the Court of Appeal ruled that the defendant could be liable only for loss to the defendant that was reasonably foreseeable.[38] In particular, though some slipping was foreseeable, as the magnitude of the slip was not foreseeable, the defendant's responsibility was significantly curtailed.

This is an interesting conclusion because, as the Court recognised,[39] the approach taken in the law of negligence holds that an injury is recoverable if it is of a kind that is reasonably foreseeable even if it is of unforeseeable extent.[40] Here, all of the claimant's injury was of a foreseeable kind. But the Court maintained that this approach was inappropriate for cases of this type, cases that it described as involving nonfeasance.[41] By this, the Court meant that the claimant's injury was caused, not by any act of the defendant's, but by its omission to act as it ought to have done in order to prevent the materialisation of a risk that it did not create. In those circumstances, the Court maintained, the appropriate standard is the 'measured duty of care' pronounced by Lord Wilberforce in *Goldman v Hargrave*.[42] Consequently, the normal approach taken in the law of negligence would not apply: the defendant would be liable only for injuries that were foreseeable both as to type and extent.

IV. Criticism of the Contemporary Approach

The approach evidenced in the cases above faces one central difficulty. It cannot explain why liability is imposed in these or in any relevantly similar cases. This is because, while the liability imposed is said to be justified at least by analogy with the law of negligence, the type of liability envisaged is in fact inconsistent with the fundamental principles of that law. In consequence, though most of the cases examined are rightly decided, they cannot have been decided for the right reasons.

Imagine that I inherit land that contains a forest that grew up naturally. I do nothing with the land, keeping it in its natural condition. You own land neighbouring mine. Seeds from the plants on my land are blown onto your land. This causes you loss, as you do not want these seeds to grow and must therefore take steps to prevent that happening. You notify me of your concerns but I refuse to remove the plants. According to the contemporary approach, as I am now aware

---

[36] ibid 847.

[37] ibid 849, 856, 858.

[38] ibid 856, 858.

[39] ibid 859–60.

[40] *Hughes v Lord Advocate* [1963] AC 837 (HL Sc). For analysis, see A Beever, *Rediscovering the Law of Negligence* (Oxford, Hart, 2007) 133–43.

[41] *Holbeck Hall Hotel Ltd v Scarborough BC* [2000] QB 836 (CA), 860.

[42] ibid.

of the issues, I will be liable to you unless the 'measured duty of care' indicates otherwise.[43]

The 'measured duty of care' may well indicate otherwise. But the point is this. It is quite unclear why, in these circumstances, I ought to be under any obligation at all. As Shaw LJ asked in *Leakey v National Trust*, 'Why should a nuisance which has its origin in some natural phenomenon and which manifests itself without any human intervention cast a liability upon a person who has no other connection with that nuisance than the title to the land on which it chances to originate?'[44]

The answer will surely be that liability is imposed because, knowing of the risk and failing to eliminate it, I am negligent. But that cannot be the right answer, at least not in itself. This is because negligence in the relevant sense, ie the failure to prevent the realisation of a foreseeable risk, is never sufficient for liability. This is most obviously brought out by considering the absence of a duty to rescue.

As we have seen, in *Goldman v Hargrave* the defendant was held liable for a fire on his land that spread to the claimant's, causing damage. The liability was said to lie in the fact that the defendant failed to eliminate a foreseeable risk. But that cannot be right. If the fire had occurred on a neighbouring public park, then the defendant would have had no responsibility, even had the risk been just as foreseeable and had it been far easier for the defendant to have extinguished the fire than it was in *Goldman v Hargrave* itself.

In the law of negligence, this is said to be the result of the fact that the defendant in such a case, though falling below the standard of care, would not owe the claimant a duty of care. And here we see the crucial sleight of hand contained in the cases above, the sleight of hand that comes from confusing the duty and the standard of care. The 'measured duty of care' is in fact a measured standard of care. Hence, even if it is appropriate to apply the so-called 'measured duty of care' to a case, it does not follow that a duty of care (or whatever the law of nuisance's equivalent should be called) was owed by the defendant to the claimant. In the cases we have examined, the courts have simply assumed that the defendant owed the claimant a duty of care (or its equivalent), but that assumption is inconsistent with the law of negligence upon which the courts pretend to derive that very duty.

The claim here is not that no duty of care was owed in the cases above. I take no stand on that matter.[45] The point rather is that the existence of a duty of care cannot be distilled by analogy with the law of negligence, because that law imposes no duty of the kind upon which the courts relied. Accordingly, the conclusion must be that the defendants' liability in the cases above cannot lie merely in the fact that they failed to eliminate a foreseeable risk and were in that sense negligent. Something more is required.

That something might appear to be that the defendants owned or occupied the land in question (in the following, I speak only of ownership). On this view, it is

---

[43] This case is modelled on, though importantly different from, *French v Auckland City Corp* [1974] 1 NZLR 340 (SC).

[44] *Leakey v National Trust* [1980] 1 QB 485 (CA), 528.

[45] Compare A Beever, *Rediscovering the Law of Negligence* (Oxford, Hart, 2007) 326–33.

the combination of ownership and negligence that generates liability. So in *Goldman v Hargrave*, the defendant was liable because he owned the land from which the fire spread and was negligent; but in the variation of that case in which the fire spread from a public park, the defendant is not liable because he was only negligent.

This thought seems to be echoed in all the cases examined and in much of the commentary. But it is also clearly insufficient. Though it is intuitive to claim that ownership makes a difference, what we are not told is why it makes the difference it is said to make. That is, we are not told why ownership generates liability in *Goldman v Hargrave* when there is no liability in the variation of that case.

Again, the claim is not that ownership does not make a difference. I will argue in the following that it can. The point is that we are not told why it makes the difference we are told that it makes. Moreover, as we will see, though it indeed makes *a* difference, it does not make *that* difference.

Somewhat ironically, as his concurring judgment was so reluctant, only Shaw LJ in *Leakey v National Trust* provided a clear answer to our question.

> The underlying theory of this approach is the correlation of control and responsibility. As the owner of land is normally in the best position to obviate or to contain or to reduce the effect of nuisances arising naturally on his land, he should be primarily responsible for avoiding the consequences of such nuisances or for compensating those who suffer by their occurring.[46]

The problem with this answer, as Shaw LJ seems to have been fully aware, is again that it is inadequate.

First, the owner of the land from which the nuisance emanates may not be in the best position to eliminate or reduce the nuisance. Frequently, the person in the best position will be the owner of the land affected by the nuisance. That was most obviously the case in *Sedleigh-Denfield v O'Callaghan*. It will also sometimes be the case that the person in the best position will be neither land owner but someone else: perhaps the fire brigade in *Job Edwards* and *Goldman v Hargrave* (at least if the facts of those cases were to reoccur today). Accordingly, if it is ownership that makes the difference, that cannot be because the owner is in the best position to prevent the risk from materialising. If we wished to attach liability to that person, then the rule would be that liability falls on the person best able to eliminate the risk and not that liability falls on the owner.

One might also extrapolate the following idea from the passage quoted above. Owning property brings benefits with it. It is only fair, then, that ownership brings responsibilities too. This also seems to have been the view of Vaughan J in *Vaughan v Menlove*: 'every one takes upon himself the duty of so dealing with his

---

[46] *Leakey v National Trust* [1980] 1 QB 485 (CA), 528. Shaw LJ claimed to find this view reflected in *French v Auckland City Corp* [1974] 1 NZLR 340 (SC). Lord Wright also linked ownership, control and responsibility in *Sedleigh-Denfield v O'Callaghan* [1940] AC 880 (HL), 905, but did nothing to explain these perceived links.

own property as not to injure the property of others'.[47] Again, however, while ownership does bring responsibilities, this argument is inadequate.

The central claim is that property brings obligations because it provides benefits. But why should that be so? There seems no reason to think that a thing that brings benefits must also bring responsibilities. Moreover, even if benefits were correlative to responsibilities, it would not follow that the benefits of property ownership brought the responsibility in question.

This point can be illustrated by imagining another version of *Goldman v Hargrave*. Imagine that fire spread to the claimant's land, not directly, but via a public park. On the modern view, the defendant would remain liable, as he knew of the risk to his neighbour, could have prevented it from materialising, did not do so, and the nuisance emanated from his land. But according to this approach, the defendant's neighbours through whose land the *lightning* passed would also be liable, as long as they could have, but did not, extinguish the fire when it spread onto the public park. But that is surely absurd.

What is perhaps even more absurd is that in *Goldman v Hargrave* itself, the only thing preventing those through whose land the lightning passed from being liable is that their actions would be judged according to the 'measured duty of care' and it would have been very difficult for them to have eliminated the risk to the claimant. That attempt to justify the absence of liability with respect to those persons is, however, a desperate move.

At this point, one can only repeat the words of Shaw LJ in *Leakey v National Trust*. 'Why should a nuisance which has its origin in some natural phenomenon and which manifests itself without any human intervention cast a liability upon a person who has no other connection with that nuisance than the title to the land on which it chances to originate?'[48] We have seen no answer to this question.

V. An Alternative Approach

I have been insisting that, while the arguments examined above do not show why ownership makes a difference, it nevertheless can make a difference. It is time to reveal that difference. I do so by reconsidering the decision of the House of Lords in *Sedleigh-Denfield v O'Callaghan*.

A. *Sedleigh-Denfield v O'Callaghan*

A trespasser laid a storm water pipe on the defendant's land and placed a grating over the pipe so that the pipe became prone to blocking, posing a risk of flooding

---

[47] *Vaughan v Menlove* (1837) 3 Hodges 51, 132 ER 490, 494.
[48] *Leakey v National Trust* [1980] 1 QB 485 (CA), 528.

to the claimant's property. The defendant was aware of the pipe and the grating and did nothing to alleviate the risk which eventually materialised. The House of Lords found for the claimant. Why?

Commentary on this case has tended to focus on Lord Wright's judgment. This is no coincidence, because that judgment is closest to the conventional view. The other judgments in the case are not only much more distant from that approach, they enunciate an alternative answer to our question. It is not surprising, then, that they are frequently ignored. They should not be. They elucidate an approach to this area of the law far superior to the one pointed to by Lord Wright. Crucially, this approach is able properly to explain the basis of the defendant's liability. What is more, it supports the outcomes of most of the modern cases, though for different reasons, and it coheres with the ratios, though not with the outcomes, of the older cases.

i. Lord Wright

We begin with Lord Wright's judgment and with two central, apparently inconsistent but in fact inconclusive passages. In the first, his Lordship maintained that negligence is not an ingredient in an action for nuisance,[49] thus suggesting that nuisance liability is strict. In the second, however, Lord Wright explicitly denied that liability in this area of the law is strict.[50] What is to be made of these claims?

The answer can only be 'Nothing'. It is quite unclear what the claims mean. In full, the first claim is:

> Negligence . . . is not a necessary condition of a claim for nuisance. What is done may be done deliberately, and in good faith and in a genuine belief that it is justified. Negligence here is not an independent cause of action but is ancillary to the actual cause of action, which is nuisance.[51]

The first two sentences of this passage appear to assert that negligence is irrelevant in nuisance. The last suggests the opposite. Moreover, while the passage could be read as saying that, although negligence is not necessary for liability in the law of nuisance *tout court*, it is sometimes necessary – thus supporting the contemporary view – alternative readings are available. It may be, for instance, that negligence is never necessary, but the presence of negligence can give evidence of something that is necessary. Furthermore, one may act in a way that creates an unreasonable risk though one acted deliberately, in good faith and out of a genuine belief that one's action was justified. The passage is inconclusive.

The second passage maintains that 'liability for a nuisance is not, at least in modern law, a strict or absolute liability'.[52] The meaning of this is again unclear. The passage may mean that the law of nuisance is fault-based, but it may mean that liability in that law does not rely on causation alone. It may mean some third

---

[49]   *Sedleigh-Denfield v O'Callaghan* [1940] AC 880 (HL), 904.
[50]   ibid.
[51]   ibid.
[52]   ibid.

possibility. The first reading seems to be ruled out by Lord Wright's immediate contention that 'If the defendant by himself or those for whom he is responsible has created what constitutes a nuisance and if it causes damage, the difficulty now being considered does not arise',[53] implying that in those circumstances the defendant would be liable. These circumstances can obtain without the defendant being at fault. It is impossible to be sure, however. Again, the passage is inconclusive.

Nor is Lord Wright's starting point entirely clear. He insists that liability is based on a view of 'what is reasonable according to the ordinary usages of mankind living in society, or more correctly in a particular society'[54] but, as was argued in chapter three, this is not identical with the conventional view.

Nevertheless, Lord Wright's focus on reasonableness led him to ask what one might reasonably expect in cases in which the nuisance came to the defendant. His answer is the one discussed above: that ownership plus negligence equals responsibility. I take this to be the point of the following passage.

> The responsibility which attaches to the occupier because he has possession and control of the property cannot logically be limited to the mere creation of the nuisance. It should extend to his conduct if, with knowledge, he leaves the nuisance on his land. The same is true if the nuisance was such that with ordinary care in the management of his property he should have realised the risk of its existence.[55]

There is, however, no logical connection here. That a person has possession or control of something does not itself entail that he is responsible for it. Nor does it follow from the fact that someone is responsible for something in some way that he is responsible for that thing in other ways. There is no argument here.

Nevertheless, Lord Wright held that if a nuisance has come to the defendant, then the defendant can be liable only if he had 'knowledge or means of knowledge' of the nuisance.[56] Drawing on previous case law, Lord Wright linked this idea to the notion that such a defendant can be liable only if he continued or adopted the nuisance: 'if the defendant did not create the nuisance he must, if he is to be held responsible, have continued it, which I think means simply neglected to remedy it when he became or should have become aware of it'.[57] This echoes the contemporary approach.

Thus, the argument is not that, as it is so ambiguous, Lord Wright's position cannot be taken to be the origin of the contemporary approach. On the contrary, it is precisely for this reason that the contemporary approach is to be seen as the offspring of Lord Wright's position. The modern view has inherited the ambiguities found in Lord Wright's judgment. Along with the ambiguity, the modern law has inherited its inability to explain the defendant's liability. An alternative must be found.

[53] ibid.
[54] ibid 903.
[55] ibid 905.
[56] ibid 904.
[57] ibid 904–05.

ii. Lord Atkin

One is found in *Sedleigh-Denfield v O'Callaghan*, in the judgments of the other judges in the case. In this regard, Lord Wright's judgment is most usefully compared with Lord Atkin's.

The key to understanding his Lordship's judgment is the following crucial passage.

> For the purpose of ascertaining whether as here the plaintiff can establish a private nuisance I think that nuisance is sufficiently defined as a wrongful interference with another's enjoyment of his land or premises by the use of land or premises either occupied or in some cases owned by oneself. The occupier or owner is not an insurer; there must be something more than the mere harm done to the neighbour's property to make the party responsible. Deliberate act or negligence is not an essential ingredient but some degree of personal responsibility is required, which is connoted in my definition by the word 'use.'[58]

This passage entirely rules out the suggestion that liability for nuisance, even when the nuisance comes to the defendant, is fault-based.[59] Lord Atkin is quite explicit: negligence is not a necessary condition for liability in this area, the relevant necessary condition is use.

Now, this does not entail that negligence is never relevant. But it does entail that if negligence is relevant, it is relevant only because it can be used to establish use. According to this view, then, the law of nuisance is use-based, not fault-based. That, of course, fits the thesis advanced in this book.

After identifying use as the basis of liability, Lord Atkin maintained that this explained the traditional view that a defendant can be liable for a nuisance that comes to him only if he continued or adopted the nuisance. If the defendant had not continued or adopted the nuisance, then the defendant had not performed a use of his land that rendered him responsible for the nuisance.

Moreover, his Lordship went on to ask:

> What is the meaning of 'continued'? In the context in which it is used 'continued' must indicate mere passive continuance. If a man uses on premises something which he found there, and which itself causes a nuisance by noise, vibration, smell or fumes, he is himself in continuing to bring into existence the noise, vibration, etc., causing a nuisance. Continuing in this sense and causing are the same thing. It seems to me clear that if a man permits an offensive thing on his premises to continue to offend, that is, if he knows that it is operating offensively, is able to prevent it, and omits to prevent it, he is permitting the nuisance to continue; in other words he is continuing it.[60]

---

[58] ibid 897.

[59] Here, I speak of fault and negligence interchangeably. The assumption that it is appropriate to do so has been questioned, an issue taken up in the following chapter. For the purposes of this discussion, 'fault' is used to mean negligence, the relationship between nuisance and negligence here being the issue.

[60] *Sedleigh-Denfield v O'Callaghan* [1940] AC 880 (HL), 897.

The crucial point is this. If a nuisance comes to a defendant, then the defendant is liable if he knows of the risk involved and can eliminate that risk but does not do so. In such circumstances, it is apposite to describe the defendant has having been negligent. But the reason he is liable is not because he was negligent *per se*. He is liable because his negligence – ie the fact that he knew about the risk and could have eliminated it – shows that his use of his land encompassed the nuisance.

Accordingly, in *Sedleigh-Denfield v O'Callaghan*, the defendant used his land in a way that interfered with the use of the claimant's land, and as the injury involved property damage, the claimant's use was more fundamental to the concept of property than the defendant's. But if the defendant had been unaware of the culvert and the grating, then he could not have been liable. This is because, while the claimant's use of his land would have been interfered with (by nature and a third party), that interference would not have been the result of the defendant's use of his land.

Note that the liability here is strict. One is liable for uses of one's land if that use interferes with a more fundamental use of another's land, whether one was at fault or not. It is just that, in certain circumstances, fault is a condition of use. This has the consequence that, in certain situations, a defendant can be liable only if he was at fault; but that is perfectly consistent with the claim that nuisance liability is in no way fault-based. In the same way, there are certain circumstances in which a person will breach a contract only if he breaks an egg over his head, but liability for breach of contract is not even in those circumstances break-an-egg-over-your-head-based.

In fact, this point was illustrated by Lord Atkin. His Lordship maintained that the act of the trespasser in *Sedleigh-Denfield v O'Callaghan*:

> created a state of things from which when the ditch was flowing in full stream an obstruction might reasonably be expected in the pipe, from which obstruction flooding of the plaintiff's ground might reasonably be expected to result: though I am not satisfied that granted this reasonable expectation of obstruction it would be necessary for the plaintiff to prove that the particular injury was such as reasonably to be expected to result from the obstruction.[61]

Again, this differs from the law of negligence. If I create an unreasonable risk of a certain type of injury to the claimant, then I am negligent. But if the injury I cause is of a different kind, then I am not liable.[62] This is because I am not at fault for creating the risk of that injury, as the unreasonable risk that I created was not an unreasonable risk of an injury of that kind.[63] But Lord Atkin held that the defendant would be liable in the relevant circumstances in the law of nuisance. This is because liability is not determined by fault. It is determined by use. It is in that sense a strict liability. It is particularly telling that this judgment was produced by one of the principal architects of the law of negligence.

---

[61] ibid 895–96.
[62] eg *Doughty v Turner Manufacturing Co Ltd* [1964] 1 QB 518 (CA).
[63] For discussion, see A Beever, *Rediscovering the Law of Negligence* (Oxford, Hart, 2007) 133–43.

Though the other judges in the case were less transparent than Lord Atkin, it is clear on reflection that their judgments at least more closely resemble Lord Atkin's than Lord Wright's. In particular, the above explains Lord Porter's claim that the defendants in the relevant circumstances are liable, 'not because they were negligent, though it may be that they were, but for nuisance because with knowledge that a state of things existed which might at any time give rise to a nuisance they took no steps to remedy that state of affairs'.[64] The negligence is evidence of use, not the basis of liability.

Moreover, all the judges held that the defendant's liability lay in the fact that he continued and adopted the nuisance,[65] a matter that Viscount Maugham linked with causation rather than a duty or standard of care.[66] Negligence was taken to be important because it constituted evidence of continuation and adoption rather than because it established liability in itself. Special mention in this regard must be made of Viscount Maugham's account of what it means to continue or adopt a nuisance.

> In my opinion an occupier of land 'continues' a nuisance if with knowledge or presumed knowledge of its existence he fails to take any reasonable means to bring it to an end though with ample time to do so. He 'adopts' it if he makes any use of the erection, building, bank or artificial contrivance which constitutes the nuisance.[67]

The discussion above reveals that this is not what it might otherwise appear to be, two disconnected ideas thrown together. Rather, they are manifestations of the same general principle found most clearly in Lord Atkin's judgment.

The passage just quoted also makes clear that if the defendant used the object that caused the nuisance, then the defendant is liable even if without fault. For instance, if the defendant in *Sedleigh-Denfield v O'Callaghan* had used the culvert and grating, then he would have been liable even if he were unaware of the risk to the claimant, could not reasonably have been aware of it, and/or could not have prevented the risk from materialising. Again, it is use that matters, not fault.

B. Further Explication

Before we re-examine the case law explored above, it is necessary further to explicate the position advanced by the majority in *Sedleigh-Denfield v O'Callaghan*, so that the concept of use can be properly employed. The following example makes the necessary point.

Imagine that someone swaps a tyre on my car for a bald one. Not knowing about this, I drive the car. In one sense, I am using the tyre. It is also fair to say that I am using a bald tyre on my car. But here we must make a distinction. Though I

---

[64] *Sedleigh-Denfield v O'Callaghan* [1940] AC 880 (HL), 920.
[65] ibid 891, 912–13, 916.
[66] ibid 892–93.
[67] ibid 894.

am using the bald tyre, I am not using the tyre *qua* bald tyre. The baldness of the tyre does not feature in the purpose to which I put it.

But if I know that the tyre is bald when I drive the car, then I am using the tyre *qua* bald tyre. The baldness of the tyre does feature in the purpose to which I put it. This is so even if I make no special allowance for the tyre's baldness – if I drive as I would do were the tyre well-treaded, for instance. If I know that the tyre is bald then, when I drive in that way, I drive as I normally would *despite the fact* that the tyre is bald. I do not do that in the first case, however.

These observations allow us to deal with the following difficulty. In *Sedleigh-Denfield v O'Callaghan*, the defendant used his land. The culvert and the grating were on his land. Therefore, the implication seems to be that the defendant used the culvert and the grating and would have done so even had he not known of their existence. This appears to entail that, on the thesis advanced here, the defendant would be liable in those circumstances. But that is not the view supported in *Sedleigh-Denfield v O'Callaghan*.

The appropriate reply is to maintain that the issue is not whether the defendant used his land, or even whether he used the culvert and the grating, in some sense. The issue is whether the defendant used his land *qua* land that contained the culvert and the grating. The defendant in *Sedleigh-Denfield v O'Callaghan* did this, but would not have done so were he unaware of the relevant facts. This point is also important when we turn to re-examine the cases explored earlier in this chapter.

VI. Revisiting the Case Law

We now revisit the case law examined above in the light of the argument of the previous section. The aim is to show how the approach promoted by the majority in *Sedleigh-Denfield v O'Callaghan* would deal with these cases.[68]

A. The Old Cases

The first case to explore is *Job Edwards*. Recall that the claimants purchased land for mining, found it to be worthless, left it unused and unoccupied, and that a third person dumped refuse on the land without the claimant's permission. The refuse caught fire and threatened to spread to the defendant's land.

Recall also that the Court of Appeal decided 2-1 that no nuisance had occurred. Because of this, *Job Edwards* is usually understood to be the last important case in favour of the rule that a person cannot be liable for a nuisance that comes to him.

---

[68] See also the very useful discussion of related cases, such as *McBryan v Canadian Pacific Railway Co* (1899) 29 SCR 359, in JW Neyers and J Diacur, 'What (is) a Nuisance?' (2011) 90 *Canadian Bar Review* 215, 224–25.

Moreover, the dissent of Scrutton LJ is said to be crucial in foreshadowing and encouraging the new approach, according to which a person can be liable for a nuisance that comes to him if he were negligent. But while there is some truth in this picture, it is misleading.

The first important point to make in this regard is that all the judges in *Job Edwards* decided the case by applying the same general principle. This is the principle that one can be liable for a nuisance that comes to one only if one continued that nuisance.[69] The difference between the judges concerned what it meant to continue a nuisance. For Banks and Astbury LJJ, a person continues a nuisance only if she fails to warn her neighbour of a risk that might emanate from her land or fails to permit her neighbour to enter her land to abate that risk.[70] For Scrutton LJ, on the other hand, a person continues a nuisance if she knows about the risk to her neighbour and fails to take reasonable care in abating that risk.[71] What we see here, then, is not a conflict over the proper principle to adopt. The judges adopt the same principle. The disagreement is over how that principle is best understood and applied.

It is this kind of disagreement, and not one over principles, that separates the cases examined in the second section of this chapter from the position taken by the majority in *Sedleigh-Denfield v O'Callaghan*. In other words, *Sedleigh-Denfield v O'Callaghan* does not call into question the principles upon which the other cases were decided. It rejects only the way in which those cases applied those principles to the facts.

The cases in question are *Giles v Walker*, *Sparke v Osborne*, *Molloy v Drummond*, *Seligman v Docker* and *Neath Rural District Council v Williams*. In all of them, the claimants failed because the courts ruled that the events of which the claimants were complaining were the result of nature. We saw, for instance, Higgins J in *Sparke v Osborne* claim that:

> I know of no duty imposed by the British common law . . . on a landowner to do anything with . . . what naturally grows on his land, in the interest of either his neighbour or himself. If he use the land, he must so use it as not thereby to injure his neighbours: *sic utere tuo ut alienum non laedas*. But if he leave it unused, and if thereby his neighbours suffer, he is not responsible. So long as he does nothing with it, he is safe. It is not he who injures the neighbour – it is Nature; and he is not responsible for Nature's doings.[72]

The principle expressed here is the same as the one promoted by the majority of the House of Lords in *Sedleigh-Denfield v O'Callaghan*. If the claimant is injured not by the defendant's use of his land but by nature, then there can be no liability. In those circumstances, it is of course impossible to say that the claimant's inju-

---

[69] *Job Edwards Ltd v Birmingham Navigations Proprietors* [1924] 1 KB 341 (CA), 352 (Banks LJ), 357 (Scrutton LJ), 365 (Astbury LJ).

[70] ibid 352, 365.

[71] ibid 357.

[72] *Sparke v Osborne* (1908) 7 CLR 51 (HCA), 75.

ries were a result of the defendant's use of his land. And clearly, in such circumstances, the defendant's use cannot be less fundamental than the claimant's.

Neath Rural District Council v Williams illustrates this point. That case was decided 11 years after *Sedleigh-Denfield v O'Callaghan* and Lord Goddard CJ was adamant that his decision was consistent with that of the House of Lords. Water from a stream that flowed over the defendant's land flooded the claimants' properties because of an obstruction. In finding for the defendant, Lord Goddard argued:

> Apart from authority, I think that the position is as follows: a landowner is not at common law under any liability to do anything with regard to a watercourse if it is a natural watercourse which flows through his land. If he creates a watercourse, or does anything to make artificial that which was previously natural, very different considerations arise, and that is why I thought at first that the recent decision in the House of Lords in *Sedleigh-Denfield v. O'Callaghan* might have a bearing on our decision here. In my opinion, however, that case does not apply because, if one reads the speech of Viscount Maugham, L.C., with care, it seems to me implicit that he is considering a case where there was a ditch into which had been inserted a pipe for the purpose of carrying off water, which pipe those on whose land it was, had allowed to get choked. I think it quite clear that he was referring throughout, and intended to refer throughout, to an artificial watercourse or to a case where works had been done to the watercourse, and not to the ordinary bed of a natural stream. I therefore do not think it necessary to discuss the principles laid down in that case, the decision in which was that if a person allows a nuisance to continue on his land, even though it had been originated by a trespasser, he nevertheless becomes liable.[73]

To use the language adopted here, the decision of the majority in *Sedleigh-Denfield v O'Callaghan* turned on whether the defendant was using the land in a way that incorporated the nuisance. The liability rests on using the land in a way that allows the nuisance to continue, not on negligently failing to prevent the nuisance. *Neath Rural District Council v Williams*, then, is quite consistent with the position taken by the majority in *Sedleigh-Denfield v O'Callaghan*.

The remaining cases are wrongly decided, as the contemporary view insists. Importantly, however, they are wrongly decided according to the principle applied in them. That is because none of the cases are correctly described as ones in which the claimant was injured by nature rather than by the defendant's use of his land.

In *Giles v Walker*, the defendant's land had originally been forest, but the forest had been cleared for cultivation. It was because the land had been cleared that thistles grew up on it and spread to the claimant's property. It is therefore not correct to regard the claimant's injury as a mere product of nature. It was the result of the use of the defendant's land.

In *Sparke v Osborne*, prickly pear spread from the defendant's farm to the claimant's. Though the weed was not brought onto the land by the defendant, the

---

[73] *Neath Rural District Council v Williams* [1951] 1 KB 115, 120–21 (citation omitted).

defendant was clearly using his land as farmland. Moreover, as he knew of the existence of prickly pear, he was using the land *qua* land that contained prickly pear. Accordingly, the claimant's injury was no mere product of nature, but was the result of the defendant's use of his land.

In *Seligman v Docker*, the large number of pheasants attracted onto the defendant's land ate the claimant's crops. These birds may have been feræ naturæ, but the defendant used his land for the purpose of hunting pheasants and attracted pheasants to the land for that purpose. Clearly, then, it is not right to say that the claimant's injury was a mere product of nature and not the consequence of the defendant's use of his land.

Molloy v Drummond raises special issues. It concerned a nuisance caused by a tree on the defendant's land. As the tree had not been planted by the defendant, the Court held that there could be no liability. That case is therefore usefully contrasted with *Davey v Harrow Corp*,[74] in which roots from the defendant's tree damaged the claimant's property. The Court refused to recognise any distinction between trees that had and had not been planted and found for the claimant.

These cases are different from those above because the object causing the nuisance remains the defendant's property.[75] When the thistle seeds in *Giles v Walker* and the prickly pear in *Sparke v Osborne* blew onto the claimant's land and germinated, they became the property of the claimants. In *Seligman v Docker*, the pheasants were never the property of either party. But in *Molloy v Drummond* and *Davey v Harrow Corp*, the tree roots, branches, etc remained the defendant's. This is why, at common law, if branches from your neighbour's tree overhang your land, you are entitled to cut them, but you are to throw the branches onto the defendant's land. Retaining the branches would be a trespass to the neighbour's property in the branches.

The distinction between these kinds of case can be captured as follows. In cases such as *Giles v Walker*, the claimant is saying, as it were: 'Your use of your land is interfering with my use of my land. Stop it.' In cases such as *Davey v Harrow Corp*, on the other hand, the claimant is saying: 'Your property is on my land. Remove it.' In the first kind of case, the court must balance the defendant's right to use his land against the claimant's right to use hers. But no such balancing is required in the second. As the defendant's property is on the claimant's land, that property must be removed. This means that the second kind of case at least fits much more closely with the law of trespass than with the law of nuisance.

This is problematic, because it was determined by the Court of Appeal in *Lemmon v Webb* that overhanging trees and the like constitute nuisance and not trespass. Because of this, it is necessary to examine that decision.

The claimant's trees overhung the defendant's land. Without giving notice to the claimant, the defendant cut the overhanging branches. The claimant maintained that this action was wrongful arguing, inter alia, that he had acquired a

---

[74] *Davey v Harrow Corp* [1958] 1 QB 60 (CA).
[75] *Lemmon v Webb* [1894] 3 Ch 1 (CA), 20.

right to overhang the defendant's land as the trees had done so for more than 20 years.

It is in this context that one must understand the Court's decision that the trees constituted a nuisance and not a trespass. The concern was this. If the overhang was a trespass, trespasses being actionable *per se*, then the legal wrong began more than 20 years ago and so the claimant may have acquired an easement through prescription to overhang the defendant's land. On the other hand, if the overhang was a nuisance, nuisances being actionable only on proof of damage, then the legal wrong began only when damage began to occur. That had transpired only recently. Hence, the Court's decision that the overhang was a nuisance rather than a trespass was motivated, not by an examination of the principles of those areas of the law, but simply in order to prevent the claimant from obtaining an easement. For that reason, the decision must be questioned.

Moreover, the Court's discussion gives further reason to hold that overhangs and the like cannot be nuisances. This is because, as the Court in fact ruled, the defendant was entitled to cut back the trees whenever he chose to do so. He did not have to wait until they caused damage to his property, interfered with his comfort or anything of the sort. In other words, the existence of the legal wrong that justifies the cutting back of the trees does not depend on damage. The tort that corresponds to that legal wrong must, therefore, be actionable *per se*. It must be trespass and not nuisance.

It may be tempting to reply that in these cases the property owner is damaged for the purposes of the law of nuisance if he has trees overhanging his property and does not want them there. Here, the damage is the failure to realise his preferences with respect to his land. If this response were adequate, it would mean that the ability to complain of or remove the branches at any stage is compatible with the idea that the legal wrong that justifies the complaint or the removal is a legal nuisance. But the response is not adequate. If the mere failure to realise one's preferences were sufficient for damage, then the distinction between torts actionable *per se* and those actionable only on proof of damage would in practice be a distinction without any difference. After all, a defendant will sue only if her preferences have not been realised.

Alternatively, it might be thought that overhanging trees and the like must be nuisances rather than trespasses because they are only gradual. But this argument has no force. It is no more of a trespass if I enter your land quickly than if I do so slowly. Nor, if I build on your land, can I defend myself on the ground that I did it only gradually.

A more promising suggestion, that can be gleaned from Kay LJ's judgment in *Lemmon v Webb*, is that the tortfeasor cannot be liable in trespass because he does not occupy the tree.[76] But it is unclear what difference occupation is meant to make. I can trespass on your land without occupying the land from which I enter yours, for instance. In fact, that the landowner is guilty of a tort even if not in

---

[76] ibid 18.

occupation of the tree suggests that the liability cannot lie in the tort of nuisance.

The judges in *Lemmon v Webb* built their position in reliance on the decision of Lord Ellenborough in *Pickering v Rudd*.[77] In that case, the defendant had attached a board to his house that overhung the claimant's land. Lord Ellenborough ruled that this was not a trespass, as the board did not touch the claimant's soil. 'I do not think it is a trespass to interfere with the column of air superincumbent on the close'.[78] His Lordship also said: 'I am by no means prepared to say that firing across a field *in vacuo*, no part of the contents touching it, amounts to a *clausum fregit*.'[79] On this view, then, overhanging branches could be trespasses only if they touch the ground. The problem is that this view no longer represents the law. The idea that a trespass is committed only by one who touches the claimant's land has long since had its day.[80]

One may nevertheless be reluctant to hold that overhanging trees and the like constitute trespasses. This is perhaps because these kinds of case resemble only distantly the historical cases from which the modern law of trespass arises. Those cases deal with what we might describe as more 'active' events. But that is not to the point. The issue is not history but whether overhanging trees are trespasses according to the principles of that law. Those principles arise from the law's history, but are not bound to it.

This is not an essay on the law of trespass. The issue, therefore, will not be settled here. Perhaps, as I have suggested, overhanging trees are trespasses. Perhaps they should be thought of as constituting a different tort. But what is clear is that it is wrong to think of them as nuisances. The wrong in these cases is of a kind that does not fit that area of the law. As indicated above, the claim with respect to these cases is not 'You are using your land in a way that is interfering with my use of mine' but 'Your property is on my land'. The action that responds to this claim should reflect the nature of it.

B. The New Cases

We turn now to re-examine the cases discussed in III. With the partial exception of *Holbeck Hall*, the aim is to show that they were rightly decided, albeit for the wrong reasons.

In *Goldman v Hargrave*, the defendant's tree was struck by lightning and caught fire. The defendant cut the tree down, but failed to extinguish the fire, which spread to the claimant's land. The Privy Council was right to hold the defendant liable. As far as the law of nuisance is concerned, this is because the defendant used the tree on his land in a way that caused a more fundamental interference with the claimant's

---

[77] *Pickering v Rudd* (1815) 4 Camp 218, 171 ER 70.
[78] ibid 70.
[79] ibid 70–71.
[80] eg *Anchor Brewhouse Developments Ltd v Berkley House (Docklands Developments) Ltd* [1987] EGLR 173; *Bernstein v Skyviews & General Ltd* [1978] QB 479.

use and enjoyment of his land.[81] Here, the wealth of the defendant etc – ie the concerns relevant to the 'measured duty of care' – are irrelevant.

In *Leakey v National Trust*, soil from the defendant's land slipped onto the claimant's. This was a use of land that interfered with the more fundamental use by the claimant of the claimant's land. This is somewhat obscured by the fact that the defendant's land in question, Burrow Mump, was a historical site and so, one is inclined to assume, left alone by the defendant. In fact, however, the defendant clearly used the land, giving grazing rights on it to a third party, for instance.[82]

Holbeck Hall is more difficult. It is, unfortunately, a disaster that worked a considerable injustice. The disaster is not unmitigated, however. The defendants and those who paid their bills may not be appeased to hear it, but *Holbeck Hall* nicely illustrates some of the most difficult problems with the conventional approach.

It is necessary to go back to the beginning. The claimant originally alleged that the defendant was guilty of three wrongs: removing support that resulted in slippage, breaching a common law duty to prevent the slippage and breach of covenant.[83] The trial judge found that the defendant was under a duty not to remove support, but did not violate that duty.[84] That claim need not concern us. More important is the judge's findings with respect to the alleged duty to prevent slippage.

In this regard, the judge began by examining 'broader issues of principle and policy' before turning to the case law.[85] He noted that the general, recent trend had been to apply principles of the law of negligence to this area,[86] what I have called the slide to negligence. Nevertheless, he then asked precisely the question that the thesis advanced in this book would have had him ask.

> I start with the proposition that there is a positive duty . . . in the case of encroachments on another's land as the result of human activity, past or present, on the defendant's land, even if the defendant was not implicated in the origin of that activity. Is there properly a distinction between that situation and some or all of those in which the origin of the harm to the plaintiff's enjoyment of possession is 'natural', in the sense of arising without human intervention?[87]

This book would have had him answer 'Yes'. Naturally, however, the judge was faced with important constraints not binding here. Of particular relevance in the judge's mind seems to have been the decision of the Privy Council in *Goldman v Hargrave*, because he went on immediately to say:

> In my view there is a significant distinction between natural events which occur randomly and at particular points, such as lightning strikes, and those which are part of a large-scale, long-term process, even if the events arising from that process are

---

[81] The defendant used the tree when he cut it down, but it is highly likely that he was in fact using it well before then.

[82] *Leakey v National Trust* [1980] 1 QB 485 (CA), 509.

[83] *Holbeck Hall Hotel Ltd v Scarborough BC* (1997) 57 Con LR 113, [22].

[84] ibid [78].

[85] ibid [35].

[86] ibid [38].

[87] ibid [41].

individually unpredictable in date, location and scale. Important examples of the second category are the effects of tectonic movement and of the advance and retreat of glaciation, including the initial upthrust and subsequent progressive degradation of mountain chains, the rise and fall of sea levels relative to the land, and the multiple movements of rock and soil at a wide range of scales and intervals which constitute and accompany these phenomena.[88]

This is an attempt to distinguish the facts of *Goldman v Hargrave* from those in the instant case, with the aim of accepting the existence of a duty in cases of the first kind while denying it in cases of the second. This was clearly the approach that the judge would have preferred to take.[89] However, in the end he felt it impossible as, in conjunction with the decided cases binding on him, it would generate significant problems.[90]

The chief difficulty in this regard was *Leakey v National Trust*. That case decided that a defendant owes a duty of care to prevent soil spilling onto the claimant's land. The judge's preferred approach in *Holbeck Hotel* would have entailed that a defendant owes no duty of care to prevent soil spilling from the claimant's land. But, the judge understandably felt, those two propositions cannot both be accepted at once. Thus, the judge held that the defendant in *Holbeck Hotel* owed the claimants a duty of care. This, therefore, is an endorsement of the conventional view, but it is another most reluctant one.

We must now turn to the claim that the defendant was guilty of breach of covenant. Originally, all the land in question had been owned by a single party. The undercliff was conveyed to the defendant in 1895. The covenant accompanying the grant contained the following:

> [(a)] That they [the grantees] will with all reasonable speed commence and carry out such works of drainage filling and banking up and other works as are in the opinion of [the grantees] or their Borough Surveyor necessary for the preservation of the said Undercliff and the public footpath therein and for the purpose of preventing the same from slipping or otherwise suffering damage

> [(b)] And will at all times thereafter use their best endeavours to maintain and preserve the said Undercliff and footpath

> [(c)] And also in the event of any damage at any time hereafter happening to the said Undercliff and public footpath by sinking slipping or from any other cause whatsoever [the grantees] will with all reasonable speed thereafter repair and make good so far as practicable such damage and reinstate so far as practicable the said Undercliff and footpath

> [(d)] Provided always and it is hereby expressly agreed and declared that [the grantees] shall not be liable for any damage that may be caused to any part of [the property retained by the grantor] owing to any slip or sinking that may take place in the said Undercliff or public footpath.[91]

---

[88] ibid [42].
[89] ibid [43]–[47].
[90] ibid [47]–[57].
[91] ibid [59]. All additions are the judge's.

The main focus was on the meaning of clause (d). The judge concluded that it meant what it appeared to mean: that the defendant would not be liable for any damage caused by slipping to the undercliff. This meant that the defendant could not be sued on the basis of breach of covenant, as the damage in question was precisely of that kind.

The judge then said:

> There remains the question whether (d) excludes or limits liability arising otherwise than from breach of covenant. Here its position and status as a proviso in [the] covenant . . . tells in the Plaintiffs' favour . . . In my view the natural construction of (d) confines its scope to the covenantors' liability under [the] covenant . . . It would require something much more specific to exclude liability for infringement of the natural right of support, even *inter partes*, while to bind successors in title would involve not merely the use of contractual words but the reservation of a right in the nature of a proprietary interest to carry out works on the grantees' land which included the removal of support for the grantor's. As to the common-law duty, that was plainly not in the contemplation of the parties in 1895 but the natural construction of the words, as expressed above, entails that it is not displaced or curtailed.[92]

The claim that clause (d) does not undermine the defendant's duty to retain support is surely correct. The point of the clause is to limit the apparent liability generated by clauses (a)–(c). Clause (d) was intended to check the legal implications of the defendant's responsibility set out in (a)–(c), not to give the defendant carte blanche to remove support from the grantor's land. As the judge rightly noted, something much clearer would have been needed for that conclusion to have been appropriate.

But the situation with respect to the 'common law duty' is quite different. As the judge rightly notes, the parties to the covenant could not have intended to have excluded this duty. That is because it did not exist in 1895 as the world had yet to hear of *Sedleigh-Denfield v O'Callaghan*, *Goldman v Hargrave* or even *Job Edwards Ltd v Birmingham Navigations Proprietors*. Thus, the parties could not have intended to exclude a duty of care that was not recognised. But it does not follow that such a duty of care 'is not displaced or curtailed' by the clause.

The point of the clause was to prevent the defendant being liable in damages for physical damage caused by slippage (unless it was caused by the defendant removing support). The duty of care imposed on the defendant is directly in conflict with the clause. It insists that the defendant will be liable for just such a thing.

To put this another way, clause (d) contains an exclusion of liability. That exclusion does not apply to damage caused by the removal of support. But that is because clause (d) does not exclude damages caused by the removal of support. In that sense, and only in that sense, clause '(d) confines its scope to the covenantors' liability under [the] covenant'. But the exclusion does apply to damage caused by slippage not caused by the removal of support. That is precisely what the parties agreed to exclude. That they thought that such liability could arise only under the

---

[92] ibid [68].

covenant does not prove that the exclusion applies only to liability that arises under the covenant.

The appropriate result in *Holbeck Hotel*, then, was to find that – as the defendant had not removed support – any potential liability was excluded by clause (d) of the covenant. That is to be borne in mind as we turn to the decision of the Court of Appeal.

Unfortunately, the issue just examined was not raised in front of that Court. The defendant's appeal centred solely on whether it owed the claimants a duty of care. As we saw in III above, the Court held in the affirmative. That is the wrong result; and it remains wrong even if we ignore clause (d) of the covenant. The defendant was not using the land. That is, the defendant was not putting the land to its purposes. It engaged with the land merely in order to fulfil its obligations under the covenant (and like covenants with other parties).[93] Its liability, therefore, should have been limited to that dictated by the covenant. It is a mark of how unsatisfactory the conventional view is that it led the courts away from the issues upon which the focus ought to have been placed to vague and undefined notions of reasonableness and duty. The litigation in *Holbeck Hotel* supports the conventional view and cannot be reconciled with the approach advanced here. I take that as a compliment.

---

[93] At least, this seems to be the appropriate conclusion to draw from the record. Matters are not entirely clear.

8

Fault and Foreseeability

I. Introduction

In an article published in 1949, still described in language such as seminal and classic, FH Newark criticised three developments in the law of private nuisance.[1] Two of these are closely linked, one might be described as the flip side of the other: the move in the law of nuisance from strict liability to fault and the separation of the tort from the action based on *Rylands v Fletcher*.[2] These issues are the subject of this and the following chapter. This chapter focuses on Newark's claim that the law of private nuisance was originally strict, that it had become increasingly influenced by notions of fault imported from the law of negligence and that this development was unfortunate.

Regrettably, we are offered no reason to accept this conclusion. Newark argues as if it followed from the fact that the law was originally strict, and that notions of fault had been 'foreign' imports, that the law should return to the *status quo ante*. But that does not follow. History is important, but it is not justification. It may be that the historical developments Newark lamented are to be welcomed. Moreover, though Newark suggests (he does no more than that) that these developments have produced a less than fully coherent law, it may be that this is because the conversion has yet to be completed. Perhaps we are living in the twilight of a coherent but morally unacceptable law, just witnessing the dawn of a coherent and justified one. And for that matter, it is in itself no argument to suggest that the law of nuisance is in danger of being enveloped by the law of negligence. Even if it is true that the 'total assimilation of nuisance into negligence'[3] may be on the horizon, that cannot constitute an objection to that development unless it is also shown that the assimilation is unwarranted. It cannot be taken for granted that we need separate laws of nuisance and negligence.

Consideration of Newark's article, therefore, presents us with three questions: Was the law of nuisance a form of strict liability? Has the law increasingly been influenced by fault-based notions imported from the law of negligence? And if so, is

---

[1] FH Newark, 'The Boundaries of Nuisance' (1949) 65 *LQR* 480.
[2] *Rylands v Fletcher* (1868) LR 3 HL 330. The third issue concerned the awarding of damages for personal injury. That issue is dealt with by implication in ch 12.
[3] S Deakin, A Johnston and B Markesinis, *Markesinis and Deakin's Tort Law*, 6th edn (Oxford, Clarendon Press, 2008) 528.

that development to be welcomed? The second question has been answered in the affirmative by the previous chapter. This chapter seeks to answer the remaining two.

II. Fault, Negligence and Foreseeability

A quarter of a century after Newark published his article, JM Eekelaar responded in what is now perhaps an even more influential paper.[4] Eekelaar maintained that Newark had misread the evidence: that although many old cases rejected concepts belonging to the law of negligence, attention to the nature of the liability imposed in those cases reveals that the liability was nevertheless fault based. According to Eekelaar, then, there has been no slide to negligence. In fact, the law always was fault based; though not fault based in quite the same way as the law of negligence.[5]

Eekelaar accepts that it is a 'cliché that "negligence is not a necessary element in nuisance"', a cliché he is happy to endorse. Thus he assents to the view, expressed by Viscount Simmonds in *Read v J Lyons & Co Ltd*, that 'if a man commits a legal nuisance it is no answer to his injured neighbour that he took the utmost care not to commit it'.[6] But he denies that Viscount Simmonds' conclusion, that 'liability is strict', follows.[7] This is because, Eekelaar maintains, one can be at fault for causing an injury that one took utmost care to prevent. If this argument were successful, it would allow Eekelaar to demonstrate that the statements upon which Newark relied to show that the law is strict are in fact compatible with the claim that the law is fault based.

Naturally enough, Eekelaar begins his argument with a definition of strict liability. He maintains that 'a person is strictly liable if he is legally responsible for a state of affairs, the causes of which he did not know nor could reasonably have known'.[8] Conversely, then, liability is fault based if a defendant cannot be liable unless he knew or ought to have known of the causes of the relevant state of affairs. As other commentators have put it, 'A defendant who has to have actual or presumed knowledge of the likely consequences of his activity can hardly be said to be liable strictly'.[9]

On this definition, liability can be fault based and yet not require negligence. This is because it is possible for a defendant to cause an injury that he knew or ought to have known would (or would be likely to) happen and yet to have taken all possible precautions to prevent that injury occurring. As Eekelaar maintains:

---

[4] JM Eekelaar, 'Nuisance and Strict Liability' (1973) 8 *Irish Jurist* 191.
[5] This may be to put things too starkly. Eekelaar acknowledges that the law is unclear in this area. His position may perhaps better be expressed by saying that the law was always – at least to a large extent – fault based. It makes no difference here whether that is so.
[6] *Read v J Lyons & Co Ltd* [1947] AC 156 (HL), 183.
[7] ibid.
[8] JM Eekelaar, 'Nuisance and Strict Liability' (1973) 8 *Irish Jurist* 191, 191–92.
[9] S Deakin, A Johnston and B Markesinis, *Markesinis and Deakin's Tort Law*, 6th edn (Oxford, Clarendon Press, 2008) 527.

It is quite consistent to deny to a defendant the defence that he has taken every precaution against an invasion yet insist that his liability depends on actual or presumed knowledge of its likelihood and indeed to hold him liable if he has such knowledge. Prevention must not be confused with detection.[10]

One is negligent only if one fails to prevent something that one should have prevented; but one is at fault if one knew or ought to have known that one's action might injure another. These conceptions are not coextensive. One can be at fault without being negligent.

It follows from this that the judicial insistence that nuisance does not depend on negligence – the insistence upon which Newark placed great emphasis – does not show that nuisance liability is strict. It is perfectly compatible with the claim that the liability is fault based.

In this context, Eekelaar examines two important examples. The first is presented in the sixteenth edition of *Salmond*.[11] A locomotive is operated in a way such that its operator 'cannot by any skill in construction or care in management be prevented from discharging sparks' that injure the claimant.[12] *Salmond* maintains that there would be liability in such a case and that this shows that such liability must be strict. Eekelaar agrees that liability would be imposed, but responds that 'plainly it does not [show that liability is strict], because [the] operator will undoubtedly be aware of the emission of the sparks'.[13] Here, then, though the operator is not negligent, he is at fault as he can foresee the claimant's injury.

Likewise, in *Rapier v London Tramways*,[14] the claimant sought an injunction against defendants who operated stables producing noise and smell. Lindley LJ said, 'if I am sued for a nuisance, and the nuisance is proved, it is no defence on my part to say, and to prove, that I have taken all reasonable care to prevent it'.[15] This had been thought to support the idea that nuisance liability is strict, but Eekelaar responds that 'Naturally [the defendants] knew of these consequences, and the persistence was deliberate'.[16] Again, then, although the defendants were not negligent, they could foresee the claimant's injury and were thus at fault.

It will help now to summarise the issue. The claim is that liability can be fault based without being negligence based and that this is because causing a foreseeable injury can be faulty and yet not negligent. If correct, then this allows us to say that the law of nuisance is and perhaps has always been fault but not negligence based. The resulting position is well summarised in the following: 'liability in nuisance is strict in the sense [and only in the sense] that a defendant may be found liable regardless of the care he took in doing what he did to avoid causing harm.

---

[10] JM Eekelaar, 'Nuisance and Strict Liability' (1973) 8 *Irish Jurist* 191, 197.
[11] RFV Heuston, *Salmond on the Law of Torts*, 16th edn (London, Sweet & Maxwell, 1973) 62.
[12] ibid.
[13] JM Eekelaar, 'Nuisance and Strict Liability' (1973) 8 *Irish Jurist* 191, 197.
[14] *Rapier v London Tramways* [1893] 2 Ch 588 (CA).
[15] ibid 600.
[16] JM Eekelaar, 'Nuisance and Strict Liability' (1973) 8 *Irish Jurist* 191, 197.

But this does not exclude . . . fault in the second sense: that is, that liability will only attach to those users of land that involve a foreseeable risk of harm'.[17]

There is something very odd about this position. It is certainly plausible to think that foreseeability and fault are connected. But it is much less clear that foreseeability is any less strongly connected with negligence. What is more, it is hard to see how foreseeability can be connected with fault except via negligence. One way of illustrating this point is to consider the seminal discussion of foreseeability in this context: Viscount Simmonds' examination of remoteness in *The Wagon Mound (No 1)*.

In relation to the law of negligence, his Lordship said:

> It is a principle of civil liability . . . that a man must be considered to be responsible for the probable consequences of his act. To demand more of him is too harsh a rule, to demand less is to ignore that civilised order requires the observance of a minimum standard of behaviour . . . For, if it is asked why a man should be responsible for the natural or necessary or probable consequences of his act (or any other similar description of them), the answer is that it is not because they are natural or necessary or probable, but because, since they have this quality, it is judged, by the standard of the reasonable man, that he ought to have foreseen them.[18]

Out of context, this passage appears to suggest that foreseeability and fault are directly linked, so that a person who could foresee that his activity would cause an injury is at fault if that injury materialises. If so, that would be a conclusion that would apply to remoteness in nuisance just as much as in negligence. But as Viscount Simmonds made clear, the role of foreseeability in relation to remoteness in the law of negligence is not freestanding. On the contrary, foreseeability is relevant here because of its connection with the negligence enquiry as a whole.

> [I]f some limitation must be imposed on the consequences for which the negligent actor is to be held responsible . . . why should that test (reasonable foreseeability) be rejected which, *since he is judged by what the reasonable man ought to foresee*, corresponds with the common conscience of mankind.[19]

> [T]he essential factor in determining liability is whether the damage is of such a kind as the reasonable man should have foreseen. This accords with the general view thus stated by Lord Atkin in *M'Alister (or Donoghue) v. Stevenson* . . .[20]

And when we turn to that case, the importance of foreseeability is clear. As Lord Atkin famously said:

> You must take reasonable care to avoid acts or omissions which you can reasonably foresee would be likely to injure your neighbour. Who, then, in law is my neighbour?

---

[17] J Murphy, C Witting and J Goudkamp, *Street on Torts*, 13th edn (Oxford, Oxford University Press, 2012) 456.

[18] *Overseas Tankship (UK) Ltd v Morts Dock & Engineering Co Ltd (The Wagon Mound, No 1)* [1961] AC 388 (PC), 422–23.

[19] ibid 423 (emphasis added).

[20] ibid 426. Compare WS Seavey, 'Mr. Justice Cardozo and the Law of Torts' (1939) 39 *Columbia Law Review* 20, 34, 'Prima facie at least, the reasons for creating liability should limit it'.

The answer seems to be – persons who are so closely and directly affected by my act that I ought reasonably to have them in contemplation as being so affected when I am directing my mind to the acts or omissions which are called in question.[21]

But why ought I reasonably to have them in contemplation? The answer is so obvious that we seldom take time to elucidate it. I ought reasonably to have them in contemplation because I can foresee that I might injure them. And that is important because, as I can foresee that my activity might injure them, I must either take appropriate steps to ensure that I perform the activity in a way that does not lead to injury or refrain from performing the activity. Thus, foreseeability in this context is important because, and only because, of its connection with prevention. If the defendant could not foresee the claimant's injury, then he is not at fault/negligent for failing to prevent it. Conversely, if the defendant could foresee the claimant's injury, then he may have been at fault/negligent for failing to prevent it.

In other words, though 'Prevention must not be confused with detection',[22] and though foreseeability does not necessarily imply negligence, the reason foreseeability leads to liability in the law of negligence is because it indicates the defendant's negligence.

A defendant who could not foresee any injury is not negligent (no breach of the standard of care). A defendant who could not foresee injury to the claimant was not negligent to the claimant (no duty of care). A defendant who could not foresee the kind of injury that the claimant suffered was not negligent for creating a risk of the injury that the claimant suffered (the injury is remote).

Note that this is not to deny that foreseeability and negligence can come apart. Eekelaar is right to claim that a defendant who can foresee but not prevent the claimant's injury is not negligent. The problem is that there is also no reason to think that such a defendant is at fault. Likewise, if liability is imposed on that defendant, that liability must be strict. The claim that a 'defendant who has to have actual or presumed knowledge of the likely consequences of his activity [to be liable] can hardly be said to be liable strictly'[23] is incorrect.[24]

It is not coincidental that this point can be demonstrated by examining the very examples used to illustrate the contrary view. Recall the example from *Salmond*. A locomotive is operated so that its driver cannot prevent it producing sparks that injure the claimant. It was suggested that because the driver cannot prevent the claimant's injury, the driver cannot be said to have been negligent. However, because the driver can foresee the injury, the driver was at fault. But the example is ambiguous in just the way that it must not be. In fact, it appears from the example

---

[21] *M'Alister (or Donoghue) (Pauper) v Stevenson* [1932] AC 562 (HL Sc), 580.

[22] JM Eekelaar, 'Nuisance and Strict Liability' (1973) 8 *Irish Jurist* 191, 197.

[23] S Deakin, A Johnston and B Markesinis, *Markesinis and Deakin's Tort Law*, 6th edn (Oxford, Clarendon Press, 2008) 527.

[24] This, of course, is not to say that the enunciated restriction would be appropriate in a tort of strict liability. It would not (see further below). The point is just that the restriction does not demonstrate that the tort is fault based.

that the driver can prevent the injury: he can refrain from operating the locomotive. Moreover, given that he can foresee that operating the locomotive will cause injury to the claimant, and given that he chooses to operate in the light of that knowledge, we can agree that he is at fault, but that is because he is negligent. He fails to prevent foreseeable injury to the claimant by deciding to operate the locomotive. Conversely, if for some reason he cannot avoid operating the locomotive, then in these circumstances he cannot be negligent, but then what ground do we have to say that he is at fault? If I am thrown off a tall building and looking down can see that I will land on you, I can foresee injury to you, but who would want to conclude that I am at fault when I do?

Recall also *Rapier v London Tramways*.[25] The claimant sought an injunction against defendants who operated stables producing noise and smell. Here, the noise and smell could not be prevented given that the defendants were operating a stable. But they did not have to operate a stable. Given that they chose to operate a stable knowing that it would produce noise and smell, it is right to conclude that they were at fault, but it is also right to say that they were negligent. In fact, this is simply two ways of saying the same thing. Alternatively, if for some reason the defendants were unable to cease operating the stable, then they were neither negligent nor at fault. If a volcano erupts on my land, I can foresee damage to my neighbours, but I am not at fault for that damage.

Foreseeability and negligence can be pulled apart, but when they are pulled apart, fault is ripped away too. Foreseeability alone implies neither fault nor negligence, but when it implies fault it also implies negligence and vice versa. Accordingly, though Eekelaar is right to insist that the judicial denial that negligence is a prerequisite to liability in nuisance does nothing to show that foreseeability is irrelevant, he is wrong to think that this undercuts Newark's claim that nuisance is, or at least was, a tort of strict liability.

III. Foreseeability and Nuisance

Nevertheless, if nuisance is a tort of strict liability, it is odd that it requires foreseeability. As we have seen, liability in negligence requires foreseeability because, in that context, foreseeability is linked to negligence. If it is not so linked in the law of nuisance – as all agree – then what is its point? The answer is that it has no point.

It is important to be clear about this matter. The issue is not whether it is possible to posit liability with a foreseeability requirement that is not fault or negligence based. Of course, such is possible – a matter examined further in the following chapter. The issue is rather whether a requirement of foreseeability makes sense in form of liability that is neither fault nor negligence based. My

---

[25] *Rapier v London Tramways* [1893] 2 Ch 588 (CA).

claim is that is cannot. If liability is strict, then there is no reason to insist that the defendant have been able to foresee the claimant's injury.

The requirement that liability in nuisance can exist only if the defendant could foresee the claimant's injury is a mistake. It is a mistake introduced into the law via two main cases, *Bolton v Stone*[26] and *The Wagon Mound (No 2)*,[27] and reinforced in *Cambridge Water Co v Eastern Counties Leather plc*.[28] I examine those cases now.

In *Bolton v Stone*, a woman was struck by a cricket ball, driven out of the defendant's ground, over a seven-foot-high fence and onto an adjacent little-used road. It was estimated that a ball was driven out of the ground on average once every five years. Given the very low probability of injury, the courts were not willing to accept that the defendant had been negligent.[29] A problem, however, was that the claimant also sued in public nuisance. She alleged that the striking of cricket balls onto the public road constituted a nuisance and that – in accordance with the preconditions for liability in that area of the law – she suffered 'special damage' for which she was entitled to recover. The Court of Appeal rejected this argument on the ground that the striking of balls onto the road was so infrequent and the inconvenience it had caused (before the claimant's injury) so trivial, that no public nuisance had occurred.[30]

This conclusion was supported by Lord Oaksey in the House of Lords.[31] However, after finding that the defendant had not been negligent, Lord Porter maintained that 'I need not discuss the alternative claim based upon nuisance, since it is admitted on behalf of the respondent that in the circumstances of this case nuisance cannot be established unless negligence is proved'.[32] That position was also advanced by Lord Reid.[33]

This appears to support the view that nuisance is or at least can be fault based, though not for the reasons suggested by Eekelaar. But it would be wrong to make much of it. The position taken by the Court is this. *If* cases of this kind are actionable in nuisance, then negligence will be a precondition for liability. This does not imply that, had this defendant been negligent, he would have been liable for committing a nuisance. Nor does it imply that cases of this kind are actionable in nuisance if the defendant has been negligent. It does not even entail that negligence is ever relevant in nuisance. There is a double conditional here. The claim is not that a defendant will be liable in nuisance *if* negligent. It is that *if* this defendant can be liable in nuisance, then he can be liable only *if* negligent. To put this another way, their Lordships' comments were intended to fend off the nuisance claim; they were not intended as commitments to the structure of the law of nuisance.

---

[26] *Bolton v Stone* [1951] AC 850 (HL).
[27] *Overseas Tankship (UK) Ltd v Morts Dock & Engineering Co Ltd (The Wagon Mound, No 2)* [1967] AC 617 (PC).
[28] *Cambridge Water Co v Eastern Counties Leather plc* [1994] 2 AC 264 (HL).
[29] For analysis, see A Beever, *Rediscovering the Law of Negligence* (Oxford, Hart, 2007) 98–103.
[30] *Stone v Bolton* [1950] 1 KB 201 (CA), 205, 208–09, 213–14.
[31] *Bolton v Stone* [1951] AC 850 (HL), 863.
[32] ibid 860.
[33] ibid 868.

Nevertheless, the comments are frequently taken as precursors of the claim that 'the tort of nuisance, uncertain in its boundary, may comprise a wide variety of situations, in some of which negligence plays no part, in others of which it is decisive'[34] and the idea that the law is fault based. The problem was made even more acute by the litigation in the *Wagon Mound* cases.

In the second of these, employees of the defendants negligently allowed a large quantity of bunkering oil to spill into the bay. The oil caught fire, causing severe damage to the claimant's ships. The trial judge found that the damage by fire was not reasonably foreseeable because it was not foreseeable that bunkering oil floating on water was flammable. Accordingly, the judge ruled that the defendant was not liable in negligence. However, the judge held the defendants liable in nuisance, maintaining that foreseeability of injury was not an essential element in that tort. This presented a problem for the Privy Council. The problem is perhaps best revealed by examining the five related cases that the Board examined.

The first was *Sharp v Powell*.[35] The defendant's employee committed an offence by washing his van in the street and allowing the water to run down the gutter towards a grating that led to the sewer. Because the grating was frozen over, the water flowed onto an uneven area where it froze. The claimant's horse slipped on the ice and broke its leg. The claimant sued the defendant, alleging nuisance.

The second case is *Pearson v Cox*.[36] A workman shook a plank, causing a tool to fall onto the passing claimant. Although the case was brought in negligence, as the Privy Council pointed out in *The Wagon Mound (No 2)*, Bramwell LJ dealt with it as involving nuisance.

The third case is *Clark v Chambers*.[37] The defendant had placed a barrier – a *chevaux de fries* – across a public road. This activity constituted a nuisance. A third party then removed part of the barrier, placing it on the footpath. The claimant, passing on the footpath at night, struck the barrier and was injured.

The fourth case is *Harold v Watney*.[38] The defendant owned a fence bordering the highway. The fence was defective and gave way when the child claimant put his foot on it. The fence was in such a condition that it constituted a nuisance.

The final case is *Farrell v John Mowlem & Co Ltd*.[39] The defendants laid a pipe across the footpath, which the claimant tripped over. Again, the claimant sued alleging nuisance.

The key feature of these cases is that, if they are nuisances at all, they are public nuisances. In all of these cases, as in *Bolton v Stone* and *The Wagon Mound (No 2)* itself, the alleged wrong occurred not on the claimant's land, but on public property.

---

[34] *Goldman v Hargrave* [1967] 1 AC 645 (PC), 657.
[35] *Sharp v Powell* (1872) LR 7 CP 253.
[36] *Pearson v Cox* (1876–1877) LR 2 CPD 369 (CA).
[37] *Clark v Chambers* (1878) 3 QBD 327.
[38] *Harold v Watney* [1898] 2 QB 320 (CA).
[39] *Farrell v John Mowlem & Co Ltd* [1954] 1 Lloyd's Rep 437.

Crucially, this area of the law overlaps the primary sphere of the law of negligence. All of the cases examined could have been, and some were, brought also on the basis of negligence. What is more, given that the law of public nuisance is very poorly defined,[40] it is in danger of undermining the law of negligence; a concern clearly expressed by the Privy Council in *The Wagon Mound (No 2)*.

The tort of public nuisance has two main prerequisites. First, the defendant must create a state of affairs that 'materially affects the reasonable comfort and convenience of life of a class of the public who come within the sphere or neighbourhood' of it.[41] Second, the claimant must suffer 'special damage', injury above that common to others. The problem is that if every circumstance that could be said to 'materially affect the reasonable comfort and convenience of life' of the public (such as imposing risk) that results in particular injury (such as personal injury or property damage) to the claimant were actionable as a public nuisance, and if the law of public nuisance were more 'claimant friendly' than the law of negligence, the latter would be ignored to death.[42]

This issue was very clearly thrown up by *The Wagon Mound (No 2)*. In both that case and in its predecessor, *The Wagon Mound (No 1)*, the Privy Council had spent a great deal of energy defining the circumstances in which an action in negligence would be available. The Court held that a claimant is entitled to recover in negligence only if his injury is a reasonably foreseeable consequence of the defendant's negligent action. But all this would have been pointless had the claimant succeeded in public nuisance. Leaking oil into the bay seems clearly to be a public nuisance and the claimants' injuries were just as clearly 'particular damage' and a result of the nuisance. But if we are to have a law that allows recovery here without negligence, there can be little point in having a law of negligence or worrying about the remoteness rules in that area of the law. Accordingly, the Privy Council felt it important to ensure that the law of public nuisance, at least in the relevant respects, was no more 'claimant friendly' than the law of negligence. Thus, they insisted that foreseeability was a requirement in both areas of the law.

But they did more than this. They went on to make two claims. The first is that, while foreseeability is a requirement in nuisance, negligence is not.[43] In this regard, they repeated the fallacy observed above. 'An occupier may incur liability for the emission of noxious fumes or noise although he has used the utmost care in building and using his premises.'[44] Yes, but if he can be liable only if he could

---

[40] An heroic attempt to make as much sense of the mess as possible is found in J Murphy, *The Law of Nuisance* (Oxford, Oxford University Press, 2010). To this reader, however, not much sense is made. This is not because of any inadequacy on the part of the author, but because of the inadequacy found in the law itself.

[41] WVH Rogers, *Winfield and Jolowicz on Tort*, 18th edn (London, Sweet & Maxwell, 2010) 709.

[42] The claim is not that there are no ways meaningfully to restrict liability in the law of public nuisance other than the ones examined here. The point now is only to understand the Privy Council's motivation for insisting that negligence was an essential element of public nuisance.

[43] *Overseas Tankship (UK) Ltd v Morts Dock & Engineering Co Ltd (The Wagon Mound, No 2)* [1967] AC 617 (PC), 639.

[44] ibid.

foresee the injury he caused the claimant, then this suggests that he was at fault, not for failing to take care in how he built the building, but for building at all. In fact, the only way to achieve the symmetry between the laws of negligence and public nuisance that the Privy Council was seeking is to ensure that, at least in the relevant contexts, a non-negligent defendant cannot be liable.

The second claim made by the Privy Council is that the discussion of public nuisance applies also to private nuisance. In fact, it is probably too kind to describe this as a claim. Rather, the Privy Council slide from examining public to private nuisance without appearing to realise that they have crossed a boundary.[45] But a boundary has most certainly been crossed.

A public nuisance is a public inconvenience that causes particular damage to a claimant. For the reasons examined above, it is easy to see why this action must at least mesh with the law of negligence. But a private nuisance is an interference with the claimant's use and enjoyment of her land. This is entirely different from the law of negligence. What is more, the two nuisance torts – if one should even refer to them in this way, wrongly suggesting that they are two parts of one entity – have an entirely different focus. Though it is clear that, given the law of negligence, public nuisance should require foreseeability, there seems no reason to apply the same rule to private nuisance. And what is more, we are offered no reason. As noted, the judgment in *The Wagon Mound (No 2)* simply slides from one tort to the other.

Likewise, in *Cambridge Water*, Lord Goff supported the view that liability in nuisance requires foreseeability, but did no more than rely on the kinds of case that we have been examining, especially, of course, *The Wagon Mound (No 2)*.[46] His Lordship claimed that 'the development of the law of negligence in the past 60 years points strongly towards a requirement that . . . foreseeability should be a prerequisite of liability in damages for nuisance',[47] a claim that is no doubt correct; but we are given no reason to think that this development should be supported and is not, as has been alleged, a mistake.

In fact, what is perhaps most notable about this whole discussion is that no major judgment or commentary, whatever position it argues for, contains any real argument on this point. Instead, its author merely relies on extrapolations from past case law and, what is more, extrapolations that have been revealed to be contentious and often dubious. This is no coincidence. It is entirely to be expected in an area of the law where the basis of liability is a mystery. In such areas, case law and opinion seem to be all that there is to go on. But the analysis presented here provides an alternative. Our task is to examine that alternative now.

---

[45] ibid.
[46] *Cambridge Water Co v Eastern Counties Leather plc* [1994] 2 AC 264 (HL), 300–01. Lord Goff also drew on his analysis of *Rylands v Fletcher*, ibid 301–06. That issue is examined in ch 9.
[47] ibid 300.

IV. Justifying Strict Liability

The current form of liability found in the law of nuisance – as far as it is possible to make sense of it – cannot be justified. As presented in *Cambridge Water*, liability in that law is strict in the sense that it does not require negligence but nevertheless requires foreseeability. That position is not coherent. Put it this way, if the point of insisting on foreseeability is not to ensure that a non-negligent defendant cannot be liable, then what is the point?

Imagine that I construct a structure on my land that, unforeseeably, after 10 years causes a subsidence that damages my neighbour's land. Here, we are told that I cannot be liable as my neighbour's injury was unforeseeable. But imagine now that a month before the subsidence occurs, but after anything can be done to prevent it, the consequence of my building comes to light. Then, we are told, I will be liable, as my neighbour's injury is now foreseeable. But it is entirely opaque how the fact that I can foresee the injury only in the second case justifies this approach.

If foreseeability is to be relevant, that can only be because of the connection between foreseeability and negligence. That is, foreseeability can be a coherent element in nuisance liability only if that liability is negligence liability. Accordingly, if foreseeability is to remain a prerequisite to liability in this area, we must come to recognise that liability is fault based – that is, negligence based. In fact, though we may wish to continue to distinguish between the kinds of damages available in the two areas of the law (though that, too, will require justification), to go down this path ultimately means the assimilation of the law of nuisance to that of negligence. If the defendant's liability rests on her negligence, then there is no good reason not to follow the principles of the area of the law that has been structured around that idea.

In that light, it is interesting to observe that commentators sometimes describe the law as heading in precisely this direction. For instance, in *Cambridge Water*, Lord Goff said that 'it is *still* the law' that nuisance liability does not require negligence,[48] implying that the law is moving towards that requirement. Similarly, it has been claimed that, though 'strict liability . . . is undoubtedly in retreat in this area . . . the total assimilation of nuisance into negligence has *yet* to occur in this field'.[49] The observations of these commentators are correct. But this is unfortunate. In this area of the law, liability should not be fault based. It must be strict.

The law of nuisance prioritises property rights so that more fundamental uses of land trump less fundamental uses. Now, one might dispute the claim that this is the key to understanding the law of nuisance given what that law is or what it

[48] ibid (emphasis added).
[49] S Deakin, A Johnston and B Markesinis, *Markesinis and Deakin's Tort Law*, 6th edn (Oxford, Clarendon Press, 2008) 528. See also C Gearty, 'The Place of Private Nuisance' [1989] *CLJ* 214, 215, 228–29.

has become, but what must be clear is that the principle just enunciated must be reflected in the law somewhere. Less fundamental rights must give way to more fundamental rights. And that principle does not refer to or imply a concern with fault or foreseeability. If my less fundamental use of my land impinges on your more fundamental use of yours, then mine must surrender to yours, regardless of fault or foreseeability. Moreover, this is because my use is, given its effect on you, wrongful. In these circumstances, your right trumps mine, but I have – possibly entirely without fault – violated yours. My activity is thus wrongful, it must stop and, if appropriate, liability in damages must follow.

None of this is to say that a defendant found liable in the law of nuisance must be blameworthy, have failed to live up to his personal responsibilities or anything of the kind. The reason that the defendant must cease the activity in question and/ or pay damages is not because of any failing on his behalf. It is because his activity interfered with a more fundamental activity of the claimant's. The issue has nothing to do with the defendant's character. It is concerned with the activities of the two parties to the dispute.

Accordingly, though the commission of a nuisance is a form of wrongdoing – the wrongdoer being the defendant, of course – the judgement that the defendant is committing a wrong is not a judgement about the defendant *per se*. Nor is it about the defendant as a person in relation to the claimant as a person. Rather, it is about the defendant's use of his land in relation to the claimant's use of his. Fault has no place here.

Though Lord Goff was right to maintain that recent developments have moved the law from imposing genuine strict liability to liability that requires foreseeability, this has been an error. If the law continues to develop in this way, it will disappear into the law of negligence. That is undesirable, because it is necessary to have an area of the law that prioritises property rights in the ways examined above.

If the law of nuisance did not exist, we would have to invent it. If the law continues its slide to negligence, we will have to reinvent it. It would be easier just understand it better.

9

The Rule in *Rylands v Fletcher*

No substantial discussion of the law of nuisance can fail to take a stand on the relationship between that law and the action based on the rule in *Rylands v Fletcher*. In this regard, two questions must be asked. First, is *Rylands v Fletcher* part of the law of nuisance or is it a separate tort? Second, what is the appropriate role of *Rylands v Fletcher* in the modern law? This chapter provides a response to those questions.

I. The Relationship between Nuisance and *Rylands v Fletcher*

Two broad schools of thought are at war over this issue. The first insists that *Rylands v Fletcher* is part of the law of nuisance. On this view, the case was relatively unimportant; significant only for making clear that an isolated event could amount to a nuisance.[1] In opposition stands the thought that, though *Rylands v Fletcher* and nuisance may be related, they are separate areas of the law resting on distinct principles.[2] In the crossfire sits the cop-out position adopted by the House of Lords in *Transco plc v Stockport Metropolitan Borough Council*: that *Rylands v Fletcher* is 'a species of nuisance', implying that it is both part of the law of nuisance and yet separate to the rest of that law.[3]

Each of these schools is able to find some support in the case law. The unfortunate reason for this is that *Rylands v Fletcher* is incoherent. In consequence, it is impossible to support one school over the other. We can only say that nothing

---

[1] eg FH Newark, 'The Boundaries of Nuisance' (1949) 65 *LQR* 480, 487–88; *Cambridge Water Co v Eastern Counties Leather plc* [1994] 2 AC 264 (HL), 297–300 (Lord Goff); M Lee, 'What is Private Nuisance?' (2003) 119 *LQR* 298, 319–22. See also R Stevens, *Torts and Rights* (Oxford, Oxford University Press, 2007) 111–13.

[2] eg PH Winfield, 'Nuisance as a Tort' [1931] *CLJ* 189, 195; JM Eekelaar, 'Nuisance and Strict Liability' (1973) 8 *Irish Jurist* 191, 196; C Gearty, 'The Place of Private Nuisance' [1989] *CLJ* 214; D Nolan, 'The Distinctiveness of *Rylands v Fletcher*' (2005) 121 *LQR* 421; J Murphy, 'The Merits of *Rylands v Fletcher*' (2004) 24 *OJLS* 643; J Murphy, *The Law of Nuisance* (Oxford, Oxford University Press, 2010).

[3] *Transco plc v Stockport Metropolitan Borough Council* [2003] UKHL 61, [2004] 2 AC 1, 9, 97. Chimpanzees are a species of ape. In that sense, they are the same as other apes. But in saying that they are *a species* of ape, one implies that they are different from all other apes.

definitive can be said about the relationship between *Rylands v Fletcher* and nuisance.

The defendant in *Rylands v Fletcher* had a water reservoir built on his land. He employed qualified engineers and consultants to do the job. However, they failed to take proper account of the fact that the reservoir was built over old mine shafts that, it was later discovered, connected with the claimant's coal mine. After a time, when the reservoir had filled, the water broke through the shafts and flooded the claimant's mine.

Donal Nolan has argued that the key to understanding *Rylands v Fletcher* is to recall that when:

> the case came before the courts, the judiciary was divided between advocates of the fault principle and proponents of an older model of strict liability. The decision in *Rylands* was an important victory for the supporters of strict liability, but while they won this particular battle their opponents eventually won the war.[4]

Because of this, as far as comprehension is concerned, the most important judgments in the case are Bramwell B's dissenting and Martin B's majority judgment in the Court of Exchequer. This is because, as we will see, only these present a coherent position with respect to this issue.

A. The Court of Exchequer

In a typical *tour de force*, Bramwell B argued:

> Now, what is the plaintiff's right? He had the right to work his mines to their extent, leaving no boundary between himself and the next owner. By so doing he subjected himself to all consequences resulting from natural causes, among others, to the influx of all water naturally flowing in. But he had a right to be free from what has been called 'foreign' water, that is, water artificially brought or sent to him directly, or indirectly by its being sent to where it would flow to him. The defendants had no right to pour or send water on to the plaintiff's works. Had they done so knowingly it is admitted an action would lie; and that it would if they did it again . . . The plaintiff's right then has been infringed; the defendants in causing water to flow to the plaintiff have done that which they had no right to do; what difference in point of law does it make that they have done it unwittingly? I think none, and consequently that the action is maintainable.[5]

This, then, is the opening salvo from the supporters of strict liability. We examine its consequences below. For the moment, our concern is with the path that this salvo cut through the other judgments.

Bramwell B's position was rejected by Martin B and Pollock CB. Martin B simply insisted that the defendant had to sue in negligence, trespass or nuisance. As the defendant had not been negligent, the first was not a possibility. As there was

---

[4] D Nolan, 'The Distinctiveness of *Rylands v Fletcher*' (2005) 121 *LQR* 421, 421.
[5] *Fletcher v Rylands* (1865) 159 ER 737, 3 H & C 263, 743.

no immediate connection between the defendant's act (the building of the reservoir) and the flooding of the claimant's mine, there could be no trespass.[6] Most importantly for our purposes, with respect to nuisance Martin B maintained:

> I think there was no nuisance in the ordinary and generally understood meaning of that word, that is to say, something hurtful or injurious to the senses. The making a pond for holding water is a nuisance to no one. The digging a reservoir in a man's own land is a lawful act. It does not appear that there was any embankment, or that the water in the reservoir was ever above the level of the natural surface of the land, and the water escaped from the bottom of the reservoir, and in ordinary course would descend by gravitation into the defendants' own land, and they did not know of the existence of the old workings. To hold the defendants liable would therefore make them insurers against the consequence of a lawful act upon their own land when they had no reason to believe or suspect that any damage was likely to ensue.[7]

Two features of this argument call for special attention.

The first is that, when considering whether a nuisance occurred, Martin B initially focused only on the building of the reservoir. Clearly, as he pointed out, that was no nuisance to the defendant. The defendant was in no way inconvenienced. But Martin B failed to consider that the flooding – ie the escape of the water – may have been a nuisance. He did turn to this issue in the second part of the passage quoted above, but here his reason for denying that a nuisance was present is entirely different. Here, the claim is not that the flooding was no inconvenience to the claimant – it was of course a major inconvenience – the claim is that the flooding was no nuisance because the defendant could not foresee it happening. This, as I have argued in the previous chapter, implies that the flooding was not a nuisance because the defendant was not negligent.

At this point, it is important to remind the reader that the issue is not whether it is possible to formulate a form of liability that is strict and requires foreseeability. Of course, such is possible. The issue is that, if liability is strict, then a foreseeability requirement cannot make sense. This is examined further in I.B.

Again, we leave the assessment of Martin B's position for the moment. For now, it suffices to say that this is the opening salvo for the proponents of fault-based liability. As we will see, it is all downhill from here.

Though Pollock CB sided with Martin B, his reasons for doing so were of a different order. His argument was as follows. If the water had entered the claimant's mine through natural fissures in the rock, the claimant would have had no cause of action. Therefore, Pollock CB concluded, it follows that the defendant cannot be liable merely because the water passed through shafts that had been the product of human endeavour. This is a hopeless argument. For a start, the premise is extremely dubious. In particular, it ignores the possible impact of the fact that the reservoir was made by the defendant. Second, the conclusion does not follow from the premise. The fact that the shafts were constructed may well make an

---

[6] ibid 745–46.
[7] ibid 745.

important difference. Pollock CB ignored what are clearly at least among the most pressing issues.

B. The Court of Exchequer Chamber

The Court of Exchequer Chamber reversed. Delivering the judgment, Blackburn J claimed that he accepted the decision of Bramwell B.[8] That is quite wrong, however. According to Blackburn J:

> the true rule of law is, that the person who for his own purposes brings on his lands and collects and keeps there anything likely to do mischief if it escapes, must keep it in at his peril, and, if he does not do so, is primâ facie answerable for all the damage which is the natural consequence of its escape. He can excuse himself by shewing that the escape was owing to the plaintiff's default; or perhaps that the escape was the consequence of vis major, or the act of God; but as nothing of this sort exists here, it is unnecessary to inquire what excuse would be sufficient.[9]

Though this is a very famous passage and though it has been extremely influential, the position it advances is incoherent.

First, the claim that the defendant must prevent (for instance) an escape 'at his peril' clearly implies strict liability. It is for this reason that this action is frequently understood as the strict liability tort *par excellence*. But it is to be noted that Blackburn J also maintained that the defendant will be liable only if the escape is likely to cause damage. Further, if an escape occurs, the defendant is only *prima facie* answerable for the damage that results. Moreover, the defendant will be liable only for damage that is the 'natural consequence' of the escape. In particular, if the escape is a result of vis major or an act of God, then the defendant will not (or may not?) be liable.

Why? Consider Blackburn J's justification for his position.

> The general rule, as above stated, seems on principle just. The person whose grass or corn is eaten down by the escaping cattle of his neighbour, or whose mine is flooded by the water from his neighbour's reservoir, or whose cellar is invaded by the filth of his neighbour's privy, or whose habitation is made unhealthy by the fumes and noisome vapours of his neighbour's alkali works, is damnified without any fault of his own; and it seems but reasonable and just that the neighbour, who has brought something on his own property which was not naturally there, harmless to others so long as it is confined to his own property, *but which he knows to be mischievous if it gets on his neighbour's*, should be obliged to make good the damage which ensues if he does not succeed in confining it to his own property. But for his act in bringing it there no mischief could have accrued, and it seems but just that he should at his peril keep it there so that no mischief may accrue, or answer *for the natural and anticipated consequences*.[10]

---

[8] *Rylands v Fletcher* (1865) LR 1 Ex 265, 278.
[9] ibid 279–80.
[10] ibid 280 (emphasis added).

Here we see a repetition of the idea that liability in this context is strict: the defendant 'is damnified without any fault of his own'. But why? Because, in part, the defendant knew (or ought to have known?) that the escape would be injurious. And why does that make a difference? We are not told, but the answer is obvious: if the defendant knew that the escape would be injurious then he should have prevented it. Given that he did not prevent it, he was negligent, perhaps for failing to prevent the escape, perhaps for bringing the dangerous item onto his land in the first place knowing that it might escape and cause injury. (Conversely, if the defendant could not have prevented the escape in any way, then the fact that he could foresee that the escape would be injurious cannot provide a reason for liability.) We are then told that the defendant will have to answer only 'for the natural and anticipated consequences'. Why? Surely, because only those consequences lie within the scope of the defendant's negligence.

Accordingly, Blackburn J's judgment is deeply inconsistent. It posits strict liability on the basis of fault. No wonder that the application of the judgment has proven to be highly problematic.

In reply, one might maintain that it is the claimant's injury given the escape that must be foreseeable, not the escape itself. In *Rylands v Fletcher*, then, the idea is that the defendant must have been able to foresee that the water would cause injury if it escaped; it is not necessary for the defendant to have foreseen that the water would escape and cause injury. The suggestion is bizarre.

I am perfectly able to foresee that if the peanuts in my house escape and are eaten by children allergic to them, the children might die. But if the peanuts grow legs, walk out the front door and jump into the mouths of children with allergies, how can the fact that I can foresee the damage they would cause if they escape justify finding me liable? If liability in this area is to be fault based, then how can I be liable? If it is to be strict, then what does it matter that I can foresee the injury? Here again we witness the inability to separate reasons that apply to one form of liability from those pertinent to its contrary.

Similarly, one might maintain that an activity may be perfectly legitimate in itself and yet pose a foreseeable risk of injury if it results in an escape (where both the escape and the injury are foreseeable). If an escape occurs, liability is justified. One may be tempted to appeal to the operation and regulation of nuclear power plants in this context, for instance.[11]

But why is liability justified in these circumstances? If the activity really is legitimate even in the face of the associated risks, then how does the fact that one of these risks has materialised into foreseeable injury show that liability for that injury is justified? One might argue that, although the activity is itself legitimate, if the activity causes injury then that is illegitimate. But why? And specifically, how can foreseeability be used to establish that the interference is illegitimate unless it

---

[11] Nuclear Installations Act 1965 (UK).

shows that the defendant was at fault? I submit that there is no answer to this question.[12]

Now, of course, various statutory protections exist that impose liability strictly for foreseeable loss. But that should not surprise us. It is not possible intentionally to create a protection for unforeseeable loss. It would be wrong to take this legislation as evincing a commitment to strict liability coupled with foreseeability. Rather, it reveals only that some potential losses, pondered because foreseeable, have attracted statutory protection.

C. The House of Lords

The defendant appealed to the House of Lords. The House of Lords sided with the claimant. The problems become even more intractable.

Again, Lords Cairns and Cranworth claimed to adopt a judgment from the court below, this time Blackburn J's.[13] To this effect, the heart of Lord Cairns' judgment is an extended quote from Blackburn J.[14] The judgment, therefore, repeats the difficulties with the one it quotes. To make things worse, Lord Cranworth implied that the liability was not only strict – hence overlooking Blackburn J's qualifications – but absolute (in the sense of liability based on *causa* alone). 'In considering whether a Defendant is liable to a Plaintiff for damage which the Plaintiff may have sustained, the question in general is not whether the Defendant has acted with due care and caution, but whether his acts have occasioned the damage'.[15]

Moreover, both of their Lordships introduced the distinction between natural and non-natural use of land. According to Lord Cairns:

> My Lords, the principles on which this case must be determined appear to me to be extremely simple. The Defendants, treating them as the owners or occupiers of the close on which the reservoir was constructed, might lawfully have used that close for any purpose for which it might in the ordinary course of the enjoyment of land be used; and if, in what I may term the natural user of that land, there had been any accumulation of water, either on the surface or underground, and if, by the operation of the laws of nature, that accumulation of water had passed off into the close occupied by the Plaintiff, the Plaintiff could not have complained that that result had taken place. If he had desired to guard

---

[12] In the case of nuclear installations, I submit that the correct understanding is this. Given the catastrophic consequences of 'nuclear escape', it is negligent – ie it poses a real risk to individuals – to operate a nuclear power plant, even though the risk of an escape is low. We think it legitimate to operate these plants, however, because of the social benefits that accrue. Our inability to distinguish between these private and public judgements means that we feel it impossible to say that the operation is both negligent (to individual persons) and legitimate (in terms of the public interest). I explore this inability in A Beever, *Forgotten Justice* (Oxford, Oxford University Press, 2013). On this approach, foreseeability is relevant, because it reveals negligence.

[13] *Rylands v Fletcher* (1868) LR 3 HL 330, 339–40.

[14] ibid.

[15] ibid 341.

himself against it, it would have lain upon him to have done so, by leaving, or by inter-posing, some barrier between his close and the close of the Defendants in order to have prevented that operation of the laws of nature.

On the other hand if the Defendants, not stopping at the natural use of their close, had desired to use it for any purpose which I may term a non-natural use, for the pur-pose of introducing into the close that which in its natural condition was not in or upon it, for the purpose of introducing water either above or below ground in quantities and in a manner not the result of any work or operation on or under the land, – and if in consequence of their doing so, or in consequence of any imperfection in the mode of their doing so, the water came to escape and to pass off into the close of the Plaintiff, then it appears to me that that which the Defendants were doing they were doing at their own peril; and, if in the course of their doing it, the evil arose to which I have referred, the evil, namely, of the escape of the water and its passing away to the close of the Plaintiff and injuring the Plaintiff, then for the consequence of that, in my opinion, the Defendants would be liable.[16]

This involves the most unfortunate choice of expression.

Readers of this case have tended to assume, as one might expect, that a natural use of land is a use of land that is natural and that, conversely, an unnatural use is a use that is unnatural. Hence, the focus of subsequent litigation and commentary has been on determining the distinction between natural and non-natural uses. Thus, some have argued that uses of land that are common or that benefit the public should be characterised as natural. Argument has been had as to whether it is natural to manufacture explosives during wartime, for example.[17] In the recent case, *Transco plc v Stockport Metropolitan Borough Council*, many different views were expressed. Lords Hoffmann,[18] Hobhouse[19] and Walker[20] argued that the rele-vant consideration was whether the defendant's use of land was dangerous. Alternatively, Lord Scott maintained that a defendant can be liable only if his use of land was extraordinary.[21] Lord Bingham argued that the defendant's use must have been dangerous and extraordinary.[22] Finally, Lord Hoffmann remarked that 'A useful guide in deciding whether the risk has been created by a "non-natural" user of land is . . . to ask whether the damage which eventuated was something against which the occupier could reasonably be expected to have insured himself'.[23] This view was opposed explicitly by Lord Hobhouse.[24] Moreover, sup-porters of the second school of thought outlined at the beginning of this section – those who maintain that *Rylands v Fletcher* and nuisance are separate torts –

---

[16] ibid 338–39.
[17] For discussion of these issues, see WVH Rogers, *Winfield and Jolowicz on Tort*, 18th edn (London, Sweet & Maxwell, 2010) 777.
[18] *Transco plc v Stockport Metropolitan Borough Council* [2003] UKHL 61, [2004] 2 AC 1, para 49.
[19] ibid para 63.
[20] ibid para 103.
[21] ibid paras 85–86. However, at para 86 Lord Scott appears to conflate extraordinariness with dan-gerousness.
[22] ibid paras 10–11.
[23] ibid para 46.
[24] ibid para 60.

point to the difference between the concepts of a natural and a reasonable use of land to support their position.[25]

But none of this connects with what Lord Cairns meant. For Lord Cairns, a 'use' is 'non-natural' if, for instance, it introduces onto the land 'that which in its natural condition was not in or upon it'. Thus, a case analogous to *Rylands v Fletcher* in which the defendant's use was 'natural' would be one where the water built up on the defendant's land and moved into the claimant's mines 'by the operation of the laws of nature' alone.[26]

Hence, in more natural language, the distinction between a 'natural use' and a 'non-natural use' is not the distinction between a use that is natural and a use that is non-natural. It is rather that between a non-use and a use. A 'natural user' of land is someone who does not use it. Land is 'naturally used' if, for instance, what is on it is there due to nature. Conversely, a 'non-natural user' of land is someone who uses it. Land is 'non-naturally used' if, for example, what is on it is there due to human endeavour.

Apart from the infelicity of Lord Cairns' expression, one reason this has not been more obvious is that, with the basis of liability in the law of nuisance so poorly defined, the relevance of such concerns has been opaque. But the discussion in chapter seven ought to have cured this. A nuisance is a use of land that interferes with another's more fundamental use. As we saw in that chapter, if the defendant does not use his land, or the alleged nuisance is not the result of the defendant's use of his land, then the defendant cannot be liable in that tort. A 'natural user' of land cannot be liable. Hence, if the water had collected on the defendant's land entirely through natural causes, and if it had flowed to the claimant's mine also entirely through natural causes, then the defendant could not have been liable. But that is not what happened. The reservoir was the product of the defendant's use of his land and, hence, so was the presence of the water. Thus, the flooding was a result of the defendant's use ('non-natural use') of his land, and thus he could be liable.

The argument just examined suggests that *Rylands v Fletcher* and nuisance are much closer than some have maintained. Nevertheless, I do not claim that *Rylands v Fletcher* is part of the law of nuisance. *Rylands v Fletcher* is not sufficiently coherent to say anything of the kind. What we can say, however, is that discussion of *Rylands v Fletcher* and of nuisance is beset by the same kinds of problems. We might say that the two torts, or the two parts of the same tort – whatever – are misunderstood in similar ways. The question, then, is not how these torts were or are related, but what role *Rylands v Fletcher* should have going forward.

---

[25] eg D Nolan, 'The Distinctiveness of *Rylands v Fletcher*' (2005) 121 *LQR* 421, 434–35; J Murphy, *The Law of Nuisance* (Oxford, Oxford University Press, 2010) 10.
[26] *Rylands v Fletcher* (1868) LR 3 HL 330, 338.

II. The Place of *Rylands v Fletcher* in the Modern Law

It will help to start again at the top, with Bramwell B's judgment in the Court of Exchequer. Its argument had the following structure.

(1) The claimant had a right to work the mines.
(2) The right is subject to the interference of nature (ie, the right is not violated when nature prevents the claimant working the mines).
(3) But the right is not subject to human interference (ie, the right is violated when human activity prevents the claimant working the mines).
(4) Thus, the defendant had no right to interfere with the claimant.
(5) Accordingly, the defendant is liable.[27]

The key feature of the argument is the nature of the right assumed in (1). We would ordinarily think of this right as a mere liberty, the absence of a duty not to work the mines. But Bramwell B thought otherwise. As (3) makes clear, the right is a genuine claim right: the presence of a duty in others not to prevent the claimant working the mines.

Now, there is no suggestion that there is anything unique about the right to work one's mines. On the contrary, the argument operates on the assumption that this specific right is generic in kind. Thus, were Bramwell B's position to succeed, it would follow that many of what we think of as liberties would become rights of this kind. Consider, for instance, the following – slightly abbreviated – argument.

(1) The claimant had a right to stand and walk unmolested/to work on his ship or wharf/to her house.
(3) That right is not subject to human interference.
(4) Thus, the defendant had no right to interfere with the claimant.
(5) Accordingly, the defendant is liable.

If this form of argument were to be accepted, then there could be no room for a law of negligence. This, of course, is particularly strongly suggested by the fact that the conclusion to this argument is inconsistent with many of that law's leading cases.[28] But what is just as important is that, even when this approach would generate liability consistent with the law of negligence, it would do so without negligence playing any role. In other words, Bramwell B's judgment calls for a universal regime of strict liability that would allow no place for a law of negligence.

---

[27] *Fletcher v Rylands* (1865) 159 ER 737, 3 H & C 263, 743.
[28] eg *Bolton v Stone* [1951] AC 850 (HL); *Palsgraf v Long Island Railroad Co* 162 NE 99 (NY 1928); *Doughty v Turner Manufacturing Co Ltd* [1964] 1 QB 518 (CA); *Overseas Tankship (UK) Ltd v Morts Dock & Engineering Co Ltd (The Wagon Mound, No 1)* [1961] AC 388 (PC); *Overseas Tankship (UK) Ltd v Morts Dock & Engineering Co Ltd (The Wagon Mound, No 2)* [1967] AC 617 (PC); *Lamb v Camden London BC* [1981] 1 QB 625 (CA); *Murphy v Brentwood District Council* [1991] 1 AC 398 (HL).

Also worth noting is that Bramwell B rejected the idea that foreseeability had a role to play in this context. Moreover, he saw why this had to be. On his view, the action here is strict. Foreseeability, on the other hand, is connected with fault and negligence. For this reason, he chose to express his conclusion by saying, 'I think that the defendants' innocence, whatever may be its moral bearing on the case, is immaterial in point of law'.[29]

I will not here make the claim that it would be wrong to replace the law of negligence with such a liability regime. For the purposes of this discussion, it suffices to say that, given that we have a developed law of negligence, Bramwell B's view cannot be accepted. If this is *Rylands v Fletcher*, then there is no place for it in our law.

However, it might be argued, we need not accept Bramwell B's position *holus-bolus*. As I have argued, the courts that heard *Rylands v Fletcher* did not. In particular, Blackburn J restricted the application of the rule to cases where the defendant 'brings on his lands and collects and keeps there anything likely to do mischief if it escapes'.[30] Hence, the idea is that this form of strict liability applies only to escapes from the defendant's land. But what could the justification for this rule possibly be?

As discussed in I.B, the reasons offered by Blackburn J appeal to the defendant's negligence. That leads to incoherence. Restricting the operation of a tort of strict liability cannot be justified on the basis that the restriction is warranted in terms of the defendant's negligence. If this is *Rylands v Fletcher*, then we cannot rationally want it.

Alternatively, previous chapters of this book have argued that it is appropriate for the law of nuisance to be strict because that area of the law is concerned to prioritise property rights. A similar argument could be made regarding *Rylands v Fletcher*, but at the cost of reducing that action to a part of the law of nuisance. If this is *Rylands v Fletcher*, then we already have it. It is called the law of nuisance.

Another possibility is to argue that liability under *Rylands v Fletcher* should be restricted to interference with the claimant's interest in land. There are two significant problems with this approach. First, as proponents of the second school of thought listed above have pointed out, there seems to be no historical warrant for a restriction of this kind.[31] More importantly, the rule is again without justification, unless it is the one connected with the law of nuisance.

The same is to be said regarding the idea that liability should be restricted to 'non-natural use'. I argued above that the view originally advanced is identical to the one found in the law of nuisance. The leading alternatives maintain that the defendant's use of his land must have been extraordinary or dangerous. The first view suggests nuisance properly understood,[32] the second suggests negligence.

---

[29]   *Fletcher v Rylands* (1865) 159 ER 737, 3 H & C 263, 744.
[30]   *Rylands v Fletcher* (1865) LR 1 Ex 265, 279.
[31]   D Nolan, 'The Distinctiveness of *Rylands v Fletcher*' (2005) 121 *LQR* 421, 432–33; J Murphy, *The Law of Nuisance* (Oxford, Oxford University Press, 2010) 9.
[32]   See *Bamford v Turnley* (1862) 3 B & S 66, 122 ER 27 and chapter three of this book.

Consider also Martin B's judgment in the Court of Exchequer. As we saw, he allowed no space for a separate tort and maintained that nuisance required fault. This view, as has been discussed in previous chapters, is widely held. It is for this reason that some claim that *Rylands v Fletcher* is to be retained. The idea is simple: we need strict liability in this area and the law of nuisance cannot provide it.

We do need strict liability in this area. Property rights can come into conflict and it is therefore necessary to prioritise them. That prioritising is to be done by focusing on the nature of the rights themselves. Fault and foreseeability are irrelevant. The more we push nuisance in the direction of negligence, the more we will feel the need for an alternative strict liability tort in this area. But we do not need to push. If the law of nuisance were properly understood, then we would have no need for *Rylands v Fletcher*. *Rylands v Fletcher* would be absorbed into the law of nuisance or, if one prefers the alternative suggestions we have examined, into the law of negligence[33] – it makes no difference. But the last thing we need is another century and a half mucking around with a tort so odd that, even after all this time, we have been unable to find a proper name for it. *Rylands v Fletcher* is a mere symptom of our misunderstanding of the law of nuisance.

---

[33] *Burnie Port Authority v General Jones Ltd* (1994) 179 CLR 520 (HCA).

10

The Parties

This chapter deals with the question: Who can sue and who can be sued? In the light of what has gone before, the answer to both parts of this question is relatively straightforward, though it is not without controversy. Again, we see that a proper understanding of the basis of liability aids comprehension of the tort in its entirety.

I. Standing: Who Can Sue?

In *Read v J Lyons & Co Ltd*, Viscount Simonds said 'he alone has a lawful claim who has suffered an invasion of some proprietary or other interest in land',[1] a position reaffirmed by the House of Lords in *Hunter v Canary Wharf*.[2]

Given the analysis of the tort above, the reason for this is clear. The tort is concerned to prioritise property rights. The claimant's complaint is that his use of his land is being interfered with. Thus, as explained in chapter three, he must complain of a use to which he has a right. A person with no 'proprietary or other interest' in the land in question cannot make such a complaint.[3]

This explains the otherwise odd-seeming case of *Pemberton v Southwark London Borough Council*.[4] The claimant was a tenant of the defendant local authority. She had fallen into arrears with her rent and the authority obtained a possession order on the property. The defendant, however, agreed not to evict the claimant, permitting her to remain in the property in return for making regular payments. This meant that she was a 'tolerated trespasser' in the property. The claimant subsequently sued the defendant in nuisance, alleging that cockroaches had entered the property from property occupied by the defendant.

The defendant argued, inter alia, that it could not be liable to the claimant as she did not have a sufficient interest in the land. The Court of Appeal rejected that argument. This was because, though the claimant could be evicted at any time by the defendant, until she was either evicted or abandoned the land, she remained

---

[1] *Read v J Lyons & Co Ltd* [1947] AC 156 (HL), 183.
[2] *Hunter v Canary Wharf* [1997] AC 655 (HL).
[3] This, of course, does not affect the rights of parties under art 8 of the European Convention on Human Rights.
[4] *Pemberton v Southwark London Borough Council* [2000] 1 WLR 1672 (CA).

in exclusive possession of it. Because of this, she had rights in the land and thus standing to sue.

This means that we are forced to reject the relevant aspects of the decision of the Court of Appeal in *Khorasandjian v Bush*.[5] In that case, the defendant had harassed the claimant by, amongst other things, telephoning her repeatedly in her home. She claimed that this constituted a nuisance. The problem was that the claimant, a girl of 18, lived in a property owned by her mother. As such, the defendant alleged, she had no standing to sue in nuisance. As Dillon LJ expressed the argument:

> the basis of the tort of private nuisance is interference with the enjoyment of a person's property, and therefore the plaintiff, as in law a mere licensee in her mother's property with no proprietary interest, cannot invoke the tort of private nuisance or complain of unwanted and harassing telephone calls made to her in her mother's home.[6]

To this claim, Dillon LJ responded:

> To my mind, it is ridiculous if in this present age the law is that the making of deliberately harassing and pestering telephone calls to a person is only actionable in the civil courts if the recipient of the calls happens to have the freehold or a leasehold proprietary interest in the premises in which he or she has received the calls.[7]

For reasons examined below, this was a most unfortunate response, not because it argues for an inappropriate conclusion, but because it occludes the real issues. And because of that occlusion, English law has suffered.

As far as it is relevant here, the decision in *Khorasandjian v Bush* was overturned by the House of Lords in *Hunter v Canary Wharf*,[8] in which the House of Lords reasserted the law's traditional approach.

What is more, Lord Goff maintained that the claimant's complaint in *Khorasandjian v Bush* was not that the defendant was committing a nuisance.

> If a plaintiff, such as the daughter of the householder in *Khorasandjian v. Bush*, is harassed by abusive telephone calls, the gravamen of the complaint lies in the harassment which is just as much an abuse, or indeed an invasion of her privacy, whether she is pestered in this way in her mother's or her husband's house, or she is staying with a friend, or is at her place of work, or even in her car with a mobile phone.[9]

The complaint, then, is not that the claimant was unable to use and enjoy the land in question. The complaint is that she did not want to be subject to harassment, harassment that it just so happened occurred in her home. Accordingly, nuisance is not the appropriate tort in which to recognise and respond to this complaint. Again, this was well put by Lord Goff.

---

[5] *Khorasandjian v Bush* [1993] QB 727 (CA).
[6] ibid 734.
[7] ibid.
[8] *Hunter v Canary Wharf* [1997] AC 655 (HL). In support, see TM FitzPatrick, 'Should Family Members have Title to Sue in Private Nuisance?' (1998) 6 *Torts Law Journal* 171.
[9] *Hunter v Canary Wharf* [1997] AC 655 (HL), 691.

In truth, what the Court of Appeal appears to have been doing was to exploit the law of private nuisance in order to create by the back door a tort of harassment which was only partially effective in that it was artificially limited to harassment which takes place in her home.[10]

The desire so to extend the tort was partly explicable because no tort of harassment or the like was then known to the law. That, no doubt, was a lacuna. But it does not follow that the appropriate way to fill the lacuna was to distort the law of nuisance. What is more, as Lord Goff also notes, an action for harassment now exists.[11]

Lord Goff further claimed that:

If a nuisance should occur, then the [person] who has an interest in the property can bring the necessary proceedings to bring the nuisance to an end, and can recover any damages in respect of the discomfort or inconvenience caused by the nuisance. Even if he or she is away from home, nowadays the necessary authority to commence proceedings for an injunction can usually be obtained by telephone.[12]

Though it is impossible to be certain as to Lord Goff's intentions, this seems to imply – correctly – that the claimant's mother in *Khorasandjian v Bush* would have been able to sue for the phone calls, even though it was her daughter who was troubled by them.

This directly contradicts Dillon LJ's claim in *Khorasandjian v Bush* that, without that decision, 'the making of deliberately harassing and pestering telephone calls to a person is only actionable in the civil courts if the recipient of the calls happens to have the freehold or a leasehold proprietary interest in the premises in which he or she has received the calls'.[13] This assumes that only the recipient of the calls can have a cause of action. That assumption is false.

As has been argued, nuisance is concerned with prioritising property rights. A nuisance occurs when the defendant uses land in a way that interferes with the more fundamental use of the claimant's. The issue is not whether the claimant is personally bothered by any of this. The action is designed to prioritise property rights, not to protect owners' or occupiers' expectations, hopes or desires (though these things are protected as a consequence of the law). In *Khorasandjian v Bush*, then, the issue is whether the defendant's actions amounted to a use of land that interfered with the more fundamental use by the claimant's mother of her land. The answer is clearly 'Yes'.

The dominance of the law of negligence in our thought can make this point difficult to understand. For that reason, it is useful to note that the position is exactly the same in the law of trespass. If I lend a car that I never use and care little about to my son (ie if I give him a licence to drive it), if he uses it as if it were his own and if you deliberately crash into it disabling it, then you inconvenience my

---

[10] ibid 691–92.
[11] Protection from Harassment Act 1997 (UK).
[12] *Hunter v Canary Wharf* [1997] AC 655 (HL), 694.
[13] *Khorasandjian v Bush* [1993] QB 727 (CA), 734.

son but not me. But I have a claim in trespass against you. And I have a claim, not merely for nominal damages, though in fact I am not at all inconvenienced. My entitlement to sue you arises from the fact that the car is mine. That it is my son who suffers the loss is neither here nor there. As usual, the modern focus on loss is a loss of focus.

Also worthy of note is Lord Goff's analysis of the academic writings that supported the position taken in *Khorasandjian v Bush*.

> I feel driven to say that I found in the academic works which I consulted little more than an assertion of the desirability of extending the right of recovery in the manner favoured by the Court of Appeal in the present case. I have to say . . . that I have found no analysis of the problem; and in circumstances such as this, a crumb of analysis is worth a loaf of opinion.[14]

As has been noted before, this is what one can expect with respect to a tort whose very basis is a mystery.

The Court of Appeal in *Khorasandjian v Bush* claimed support from the decision of the Alberta Supreme Court in *Motherwell v Motherwell*.[15] That support was examined in *Hunter v Canary Wharf*. In *Motherwell v Motherwell*, the defendant made frequent, harassing telephone calls to the three claimants: the defendant's father, brother and sister-in-law. We are concerned only with the claim as between the defendant and her sister-in-law. Though the calls were made to that claimant's home, only her husband held title to the land. Nevertheless, the Alberta Supreme Court found for the claimant.

In doing so, the Canadian Court in turn relied on the decision of the English Court of Appeal in *Foster v Warblington Urban District Council*.[16] In that case, the claimant had purchased and used oyster ponds on the foreshore of a creek near the sea. The defendant was responsible for sewage discharged into the claimant's oyster ponds. The claimant's title to the ponds was disputed, but this was held not to be decisive. Vaughan Williams LJ maintained:

> But, even if title could not be proved, in my judgment there has been such an occupation of these beds for such a length of time . . . as would entitle the plaintiff as against the defendants, who have no interest in the foreshore, to sustain this action for the injury which it is alleged has been done by the sewage to his oysters so kept in those beds.[17]

Commenting on this in *Motherwell v Motherwell*, Clement JA said:

> There is authority that a claim in nuisance is not necessarily restricted to an occupier who has some legally demonstrable and enforceable right of occupation. In *Foster v. Warblington Urban Council*, . . . a substantial de facto occupation was recognized as sufficient.

[14] *Hunter v Canary Wharf* [1997] AC 655 (HL), 694.
[15] *Motherwell v Motherwell* (1976) 73 DLR 62 (Alberta SC).
[16] *Foster v Warblington Urban District Council* [1906] 1 KB 648 (CA). For a similar case, see *Newcastle-Under-Lyme Corpn v Wolstanton Ltd* [1947] Ch 427.
[17] *Foster v Warblington Urban District Council* [1906] 1 KB 648 (CA), 659–60.

Thus, a distinction is drawn between one who is 'merely present' and occupancy of a substantial nature. In the latter case it is the fact of the occupation that supports the action, although admittedly the legal aspect of an occupation may well have an influence on the conclusion. I would not think trespass, even if persisted in, would ground an action in nuisance.[18]

In *Hunter v Canary Wharf*, Lord Goff insisted that this was in error.

[The] conclusion [in *Motherwell v Motherwell*] was very largely based on the decision of the Court of Appeal in *Foster v. Warblington Urban District Council* . . . which Clement J.A. understood to establish a distinction between 'one who is "merely present"' and 'occupancy of a substantial nature,' and that in the latter case the occupier was entitled to sue in private nuisance. However, *Foster v. Warblington Urban District Council* does not in my opinion provide authority for the proposition that a person in the position of a mere licensee, such as a wife or husband in her or his spouse's house, is entitled to sue in that action. This misunderstanding must, I fear, undermine the authority of *Motherwell v. Motherwell* on this point; and in so far as the decision of the Court of Appeal in *Khorasandjian v. Bush* is founded upon *Motherwell v. Motherwell* it is likewise undermined.[19]

Neither the Court of Appeal in *Khorasandjian v Bush* nor the House of Lords in *Hunter v Canary Wharf* understood the decision in *Motherwell v Motherwell*.

Lord Goff was quite right to note that *Foster v Warblington Urban District Council* did not establish that 'a person in the position of a mere licensee . . . is entitled to sue'. In that case, the claimant was found to be the legal occupier, that is, the legal possessor, of the oyster pools in question, even on the assumption that he could not prove title. Thus, Lord Goff was right to insist that the case does not support the proposition he examines. But Clement JA did not make it. His claim was that *Foster v Warblington Urban District Council* supports the idea that occupation or possession is sufficient for standing.

With that claim, Lord Goff would have had no quarrel. But he would have thought it irrelevant, as the claimants in the cases we are examining were not occupiers and were not in possession. But it was that, and not the traditional rule under consideration now, that Clement JA was disputing. In his view, those claimants were in possession.

Thus, Clement JA accepted that a mere licensee could not recover.[20] However, he insisted that the claimant was no mere licensee. 'In the case at bar the brother is, as I infer, the owner of the premises *he occupies with his wife*, the sister-in-law, and their family.'[21] Accordingly:

Here we have a wife harassed in the matrimonial home. *She has a status, a right to live there* with her husband and children. I find it absurd to say that her occupancy of the

---

[18]   *Motherwell v Motherwell* (1976) 73 DLR 62 (Alberta SC), [60]–[61].
[19]   *Hunter v Canary Wharf* [1997] AC 655 (HL), 691.
[20]   *Motherwell v Motherwell* (1976) 73 DLR 62 (Alberta SC), [59].
[21]   ibid (emphasis added).

matrimonial home is insufficient to found an action in nuisance. In my opinion she is entitled to the same relief as is her husband, the brother.[22]

Consider also the decision of the New Brunswick Court of Appeal in *Devon Lumber Co Ltd v MacNeill.*[23] The claimants complained of wood dust entering their house from the defendant's mill. Two of the claimants were the husband and wife owner of the property. The other two were the owner's children. Stratton CJNB allowed the children's claim, arguing:

> In the present case, it was established at trial that Mrs. MacNeill was a joint owner of the property with her husband and that they and their children lived together in the family home when the nuisance complained of occurred. Thus, at all relevant times, the MacNeills were *sharing possession* of the family home with their children and at the same time *the children had a right to occupy the home* with their parents . . . I would accordingly conclude and hold that even though the children lacked any legal title to the property they *had a right of occupation* sufficient to support an action on their behalf for damages for any unreasonable and substantial interference with their lawful use or enjoyment of the family residence.[24]

This, it must be stressed, is not a rejection of the traditional rule outlined in *Read v J Lyons & Co Ltd* and reasserted by the House of Lords in *Hunter v Canary Wharf.* The Canadian courts all accept that 'he alone has a lawful claim who has suffered an invasion of some proprietary or other interest in land'.[25] The difference is that, in the kinds of cases under examination, the Canadian courts were prepared to recognise such interests.

This, it must also be stressed, does not involve a different approach to the law of nuisance. The difference, rather, concerns the underlying primary rights. In short, the difference directly concerns, not tort, but property law. The English courts were not prepared to recognise any right to property in persons such as a spouse or child of the title holder unless that right arises through legislation.[26] The Canadian courts, however, were more generous. Again, with respect to the law of nuisance, both jurisdictions apply the same principles; the difference is that they apply those principles to different underlying sets of primary rights.

Note that this is not the difference claimed by the English Court of Appeal in *Khorasandjian v Bush.* Dillon LJ's judgment suggested that the decision in *Motherwell v Motherwell* was policy based, founded on the desire to keep the law of nuisance 'up to date'.[27] That is an altogether too shallow reading of that case.

Because the division between the English and Canadian courts concerns the law of property rather than the law of nuisance proper, this is not the place to discuss it fully here. Nevertheless, the following comments seem pertinent.

---

[22] ibid [62] (emphasis added). Hence, TM FitzPatrick, 'Should Family Members have Title to Sue in Private Nuisance?' (1998) 6 *Torts Law Journal* 171 is wrong to suggest that the court is trading on the ambiguity between legal and merely factual possession.

[23] *Devon Lumber Co Ltd v MacNeill* (1987) 45 DLR (4th) 300 (New Brunswick CA).

[24] ibid [14] (emphases added).

[25] *Read v J Lyons & Co Ltd* [1947] AC 156 (HL), 183.

[26] eg the Matrimonial Homes Act 1967 (UK) and the Family Law Act 1996 (UK).

[27] *Khorasandjian v Bush* [1993] QB 727 (CA), 734.

It is surely quite bizarre that, at least as far as English law is concerned, persons such as children living in their parents' house are considered mere licensees. This is not only because, before the children are of age, the licence cannot be revoked at will as it could be for, say, a guest. It is because the status of a licensee is entirely inconsistent with the child's relationship to the property. This is not only because the child will be naturally attached to his home. It is also because, and indeed more fundamentally because (unless speaking specifically of the law of property), we recognise the home as *belonging* to the child. That is, after all, what we say. It is *his* home. And we recognise violations of the home as violations of what belongs to the child.[28]

There is no good reason for this belonging not to be recognised in property law. Of course, the right of the child must not trump the rights of the parents. But in a legal system used to recognising degrees of property, this poses no difficulty. Parents should have rights superior to their children, but that does not prevent children having rights superior to strangers.[29]

That the call is for a change to the law of property, and not to the law of nuisance, is indicated also by the fact that the change, if implemented, would affect the operation of the law of trespass as well. It is surely wrong that child occupants of their home have no right of action against trespassers. Parents should have rights superior to their children, but that does not prevent children having rights superior to trespassers.

In that light, it can be seen that the position taken by the English Court of Appeal in *Khorasandjian v Bush*, by Lord Cooke in *Hunter v Canary Wharf* and by the majority of commentators, is timorous in recognising the rights of children (to continue our focus on that category of person). Certainly, children should be protected from nuisances. But that is not because they need looking after by the private law, pushed, perhaps, to do so by human rights instruments.[30] It is because their private rights to their home ought to be recognised. To put this another way, the injustice worked by the current English position is not cured by treating children (and others) as passive recipients of our generosity in extending actions to protect their interests; it is cured by recognising their moral personality and the primary rights that arise from it.

---

[28] For the record, I do not regard these comments as non-legal or accept that these points have been made from outside the legal point of view.

[29] This is given all the more impetus by art 8 of the European Convention on Human Rights, given effect in UK law by the Human Rights Act 1998. But it would be quite wrong to base the argument on such. Family members should not need these instruments in order to have their private rights recognised, though they may find that these tools are the best available.

[30] Here, I mean especially to criticise the judgment of Lord Cooke in *Hunter v Canary Wharf* [1997] AC 655 (HL). One anonymous reviewer asks why I do not at this point examine recent scholarship relating to the special status of 'the home' or the impact of human rights instruments. The reason is that I think that this material approaches the issues from the wrong end. For my views about human rights in particular, see A Beever, 'Our Most Fundamental Rights' in A Robertson and D Nolan (eds), *Rights and Private Law* (Oxford, Hart, 2011). I am, therefore, also distressed by the decision of the Court of Appeal in *Dobson v Thames Water Utilities Ltd* [2009] EWCA Civ 28, [2009] 3 All ER 319 (CA).

II. Identifying the Defendant: Who Can be Sued?

Who can be sued? The textbooks give a standard answer: The general rule is that the creator of a nuisance and the occupier of the land from which the nuisance emanated are liable.[31] However, textbooks also tell us that there are a great many exceptions to this rule, so many that it is hard to see in what sense the rule can be said to exist at all.[32] Thus, once more, a new approach is called for: an approach that does not classify or pigeonhole according to evidently inadequate criteria, but that possesses genuine explanatory power.

The law of nuisance is concerned to prioritise property rights. It does so by insisting that the exercise of more fundamental rights trumps the exercise of less fundamental rights. It follows from this, as we have seen in chapter seven, that a defendant can be liable only if she uses the land in question in a way that encompasses the nuisance. Otherwise, no matter how much of a nuisance in colloquial terms the complained-of situation is, and no matter how much the defendant interferes with the claimant's use and enjoyment of his land, the defendant cannot be committing a nuisance. Of course, that does not mean that she acts legally. It may well be that she commits a different tort or a crime. But that is another matter.

This point is sometimes expressed by saying that the nuisance must emanate from the defendant's land. That formulation is too narrow, however. It is better to say that the nuisance must emanate from land over which the defendant exercises control. This is because the defendant cannot be using the land unless she has control over it. In other words, control here is a synonym for use. But as we will see, even this is not quite correct. In accordance with the principle argued for in this book, the issue is whether the nuisance relates to the use by the defendant of the relevant land. As we examine in the exploration of *Halsey v Esso Petroleum*[33] at the end of this chapter, it is possible to use one's land in a way that causes a nuisance to emanate from outside one's land. Liability for such activities is supported by the argument advanced here.

It is for this reason that occupiers are liable, even if they do not create the nuisance, as long as the nuisance relates to their use of land. So, for instance, an occupier is liable for the nuisances committed by those who are lawfully on the occupier's land. In these circumstances, the creation of the nuisance must at least by implication be licensed by the occupier (or the activity in question would exceed the licence and thus be an act of trespass), and so relates to the occupier's use of the land. However, as we saw in chapter seven, a defendant cannot be liable for a nuisance created on her land by a trespasser or by an act of nature, unless she continues or adopts that nuisance. This is because, as discussed, without continuation or adoption, the nuisance does not relate to the defendant's use of his land.

[31] See, eg, WVH Rogers, *Winfield and Jolowicz on Tort*, 18th edn (London, Sweet & Maxwell, 2010) 734–44.

[32] Again, see, eg, ibid.

[33] *Halsey v Esso Petroleum* [1961] 1 WLR 683.

Thus, the law's approach with respect to occupiers is an immediate consequence of the issues examined in chapter seven.[34] As such, it does not itself need to be explored further here. However, it is important to stress that this has nothing to do with vicarious liability.

If a third party creates a nuisance on the defendant's land in a way that relates to the defendant's use of that land, then the defendant is liable, not because he is vicariously liable for the actions of the third party, but because he is using his land in a way that interferes with the more fundamental use of the claimant's.[35]

Unfortunately, this issue is muddied by the decision of the English Court of Appeal in *Matania v National Provincial Bank*.[36] Independent contractors, hired by the defendant, created a great deal of noise and dust in the claimant's premises. In finding for the claimant, Romer LJ said:

> if the Elevenist Syndicate had done this work themselves, in view of the conclusions of fact to which we have come, the syndicate would plainly have been responsible to Mr Matania for the damage that he sustained by reason of the syndicate not having taken reasonable and proper precautions to minimise that damage, but it is said by them, and said truly: 'The work was not done by us, but by our co-defendants, Messrs. Adamson, who were independent contractors.' It is, of course, true that in general a person is not liable for damage caused to another by the negligence of his independent contractor [as vicarious liability holds in this situation], but to that rule there is an exception . . . The exception, as I understand it, is this, that where a man employs an independent contractor to do work which of its very nature involves a risk of damage being occasioned to a third party, that person is responsible to the third party if such damage be occasioned and cannot shelter himself under the general principle of non-liability for the negligence of an independent contractor. Now apply that principle to the present case. It appears to me that the syndicate must be held liable.[37]

According to this view, the defendant was vicariously liable for the tort committed by the contractor. The reason for this is that, although vicarious liability would not normally hold where the primary tortfeasor was an independent contractor, this case falls under an exception to that rule. This sort of reasoning has led to the view that 'it may be that it is the general rule in nuisance that the occupier is liable for his contractor's negligence'.[38]

Romer LJ's analysis is odd. If I hire a person to commit a tort, and that tort is committed, I am no doubt liable. But that is not because the tort was committed by my employee acting in the course of his employment. It is because, in hiring

---

[34] eg *Sedleigh-Denfield v O'Callaghan* [1940] AC 880 (HL).

[35] This view must also be distinguished from the view of vicarious liability promoted in R Stevens, *Torts and Rights* (Oxford, Oxford University Press, 2007) 257–74. Stevens argues, in my view correctly, that so-called vicarious liability is not really vicarious. Rather, in the relevant cases, *in law*, the defendant – often a legal rather than a natural person – has committed the tort through the actions of another. In the cases under discussion here, however, it is often only the defendant who is committing the tort. This should become clear in the following. This is not to criticise Stevens' position in any way. It is to say only that it does not apply to these cases because vicarious liability is not relevant here.

[36] *Matania v National Provincial Bank* [1936] 2 All ER 633 (CA).

[37] ibid 648. See also ibid 645–45 (Romer LJ).

[38] WVH Rogers, *Winfield and Jolowicz on Tort*, 18th edn (London, Sweet & Maxwell, 2010) 736.

the person to commit the tort, I commit it when it is committed. In the language of the criminal law, my liability is secondary, not vicarious.[39] Thus, the liability of the defendant in *Matania v National Provincial Bank* is best understood, not as vicarious, being based on an exception to the normal rules of vicarious liability, but as secondary. The independent contractor was hired by the owner to commit the tort, and thus the owner was liable for committing the tort, not vicariously for the commission of the tort by another. The defendant in *Matania v National Provincial Bank* used his property (through another) in a way that interfered with a more fundamental use of the claimant's land. Thus, the defendant was liable.

Another somewhat unfortunate case in this regard is *Bower v Peate*.[40] The defendant hired a contractor to excavate his property. The excavation removed soil supporting the claimant's land, thereby causing a subsidence on that land and damaging the claimant's house. Cockburn CJ allowed the claim, basing the relevant part of his decision on two grounds. The second of these was the following:

> A man who orders a work to be executed, from which, in the natural course of things, injurious consequences to his neighbour must be expected to arise, unless means are adopted by which such consequences may be prevented, is bound to see to the doing of that which is necessary to prevent the mischief, and cannot relieve himself of his responsibility by employing some one else . . . to do what is necessary to prevent the act he has ordered to be done from becoming wrongful.[41]

This suggests that the defendant's liability rests on a non-delegable duty, often itself thought to be an instance of vicarious liability.[42]

This kind of appeal to a non-delegable duty is uninformative. What we need to know is what the duty is and why it is of such a nature that it cannot be delegated. Moreover, if we do know that, then we do not additionally need to be told that the duty is non-delegable. In short, the claim that a duty is non-delegable is an assertion masquerading as an argument. What is the argument?

First let us ask: What is the defendant's duty? The answer cannot be that the defendant had a duty to ensure that the soil remained to support the claimant's land. As we see below, if a trespasser had removed the soil unknown to the defendant, he would not have been liable. The duty must rather have been a duty not *to remove* the soil, given that removal would cause the subsidence. But now that is the issue. Did the defendant remove the soil?

The answer is 'Yes'. The defendant employed the contractor to remove the soil. Again, then, he removed it, though of course not physically. His liability is secondary, not vicarious. The removal of the soil was a use of the land by the defendant (through another) and so, as it interfered with a more fundamental use of the claimant's land, the defendant was liable.

---

[39] *cf* the discussion of this matter in *OBG Ltd v Allan* 2007 UKHL 21, [2008] 1 AC 1 (HL), though I think that concept misplaced in that context.

[40] *Bower v Peate* (1876) LR 1 QBD 321.

[41] ibid 326.

[42] For criticism of this view, see R Stevens, 'Non-Delegable Duties and Vicarious Liability' in JW Neyers, E Chamberlain and SGA Pitel (eds), *Emerging Issues in Tort Law* (Oxford, Hart, 2007).

However, as Cockburn CJ noted, the defendant's position would have been different were he:

> in the position of a man who has simply authorized and contracted for the execution of a work from which, if executed with due care, no injury can arise, and who is therefore not to be held responsible if, while the work is going on, injury arises from the negligence of the contractor or his servants.[43]

This is because, in those circumstances, the defendant would (or may) not have been using his land in the relevant way. In those circumstances, the use would have been only by the contractor. Thus the defendant would not be liable.

As noted at the beginning of this section, the conventional view holds that, in general, an occupier is liable for nuisance created on her land. This appears to suggest that a landlord, not in occupation, will not be liable. In fact, however, that is not so. There are circumstances in which a landlord will be liable. Again, this occurs when the nuisance can be described as relating to the landlord's use of the land.[44]

The most obvious case is if the landlord has authorised the nuisance. Thus, when the defendant in *Tetley v Chitty* leased land to a go-kart club in order to operate a go-kart track, he was found liable for the noise created by the racing carts.[45] As the lease between the landlord and the tenant was for the purposes of go-kart racing – that is, that was a common purpose as stated in the lease – it was correct to say that the go-kart racing was an exercise of the landlord's (and the tenant's) rights in the land and thus was a use of the land by the landlord (and the tenant).

The position is the same if the landlord knew that the land would be used by the tenant in the relevant way. There again, as the lease was taken out with this knowledge, the nuisance is committed in accordance with the exercise of the landlord's rights in the land and is therefore a use by the landlord.

The position is also the same if the nuisance arises in relation to something over which the landlord retains a right. In practice, this issue has arisen when a nuisance arises as the result of something that the landlord has covenanted to repair or has the right to enter and repair.[46] So, for instance, if the terms of the lease permit the landlord to enter the property in order to repair, say, a water tank, and the tank leaks onto the claimant's property causing damage, then this nuisance can be described as the result of an exercise of the landlord's rights in the land in question and hence of the landlord's use of the land.

This position also supports the much criticised rule, if little else, advanced by the English Court of Appeal in *Hussain v Lancaster CC*.[47] The claimants owned a shop on a council housing estate where they were subject to serious harassment

---

[43] *Bower v Peate* (1876) LR 1 QBD 321, 326.
[44] Note that the conclusions reached here are quite independent of the Defective Premises Act 1972.
[45] *Tetley v Chitty* [1986] 1 All ER 663.
[46] See, eg, *Payne v Rogers* (1794) 2 HBl 350; *Mint v Good* [1951] 1 KB 517 (CA).
[47] *Hussain v Lancaster CC* [2000] QB 1 (CA).

by persons living on the estate. They sued the local council, who owned both the highway upon which the harassment was committed and most of the property in the housing estate. Perhaps unfortunately, as it appears to have confused the issues and led to their claim being rejected in total, the claimants sought damages and injunctions requiring the council to take steps to avert the nuisance or to remove the perpetrators.

In finding for the defendant, the Court ruled that a nuisance is not committed unless it results from the defendant's use of the defendant's land.[48] If we understand 'defendant's land' in this formulation to mean land of which the defendant is in legal possession, then this statement is to be supported. Its basis is provided by the account advanced here. However, that principle was misapplied in *Hussain v Lancaster CC*. And it was misapplied, in part, because of the misunderstandings we have been examining.

According to Hirst LJ, the defendant could not be liable as, although 'the acts complained of unquestionably interfered persistently and intolerably with the plaintiffs' enjoyment of the plaintiffs' land, . . . they did not involve the tenants' use of the tenants' land and therefore fell outside the scope of the tort'.[49] This assumes that the defendant's liability could only be vicarious. The idea was that, in order to find the defendant liable in nuisance, it was necessary to show that the tenants had committed a nuisance; but that was impossible as the harassment was not the result of the tenants' use of their land. This approach is wrong. In *Hussain v Lancaster CC*, it was at least arguable that the harassment suffered by the claimants was the result of the exercise of the defendant's rights in its land – the land in question here being the highway, not the apartments in the estate. Accordingly, the case should have been allowed to go to trial.[50]

In that regard, *Hussain v Lancaster CC* is usefully compared with the decision of the same Court, almost exactly one year later, in *Lippiatt v South Gloucestershire Council*.[51] Travellers had camped on the defendant council's land, neighbouring the claimants'. The travellers had committed frequent acts of trespass on, had left refuse on, had obstructed access to, had stolen items from and had damaged the claimants' property. They had also acted belligerently towards the claimants and their families, employees and neighbours. Importantly, though the travellers were trespassers on the defendant's land, the defendant not only tolerated their presence but provided amenities such as toilets and water.[52]

The Court held that the claim should not be struck out and that, if the facts were as alleged, the claimants should succeed. This cannot have been because the

---

[48] ibid 23.

[49] ibid.

[50] This is not to say that the claimants ought to have succeeded. Liability should flow only if the defendant's use of land encompassed the tenant's harassment of the claimants. That was the matter that needed to be litigated.

[51] *Lippiatt v South Gloucestershire Council* [2000] QB 51 (CA). See also *Page Motors Ltd v Epsom and Ewell* (1981) 80 LGR 337 (CA).

[52] *Lippiatt v South Gloucestershire Council* [2000] QB 51 (CA), 55.

defendant would be vicariously liable for the nuisance committed by the travellers. It is because the defendant would be liable for its use of its land.

That point, however, does not seem to have been fully appreciated by the Court. It distinguished *Hussain v Lancaster CC* on the ground that the earlier case involved no private nuisance as the harassment did not emanate from the harassers' land; whereas in *Lippiatt*, 'the allegation is that the travellers were allowed to congregate on the council's land and that they used it as a base for the unlawful activities of which the plaintiffs, as neighbours, complain'.[53] For the reason noted above, that principle may well apply to *Hussain v Lancaster CC*.

The problem is that, while the Court in *Lippiatt* correctly held that the defendant's liability in that case would be secondary and not vicarious, it distinguished *Hussain v Lancaster CC* in a way that requires this kind of liability to be vicarious rather than secondary. The better position is to hold that, though the rule enunciated in *Hussain v Lancaster CC* is correct, it was not correctly applied in that case.

Note also that *Lippiatt* supports the position advanced here. If, as the Court in *Lippiatt* maintained, the harassers in *Hussain v Lancaster CC* could not be liable in private nuisance, because their harassment did not emanate from their land,[54] then the travellers also could not be liable for nuisance (though of course they could be liable in other ways) *unless* their presence on the land in question generated in them rights to the use of that land.

The rule that a defendant can be liable only if she uses the land in question in a way that encompasses the nuisance is sound. But it has been much criticised. It will be instructive to examine one important example of this criticism.

According to WVH Rogers:

> In *Hussain v Lancaster CC* . . . the Court of Appeal said that there was no nuisance because the acts did not involve the wrongdoers' use of their land, even though it affected the claimants' enjoyment of theirs. With respect, this seems an unnecessary restriction: to say that nuisance is a tort to the claimant's land does not require the additional proposition that it must involve the defendant's use of his land. Suppose, for example, that D, in pursuit of a vendetta against C, repeatedly disturbs C in his remote farmhouse by parking outside, shining his car headlights through the windows and playing his music system at full volume. That is not a public nuisance because it does not affect a 'class' of people. Is there any reason why it should not be a private nuisance? Of course, such conduct might now be a tort under the Protection from Harassment Act 1997 but it is surprising that it was not a nuisance before the Act. The approach in *Hussain* would insulate from liability persons like independent contractors who may create a nuisance affecting the land of C while working on the land of B but have no possession of the latter.[55]

The first thing to say about this passage is that, to its author, the rule 'seems an unnecessary restriction' because of the influence of the conventional approach. It

[53] ibid 61.
[54] ibid.
[55] WVH Rogers, *Winfield and Jolowicz on Tort*, 18th edn (London, Sweet & Maxwell, 2010) 734–35 (citations omitted).

is because liability in nuisance is thought to rest on the unreasonableness of the defendant's conduct and/or the interference with the claimant and, in this case, both the defendant's behaviour and the interference with the claimants seems unreasonable. Taking the second half of this view, *Hussain v Lancaster CC* appears to be a case in which the claimants' enjoyment of their land was unreasonably interfered with.

That just shows the limitations of this approach. No doubt, the interference with the claimants' use of land – that is, the harassment – was unreasonable. But that in itself can do precisely nothing to show that the defendant ought to be liable. This is particularly clear in this case when the defendant was not doing the harassing. The general point is that it is impossible to decide whether one person should be liable to another by focusing only on the position of one of the parties.

Moreover, why might we think that the defendant in the farmhouse example is committing a wrong? The notion that the defendant is engaged in a vendetta suggests that it is because the defendant is harassing the claimant. Now, it is surprising that it was not a recognised legal wrong before the passage of the Protection from Harassment Act, but that is surely because it is surprising that we needed that Act in order to recognise harassment as a wrong; not, it must be stressed, as a nuisance, but as an act of harassment.

What is more, it is important to recognise that the answer to the question 'Is there any reason why it should not be a private nuisance?' is very likely to be 'No'. But if there is a nuisance here, it is not being committed by the defendant. It is being committed by the person who owns (or controls) the land upon which the defendant is parked, assuming that the person knows, perhaps as a result of being told, what is going on.

And this seems the right approach. Change the example slightly. Imagine that the claimant is seriously being disturbed by lights shining into his bedroom from cars passing over a hill on an adjacent road. Is each and every driver guilty of a nuisance? Surely the answer is 'No'.[56] If the claimant has an action, he has an action against the owner of the road, who must erect a barrier or the like. Again we can see that it is the defendant's intention in the original case, his desire to inflict revenge, that makes us feel that he is a wrongdoer. That wrong must therefore be harassment rather than nuisance.

Finally, it is not clear that the rule in question will 'insulate from liability' persons such as the independent contractor imagined. This position seems wrongly to assume that liability in this area must be vicarious or at least linked to vicarious liability. Independent contractors in these circumstances may in fact be exercising rights in the land in question. Furthermore, even if the person cannot be sued in nuisance, he is very likely to be able to be sued in other torts and nothing here insulates the occupier of the land from nuisance liability.

---

[56] And note that this cannot be because the interference caused by each individual driver is insufficient to constitute a nuisance. *Lambton v Mellish* [1894] 3 Ch 163.

As Rogers also notes, in *Le Jones (Insurance Brokers) Limited v Portsmouth CC*, Dyson LJ appeared to hold that there was no authority for the rule 'that a person cannot be liable in nuisance unless he is in occupation of the land or has some legal interest in it'.[57] The difficulty is that this claim is patently incorrect. Not only do *Hussain v Lancaster CC* and *Lippiatt v South Gloucestershire Council* stand opposed but, as Rogers acknowledges, *Transco plc v Stockport Metropolitan Borough Council* 'is replete with statements like [nuisance is an] "interference by one occupier of land with the right in or enjoyment of land by another occupier of land"'.[58] Rogers replies that 'this is the position in the vast majority of cases and . . . nothing turned on the defendant's status [in *Transco*] since it plainly was an occupier'.[59] However, while this is true, it does not undermine the force of the claims in *Transco*. Why, after all, repeatedly say that a nuisance is an 'interference by one occupier of land with the right in or enjoyment of land by another occupier of land' if one means only that a nuisance is an interference with 'the right in or enjoyment of land by anyone'? Perhaps this was just a verbose slip on the part of the House of Lords in *Transco* but, *if* so, then it was a Freudian one in which the judges revealed more than they knew.

What, then, should be said about *Le Jones (Insurance Brokers) Limited v Portsmouth CC*? The claimant suffered damage when roots from trees on land owned by Hampshire County Council encroached onto his property.[60]

> At all material times, [the defendant] was acting as agent for Hampshire County Council . . . pursuant to an agency agreement [between the defendant and HCC, by which the defendant] agreed to carry out inter alia the functions of 'planting and maintenance of trees and shrubs and grass verges' [and] control, ordering and supervision of routine maintenance.[61]

In finding for the claimant, Dyson LJ said:

> In my view, the basis for the liability of an occupier for a nuisance on his land is not his occupation as such. Rather, it is that, by virtue of his occupation, an occupier usually has it in his power to take the measures that are necessary to prevent or eliminate the nuisance. He has sufficient control over the hazard which constitutes the nuisance for it to be reasonable to make him liable for the *foreseeable* consequences of his failure to exercise that control so as to remove the hazard.[62]

---

[57] *Le Jones (Insurance Brokers) Limited v Portsmouth CC* [2002] EWCA Civ 1723, [2003] 1 WLR 427 (CA), [13]. See also *Southport Corp v Esso Petroleum Co Ltd* [1953] 3 WLR 773, 776. This case, however, clearly involves a *public*, not a private, nuisance. As Devlin J says: 'An action for a public nuisance of this type cannot in principle depend upon contiguity to the highway'.

[58] WVH Rogers, *Winfield and Jolowicz on Tort*, 18th edn (London, Sweet & Maxwell, 2010) 735 n 192; *Transco plc v Stockport Metropolitan Borough Council* [2003] UKHL 61, [2004] 2 AC 1, [9].

[59] WVH Rogers, *Winfield and Jolowicz on Tort*, 18th edn (London, Sweet & Maxwell, 2010) 735.

[60] Here I will ignore the claim made in ch 7 that such liability does not properly lie in the law of nuisance.

[61] *Le Jones (Insurance Brokers) Limited v Portsmouth CC* [2002] EWCA Civ 1723, [2003] 1 WLR 427 (CA), [4].

[62] ibid [11] (emphasis added).

As must now be clear, this is to accept the slide to negligence. Here, the liability is understood to lie in the defendant's failings, indeed in the defendant's fault. Given this approach, it is entirely unsurprising that Dyson LJ came to the conclusion that it was irrelevant whether the defendant was in occupation of the land in question. The defendant had caused a foreseeable injury to the claimant and thus was liable. It was also entirely unsurprising that Dyson LJ also held that the defendant was liable in negligence.

Consider the following.

> In my judgment, it is not necessary to decide whether Portsmouth was an occupier of the highway in this case. What matters is that it had the right and duty to maintain the trees, and that this included, where necessary, the right and duty to reduce their height so as to prevent damage being caused to nearby properties. The agency agreements gave it sufficient control over the trees, both in fact and in law, to prevent any nuisance from occurring, and to eliminate any nuisance that did occur. Mr Bebb [for the defendant] submitted that the control exercised by Portsmouth arose from the performance of its contractual obligations to HCC. This is true, but in my view irrelevant. What matters is that it exercised control, not the legal basis on which it came to do so. I am in no doubt that the degree of control exercised by Portsmouth over the trees was sufficient for it to be reasonable to fix it with liability for the nuisance.[63]

This is to say that the defendant's liability lies in the fact that it had sufficient control over the growth of the trees that it was able to prevent the claimant's injury and so, as that injury was foreseeable and the defendant did not prevent it, the defendant was liable. This just means that the defendant was guilty of negligence.

I submit that *if*, as Dyson LJ is prepared to assume, the defendant was what we might call a bare licensee – that is, a person with no more than a permission to be on the land and hence no entitlement to use the land – and did not use the land, then with respect to the law of nuisance, *Le Jones (Insurance Brokers) Limited v Portsmouth CC* is wrongly decided. But there is surely significant evidence to suggest that the defendant was no bare licensee and did use the land. As we are told, 'At all material times, [the defendant] was acting as agent for Hampshire County Council', exercising control over, not only the trees, but all the land in question.[64] It is far from unlikely, then, that the defendant was exercising rights, and not merely contractual rights, over the land in question and so was rightly held liable in nuisance. It is not necessary to collapse the law into negligence to get this result.

Before we can leave these issues behind, it is necessary to discuss the following four examples that are apparently inconsistent with the position advanced here.[65] The first is the decision of the Supreme Court of New Zealand in *Clearlite Holdings Ltd v Auckland City Corp*.[66] In the words of Mahon J, 'In this case the plaintiff company seeks to recover its monetary loss sustained by reason of structural damage

---

[63] ibid [12].
[64] ibid [4].
[65] As claimed, for instance, in K Barker and others, *The Law of Torts in Australia*, 5th edn (Melbourne, Oxford University Press, 2012) 199.
[66] *Clearlite Holdings Ltd v Auckland City Corp* [1976] 2 NZLR 729 (SC).

caused to its factory building by a tunnel excavated under that building'.[67] The problem for the claimant was that this appeared to show that the nuisance had emanated from the claimant's own land.[68]

Mahon J, however, ruled in favour of the claimant, dismissing in the process the claim found in the 16th edition of *Salmond on Torts*, that 'As nuisance is a tort arising out of the duties owed by neighbouring occupiers, the plaintiff cannot succeed if the act or omission complained of is on premises in his occupation. The nuisance must have arisen elsewhere than in or on the plaintiff's premises'.[69]

In fact, however, this decision is perfectly consistent with the position advanced here. As Robert Chambers has pointed out, the defendant was a statutory licensee with an exclusive right of control over the subsoil through which the tunnelling was done and the nuisance emanated from this land.[70] *Clearlite Holdings*, then, is an illustration of, not an exception to, the principle enunciated here.

Similar comments are to be made regarding the suggestion of Neale J in *Halsey v Esso Petroleum*[71] that the noise caused by the use of heavy vehicles on the public highway outside the defendant's terminal could constitute a nuisance. This is correct as that noise, though caused by vehicles outside the defendant's land, can nevertheless be represented as the result of (strictly: encompassed by) the use of the defendant's terminal. Here we see why it is too narrow to maintain that the nuisance must emanate from the defendant's land or even land which the defendant controls.

A different response must be given to *Paxhaven Holdings Ltd v AG*,[72] also a decision of Mahon J on the Supreme Court of New Zealand. The defendant had leased a portion of the claimant's land for carrying out fire-fighting exercises. The defendant left a barrel of fuel oil on the land. The claimant's cattle drank the fuel oil and died. The claimant alleged that the defendant was guilty of committing a nuisance. Mahon J agreed.

This, however, cannot be correct. The proper action in this case is breach of contractual licence or trespass. It seems plain that leaving the barrel of oil on the land was both a breach of the defendant's licence and therefore a trespass. Thus, that is the basis on which the claimant ought to have proceeded. Alternatively, if the contract permitted the defendant to leave the barrel of oil on the claimant's land, then there can be no action for breach of licence or trespass, but there can in those circumstances be no nuisance either, as the alleged nuisance was, *per hypothesis*, permitted by contract.

Likewise, though the decision of the Victorian Court of Appeal in *Animal Liberation (Vic) Inc v Gasser*[73] is sometimes thought to have ended the rule that a

---

[67] ibid 731.
[68] ibid.
[69] ibid.
[70] RS Chambers, 'Nuisance – Judicial Attack on Orthodoxy' [1978] *New Zealand Law Journal* 172.
[71] *Halsey v Esso Petroleum* [1961] 1 WLR 683.
[72] *Paxhaven Holdings Ltd v AG* [1974] 2 NZLR 185.
[73] *Animal Liberation (Vic) Inc v Gasser* [1991] 1 VR 51 (CA).

private nuisance must emanate from the defendant's land in Australia, that case tells us nothing about the law of private nuisance.

In *Animal Liberation (Vic) Inc v Gasser*, members of the defendant organisation protested against the use of animals in the claimant's circus. The protests included demonstrations outside the circus aimed at persuading members of the public not to attend. It was alleged that the protestors in this regard engaged in acts of 'intimidation', such as shouting and abuse. The claimant maintained that these actions constituted a nuisance and obtained an interim injunction against which the defendant appealed. The Court found for the claimant, maintaining that, on the facts as alleged, the protestors were guilty of a nuisance. The nuisance, however, was clearly not occurring on the defendant's land.

The Court in *Animal Liberation (Vic) Inc v Gasser* drew on a number of older cases, all of which involved parties who were found to have committed a nuisance by engaging in picketing. The first such case was *J Lyons & Sons v Wilkins*, in which Lindley MR said that 'Such conduct seriously interferes with the ordinary comfort of human existence and ordinary enjoyment of the house beset, and such conduct would support an action on the case for a nuisance at common law'.[74] Lindley then went on to cite a number of private nuisance cases in support of this view. This, of course, suggests that the nuisance in question is private nuisance. But it is also worth noting that none of the judges in the case can be said to have given the matter serious consideration, it not being a crucial aspect of the case. And as we see, later cases suggest that the nuisance in *J Lyons & Sons v Wilkins* was public, not private, nuisance.

Thus, in *Sid Ross Agency Pty Ltd v Actors and Announcers Equity Association of Australia*, Mason JA said:

> At common law, picketing is not necessarily a nuisance and unlawful as such, but it becomes so if it involves *obstruction* and besetting ... Here the pleading makes it abundantly clear that the form of picketing threatened involved *obstruction of the thoroughfares* and besetting of those who wished to enter the clubs [of third parties], thereby constituting a nuisance and an interference with *their* rights.[75]

This suggests that the wrong threatened by the defendants was an intimidation of third parties that amounted to a *public* nuisance suffered by the defendant.

Similarly, in *Dollar Sweets Pty Ltd v Federated Confectioners Association of Australia*, Murphy J said

> I am also satisfied that the acts of all the defendants which have now been repeatedly performed over many months cannot be considered to be a lawful form of picketing, but amount to a nuisance involving, as they do, obstruction, harassment and besetting. The form of picketing which the evidence discloses here is not peaceful but amounts clearly to an interference with the rights of a person wishing to enter or at least to proceed and make deliveries or take supplies to or from the plaintiff's premises. In fact, so

---

[74] *J Lyons & Sons v Wilkins* [1896] 1 Ch 255 (CA), 267.
[75] *Sid Ross Agency Pty Ltd v Actors and Announcers Equity Association of Australia* [1971] 1 NSWLR 760 (CA), 767 (emphases added).

often as they are able, the defendants physically prevent persons and vehicles from approaching and entering the plaintiff's premises. This, as I have said, is done by obstruction, threats and besetting, the latter meaning, in this context, to set about or surround with hostile intent. Besetting is appropriately a term applied to the occupation of a roadway or passageway through which persons wish to travel, so as to cause those persons to hesitate through fear to proceed or, if they do proceed, to do so only with fear for their own safety or the safety of their property. This is exactly what has occurred in this case, and is continuing to occur as a consequence of the picket, and its operation.[76]

Again, the defendant's wrong was an intimidation of third parties that amounted to a *public* nuisance suffered by the defendant.

Exactly the same is to be said of *Animal Liberation (Vic) Inc v Gasser*. The protestors' actions were described to have produced the following state of affairs.

For the people to enter the circus they had to walk past the ticket office and the 35 to 40 chanting protesters ... The demonstrators ... were on both sides of the entrance to the circus tent which is through a caravan referred to as the ticket office. (They) were carrying placards and handing out leaflets. They were intimidating the patrons and were intent on obstructing their entry to the circus. Some of the demonstrators engaged the patrons in discussion and I saw at least one argument. The demonstrators were aggressive in their manner and obstructed access to the circus tent by locating themselves around the ticket office.[77]

The Court commented:

It is one thing to attempt to dissuade another from a course which he/she wishes to pursue, by spoken words, and by holding up placards and signs, and/or by some play acting. It is quite another thing to attempt the dissuasion by putting the other person, and or the children accompanying him/her, in fear of personal safety, or by driving them away by making the surroundings intolerable, as by loud noise or unpleasant odours, or express or implied threats.[78]

Once again, whatever the Court may have intended, the clear implication is that the wrong is an act of intimidation that causes a public nuisance.

Given that, *Animal Liberation (Vic) Inc v Gasser* is irrelevant to our investigation. Naturally, a public nuisance does not have to emanate from the defendant's land. But that gives us no reason to think that this is not a requirement for a private nuisance. A private nuisance is an 'interference by one occupier of land with the right in or enjoyment of land by another occupier of land'.[79]

---

[76] *Dollar Sweets Pty Ltd v Federated Confectioners Association of Australia* [1986] VR 383, 388.
[77] *Animal Liberation (Vic) Inc v Gasser* [1991] 1 VR 51 (CA), 58.
[78] ibid.
[79] *Transco plc v Stockport Metropolitan Borough Council* [2003] UKHL 61, [2004] 2 AC 1, [9].

11

Statutory Authority

This chapter deals with the issue of statutory authority as it operates to negative a cause of action that would otherwise be possessed by the claimant. This issue is in fact so small that it barely deserves its own chapter. However, a certain amount of confusion has arisen in this regard that it is necessary to eliminate.

The operative principle is simple. In order for a nuisance to exist, the activity complained of must be illegal. But if a statute determines that the activity is legal, then there can be no nuisance.

In *Allen v Gulf Oil Refining Ltd*,[1] the claimant complained of the noise, vibration and smell caused by the defendant's construction of an oil refinery on the defendant's land. Ordinarily, accepting the claimant's allegations of fact, this would constitute a nuisance. In other words, the activity would be illegal. But the defendant maintained that the activity was authorised by the Gulf Oil Refining Act 1965. The majority of the House of Lords agreed. Thus, Lord Wilberforce maintained, 'I cannot but regard [the statute] as an authority . . . to construct and operate *a refinery* upon the lands to be acquired'.[2] As the inconveniences complained of were the inevitable consequences of the construction of a refinery – that is, because they were the result of the activity that the statute authorised – it followed that the activity and its consequences could not be illegal. There could therefore be no nuisance.

This analysis is usefully distinguished from the one provided by Lord Scott in *Transco plc v Stockport Metropolitan Borough Council*.

> [I]t is, I think, worth reflecting on why it is that an activity authorised, or required, by statute to be carried on will not, in the absence of negligence, expose the actor to strict liability in nuisance or under the rule in *Rylands v Fletcher*. The reason, in my opinion, is that members of the public are expected to put up with any adverse side-effects of such an activity provided always that it is carried on with due care. The use of the land for carrying on the activity cannot be characterised as unreasonable if it has been authorised or required by statute. Viewed against the fact of the statutory authority, the user is a natural and ordinary use of the land.[3]

---

[1] *Allen v Gulf Oil Refining Ltd* [1981] AC 1001 (HL).
[2] ibid 1012.
[3] *Transco plc v Stockport Metropolitan Borough Council* [2003] UKHL 61, [2004] 2 AC 1. Witness also the claim that 'A plea of statutory authority is in substance a plea of public interest': K Barker and others, *The Law of Torts in Australia*, 5th edn (Melbourne, Oxford University Press, 2012) 203.

This is in line with the conventional view of the law of nuisance outlined in chapter two. According to this account, the law of nuisance is based on the reasonableness of the defendant's use of his land. Given that, it seems right to say that if Parliament has determined that the defendant may or must use his land in a certain fashion, then that use cannot be, or cannot be found by the courts to be, unreasonable.

However, even putting aside the criticism of the conventional view made elsewhere in this book, this is an unnecessarily convoluted analysis. If the legislature has authorised an activity, it follows immediately that the activity cannot be illegal. We can get to the same result more circuitously by reasoning as did Lord Scott, but it is unnecessary to do so.

Moreover, we should not do so. Lord Scott's position does not take sufficient account of the impact of legislation and is thus not sufficiently respectful of the legislature. When the legislature passes legislation that authorises an activity, it is appropriate to assume that the legislature regards the activity as reasonable, but the primary impact of the legislation is not to advise that the activity is reasonable but to determine that it is legal. An appropriately respectful response to such legislation on the part of judges, then, is not to take it as advice – even as advice that must be accepted – that the defendant's actions are reasonable, but to take it as showing that the defendant's actions are legal regardless of the issue of reasonableness or anything else. As Blackburn J said in *Hammersmith and City Railway Co v Brand*, 'if the Legislature authorizes the doing of an act . . . no action can be maintained for that act, on the plain ground that no Court can treat that as a wrong which the Legislature has authorized'.[4] That the conventional view has led to an alternative approach is another mark of its inadequacy.[5]

In *Allen v Gulf Oil Refining Ltd*, Lord Wilberforce said:

> It is now well settled that where Parliament by express direction or by necessary implication has authorised the construction and use of an undertaking or works, that carries with it an authority to do what is authorised with immunity from any action based on nuisance. The right of action is taken away.[6]

This is correct, but the principle is not best expressed in this manner. Reference to immunity and to removing rights of action suggests that statutory authority removes only the claimant's secondary rights; that is, that it only prevents the claimant successfully bringing suit. In fact, however, the statutory authority destroys the claimant's primary rights vis-à-vis the defendant. The reason that the claimant cannot successfully bring suit is not because his action is barred, it is because the defendant's activity was legal. That must mean that, given the statute, the claimant had no relevant primary right that it held as against the defendant.

---

[4] *Hammersmith and City Railway Co v Brand* (1869–1870) LR 4 HL 171, 196. See also *Geddis v Proprietors of Bann Reservoir* (1877–1878) LR 3 App Cas 430 (HL), 455–56.
[5] For a similar and instructive analysis, see JW Neyers and J Diacur, 'What (is) a Nuisance?' (2011) 90 *Canadian Bar Review* 215, 236–37.
[6] *Allen v Gulf Oil Refining Ltd* [1981] AC 1001 (HL), 1011.

In consequence, according to the analysis presented here, statutory authority results in the confiscation of the claimant's property rights. Thus, in accordance with constitutional principle, it should not be done lightly or without compensation.[7]

Lord Keith dissented in *Allen v Gulf Oil Refining Ltd*. He argued that the defendant's activity was not authorised by the statute. In his view, it was necessary to distinguish between what the Gulf Oil Refining Act authorised the defendant to do and why it authorised the defendant to do it. Specifically, Lord Keith argued that the defendant was authorised to do certain things, such as compulsorily purchase land, in order to build a refinery; but the Act did not authorise the building of the refinery. As such, Lord Keith maintained that the inconvenience complained of by the claimant was not the result of an activity authorised by statute.[8]

The majority's position, on the other hand, was that, as the defendant was authorised to do certain things in order to build a refinery, the natural implication was that the Act did authorise the building of the refinery. Accordingly, the majority held that the inconvenience complained of by the claimant was the result of an activity authorised by the statute.

The disagreement between the majority and Lord Keith was highly significant, but it does not concern the law of nuisance as such. Rather, it concerns statutory interpretation. In other words, the disagreement was not about how the law of nuisance should be understood but about how statutes should be read. This book is not concerned with statutory interpretation and it takes no stand on how the debate above should be decided. Nevertheless, it is not possible to discuss this topic further and avoid this issue entirely. Accordingly, the material below utilises concepts of statutory interpretation to an extent. No controversial claims are made in this regard, however.

The approach enunciated above enables us to solve an outstanding problem relating to planning permission. In short, the problem is this. In *Gillingham v Medway (Chatham) Dock Co Ltd*,[9] a case of public nuisance though decided on the basis that the law was in this regard identical with private nuisance, the Court held that planning permission can constitute a defence. In *Wheeler v Saunders Ltd*,[10] the Court of Appeal held that it could not, though without overruling *Gillingham*. This has led to significant confusion. But the solution is to understand first that planning permission presents no special problem. The issue is simply one of the ambit of the statutory authority.

In *Gillingham*, supporting the view that the defendant was protected by statutory authority, Buckley J said:

---

[7] For more discussion of these theme, see D Campbell, 'Of Coase and Corn: A (Sort of) Defence of Private Nuisance' (2000) 63 *MLR* 197.

[8] *Allen v Gulf Oil Refining Ltd* [1981] AC 1001 (HL), 1019–20.

[9] *Gillingham v Medway (Chatham) Dock Co Ltd* [1993] QB 343.

[10] *Wheeler v Saunders Ltd* [1996] Ch 19 (CA). See also *Ports of Auckland v Auckland City Council* [1999] 1 NZLR 600.

Doubtless one of the reasons for this approach is that Parliament is presumed to have considered the interests of those who will be affected by the undertaking or works and decided that benefits from them should outweigh any necessary adverse side effects. I believe that principle should be utilised in respect of planning permission.[11]

This is ambiguous between two very different positions. It could imply the view advanced by Lord Scott in *Allen v Gulf Oil Refining Ltd* criticised above. On this understanding, liability is negatived because, in the light of the planning permission, the court must accept that the defendant's activity is in the public interest. This view is objectionable for the reasons noted earlier. What is more, it will prevent us from finding the solution to the problem now under consideration.

An alternative reading is available, however. On this view, the relevance of the fact that 'Parliament is presumed to have considered the interests of those who will be affected by the undertaking or works and decided that benefits from them should outweigh any necessary adverse side effects' is that, given this presumption, the statutory authority must be understood to extend to the defendant's activity and its impact on the claimant. Witness also this passage, in which Buckley J describes the relevant planning regime:

> Parliament has set up a statutory framework and delegated the task of balancing the interests of the community against those of individuals and of holding the scales between individuals, to the local planning authority. There is the right to object to any proposed grant, provision for appeals and inquiries, and ultimately the minister decides. There is the added safeguard of judicial review. If a planning authority grants permission for a particular construction or use in its area it is almost certain that some local inhabitants will be prejudiced in the quiet enjoyment of their properties.[12]

Here, the idea seems to be that this conflict between the defendant's and the claimant's use of land was a matter considered by the planning authority. If that is so and if the permission is consequently granted, then that indicates that the permission incorporates an authorisation to perform the action *despite the fact* that it is inconsistent with the claimant's private rights. Here there is permission to act inconsistently with the claimant's private right.

Not all forms of planning permission will be of this kind, however. Compare what Staughton LJ said of the planning permission in *Wheeler v Saunders Ltd*:

> [T]he planning authority may not have had the full picture as to the effect of its decisions, and in particular the planning authority may reasonably have believed that any nuisance resulting from its decision would not be new but only a continuation of what had existed and been tolerated in the past.[13]

Here, given that the authority did not (or may not have) considered the claimant's private rights, one cannot conclude that the permission incorporates an authorisation to perform the action despite the fact that it is inconsistent with the

[11] *Gillingham v Medway (Chatham) Dock Co Ltd* [1993] QB 343, 359.
[12] ibid.
[13] *Wheeler v Saunders Ltd* [1996] Ch 19 (CA), 29.

claimant's private rights. One can conclude only that the permission authorises the defendant to perform an action where, as it turns out, this action is inconsistent with the claimant's private rights. Here there is no permission to act inconsistently with the claimant's right.

Accordingly, much turns on the enquiry conducted by the planning authority. To the extent that it considers the impact on the private rights of the claimant, it will tend to show that the planning permission constitutes a defence. Conversely, to the extent that this issue is ignored, the permission will be irrelevant. This is a matter, broadly, of construction.

Also relevant is the ambit of the authority given to the planning body. As Staughton LJ said:

> I do not consider that planning permission necessarily has the same effect as statutory authority. Parliament is sovereign and can abolish or limit the civil rights of individuals . . . Parliament cannot be irrational just as the sovereign can do no wrong. The planning authority on the other hand has only the powers delegated to it by Parliament. It is not in my view self-evident that they include the power to abolish or limit civil rights in any or all circumstances.[14]

Again, this is ultimately a matter of construction.[15]

The analysis advanced here also accounts for features of the law often thought to constitute additions or exceptions to the ordinary approach. So, for instance, in order to rely on statutory authority, it is said that the defendant's activity must be *intra vires* the statute in question. That, of course, is an immediate consequence of the principle enunciated above.

Moreover, the defendant will succeed only if the inconvenience complained of was an 'inevitable consequence' of the authorised activity. Being a reasonable consequence, or the like, is not sufficient. This rule rests on the idea that the legislature cannot be presumed to have intended to extinguish private rights. Rather, legislation will be read to extinguish these rights only if such is express or clearly implied. It follows that if the inconvenience of which the claimant complains is not the inevitable consequence of the authorised activity, then the legislature cannot be taken to have authorised the specific activity that caused the inconvenience. An example should clarify the point.

In *Allen v Gulf Oil Refining Ltd*, the majority of the House of Lords held that the defendant was authorised to build and operate an oil refinery. If, however, it was possible to have built and operated the refinery without creating the noise, vibration and smell complained of by the claimant, then the specific activity connected with the claimant's complaint – namely, building and operating a refinery *in a way* that caused noise, vibration and smell – would not have been authorised by the legislature. That is, if the defendant could have built and operated the refinery

---

[14] ibid 28.
[15] One important feature of this passage, and it is one that conflicts with the judgment in *Gillingham v Medway (Chatham) Dock Co Ltd* [1993] QB 343, is that the presumption must be that Parliament does not intend to remove private rights or to delegate the authority to do so.

without disturbing the claimant's rights, then the legislation would have been read to have authorised the defendant to build and operate a refinery, but only in a way that did not violate the claimant's rights. In *Allen v Gulf Oil Refining Ltd* itself, however, the defendant could not build or operate a refinery without causing the inconveniences of which the claimant complained. Thus, as the building and operating was authorised by statute, it follows that those inconveniences cannot have been illegal.

For the same reason, statutory authority does not protect a defendant who interferes with the claimant as a result of negligence. This is not, as Lord Wilberforce maintained, a 'qualification' on or 'condition' to the general approach;[16] it is a straightforward consequence of that approach. Unless the statute says so or clearly implies such, an authorisation to undertake an activity is not an authorisation to undertake the activity negligently. A defendant who acts negligently, then, acts outside the scope of the authorisation.

Likewise, legislation that permits the defendant to carry out an activity, though not necessarily an activity that causes a nuisance, can provide no defence. So, for instance, had the Gulf Oil Refining Act authorised the defendant to build and operate a refinery *somewhere*, and had it been possible for the defendant to have built and operated the refinery at a location that would not cause the kinds of inconvenience complained of, then the defendant would not have been able to rely on the Act. As Lord Selborne said in *Managers of the Metropolitan Asylum District v Hill*, an Act does not authorise the creation of what would otherwise be a nuisance if the Act 'does not necessarily require anything to be done under it which might not be done without causing a nuisance . . . [and] there is no evidence on the face of the Act that the Legislature supposed it to be impossible for any of them to be done (if they were done at all) somewhere and under some circumstances, without creating a nuisance'.[17] This is because, in those circumstances, 'the Legislature has manifested no intention that any of these optional powers . . . should be exercised at the expense of, or so as to interfere with, any man's private rights'.[18]

Again, for the same reason, legislation that confers discretion on the defendant must be divided into two kinds: legislation that provides discretion in relation to the performance of an activity that might cause a nuisance and legislation that provides discretion in relation to the performance of (what would otherwise be) a nuisance. A statute that gives a body the authority to build a sewer, conferring on the body the discretion as to how best to build the sewer is an example of the former. Here, the defendant cannot rely on the statute, unless the sewer cannot be built without causing a nuisance. But a statute that said or implied that the body possessed a discretion to determine how the sewer should be built, including the discretion to determine whether and how activities should be performed that will generate nuisances, is an example of the latter. Here, the statute will constitute a defence.

[16] *Allen v Gulf Oil Refining Ltd* [1981] AC 1001 (HL), 1011.
[17] *Managers of the Metropolitan Asylum District v Hill* (1880–1881) LR 6 App Cas 193 (HL), 201.
[18] ibid.

Of course, many issues of statutory interpretation remain. What is important now, however, is that the principle as it applies to the law of nuisance is clear and simple, even if applying it to particular cases can be difficult.

Before we finish, it will be useful to examine the instructive decision of the Supreme Court of Canada in *Tock v St John's Metropolitan Area Board.*[19] The claimant's basement was flooded due to a blockage in the storm water drains operated by the defendant. The defendant maintained that any possible action in nuisance was negatived by the Municipalities Act 1979. Though the Court unanimously held for the claimant, it was deeply split as to why.

According to Wilson J, with whom Lamer and L'Heureux-Dube JJ concurred, though the Act 'authorize[d] the [defendant] to construct and continue to operate and maintain the sewage system in question',[20] it was possible for the defendant to do these things without causing the flooding of the claimant's basement. Thus, the statute did not constitute a defence. This is of course entirely in line with the argument presented here.

La Forest J, with whom Dickson CJ somewhat remarkably concurred, came to the same result for different reasons.

Constraints of time and money will always militate against the building of absolutely failsafe systems (on the assumption that such systems are possible) and the maintaining of the best conceivable inspection system. Accordingly, a public authority charged with operating any service will inevitably have to strike a balance between the need to give due consideration to factors bearing on efficiency and thrift, and the need to protect persons and property from damage that the system in question is likely to cause. In a word, it will be necessary to make compromises, and I have no reason to doubt that these compromises will take into account the possibility of a certain amount of inevitable damage. This, it seems to me, is bound to occur where the costs of preventing predictable damage far outweigh the actual costs of that damage. To take one example, a public authority, depending on the nature of the threat posed to life and limb, might incur considerable difficulty in justifying to its ratepayers a decision to disburse annually an extra million dollars for a program of inspection that stood merely to forestall damage of one hundred thousand dollars. But the decision not to inspect in such circumstances does not change the fact that the resultant damage should properly be viewed as a cost of running the system . . . To my mind, the flaw in the inevitability test, as traditionally expressed, is that it does not take due account of the fact that 'inevitable' damage is often nothing but a hidden cost of running a given system.

In short, I question the applicability to the facts of the instant case of the defence of statutory authority as it is conventionally formulated. Where, as here, the authorizing statute does not specifically provide that a right of action in nuisance is taken away . . . I see no point in donning the cloak of a soothsayer to plumb the intent of the Legislature. After all, if the Legislature wishes to shift the risk from a public authority to the individual, it can do so in express terms. I see no reason why it should be presumed to be authorizing a serious nuisance. Nor do I accept that any weight should be accorded a showing by the public body that damage was inevitable. The determination that damage was inevitable,

---

[19] *Tock v St John's Metropolitan Area Board* [1989] 2 SCR 1181.
[20] ibid [7].

in the sense in which the term was defined earlier, does not provide a rationale for con-
cluding that it is reasonable to demand of the person whom misfortune has singled out
that he or she pay for the damage concerned. The costs of damage that is an inevitable
consequence of the provision of services that benefit the public at large should be borne
equally by all those who profit from the service.[21]

This led La Forest J to conclude that the defendant ought to be liable, so that the
defendant could pass the relevant costs on to those who benefit from the presence
of the sewer.

Two responses are pertinent. The first is that, on La Forest J's view, the issue
of the legality of the defendant's activity is irrelevant.[22] La Forest J did not argue
that the defendant committed a wrong. He rather argued that the best result is to
hold the defendant liable, as the defendant will function as a convenient conduit
through which an appropriate transfer can be made from the public to the claimant. Because of this, it follows on this picture that if a more convenient conduit
could be found, then that person ought to be liable. That is unacceptable.

Moreover, imagining that the flooding was inevitable, La Forest J's argument
would apply with equal force. Taking the argument seriously, then, would mean
that a defendant in those circumstances would also be liable.[23] But that cannot be
so, as in that case the legislation determines that the defendant's activity was legal.
The fundamental problem with La Forest J's analysis is that it is not a legal analysis.

Second, La Forest J misunderstood the significance of inevitability. As he
understood it, an inconvenience that is an inevitable consequence of an authorised activity is generally thought not to be actionable because it is assumed that
the legislature intended it not to be. In fact, however, the reason is that, as the
inconvenience was an inevitable consequence of an authorised activity, and as the
legislature authorised the activity, the causing of the inconvenience by the activity
cannot be illegal. This conclusion does not depend on the idea that the legislature
intended to authorise the inconvenience. As La Forest J rightly maintains, that
will seldom be the case.

---

[21] ibid [80]–[81]. *cf Marcic v Thames Water Utilities Ltd* [2002] 2 All ER 55 (CA), [113].

[22] One might prefer to express the point by saying that legality is reduced to the relevant economic
concerns.

[23] However, it is not clear that La Forest J took the argument seriously. *Tock v St John's Metropolitan
Area Board* [1989] 2 SCR 1181, [83].

12

Remedies

This chapter examines two issues: the basis upon which a court will issue an injunction preventing future acts of nuisance and remoteness of damage. The latter assumes prominence because of the rejection of foreseeability as an element of the action in chapter eight.

I. Injunctions

A. Principle and Discretion

It is customary to begin discussing injunctions by saying that they are a discretionary remedy.[1] The custom is unfortunate. The claim is at best deeply misleading.

If the claim means that the decision to award an injunction is arbitrary, that there are no rules or principles to guide a judge's decision, then the claim is straightforwardly false. Relevant principles exist to guide judicial decision making. Those principles are examined below. Alternatively, if the claim means that the principles in question guide but do not 'mechanically' determine outcomes, then the claim is correct. But as the same is true of all but the most exceptional areas of law, it is misleading at best to designate this one as peculiarly discretionary.

Frequently, a contrast is made between injunctions, which are said to be discretionary, and damages, which are said to be as of right. This contrast is genuine, but it is not well captured by the terminology under consideration. If the claimant proves that she has suffered actionable damage as the result of the defendant's nuisance, then it follows automatically that the claimant is entitled to damages. That is because the principles relating to the recovery of damages determine that there are no circumstances in which a claimant in the relevant situation would not be entitled to damages. However, if the claimant proves the existence of a continuing nuisance, it does not necessarily follow that the court will award an injunction. As we will see, the courts have the power to award damages in lieu of an injunction. But that is not because injunctions are a discretionary remedy. Rather, it is because the principles relating to the issuing of an injunction determine that there are

[1] Compare K Oliphant (ed), *The Law of Tort* (London, Butterworths, 2007) 383–84; J Murphy, *The Law of Nuisance* (Oxford, Oxford University Press, 2010) 115.

circumstances in which a claimant in the relevant situation would not be entitled to an injunction. The fact that an award is not automatic or inevitable does not show that it is awarded on a discretionary basis.

Of course, injunctions are described as discretionary because the award has its origin in equity rather than common law, and equity was, for a portion of its past, a discretionary jurisdiction. But modern equity is an altogether different creature. It is as principled as the law in general. In fact, it seems far more so in practice than, say, the modern law of negligence.

The starting point for discussion of the award must be the Chancery Amendment Act 1858, more commonly known as Lord Cairns' Act, which gave the Court of Chancery the power to award damages in lieu of an injunction. On the face of it, this gave the courts the discretion to refuse to award an injunction and to insist on damages instead. However, in accordance with their role as legal bodies, when presented with an apparent discretion of this kind, the courts 'structured their discretion' by developing principles. In ordinary language, this means that the courts abolished any apparent discretion that they were given, discretion in the proper sense being inconsistent with law. However, it may be best not to put too much emphasis on terminology.

In *Shelfer v City of London*, AL Smith LJ said:

In my opinion, it may be stated as a good working rule that –

(1.) If the injury to the plaintiff's legal rights is small,
(2.) And is one which is capable of being estimated in money,
(3.) And is one which can be adequately compensated by a small money payment,
(4.) And the case is one in which it would be oppressive to the defendant to grant an injunction: –

then damages in substitution for an injunction may be given.[2]

Unless the entirety of the common law is discretionary, this is not.

The focus now turns to the content of this principle. It is important to elucidate its justification. In this regard, two questions are pertinent. First, why does the law restrict the ability of the defendant to pay damages in lieu of an injunction? Second, why does the law permit the defendant to pay damages in lieu of an injunction when it does?

AL Smith LJ's answer to the first question is neatly stated in the following. A 'person by committing a wrongful act . . . is not thereby entitled to ask the Court to sanction his doing so by purchasing his neighbour's rights, by assessing damages in that behalf, leaving his neighbour with the nuisance'.[3] In short, as this issue only arises when a nuisance is being committed, awarding damages in lieu of an injunction would allow the defendant to pay in order to continue to violate the claimant's rights. Unless the claimant consents or the unusual circumstances examined in I.D obtain, that is an injustice.

---

[2] *Shelfer v City of London* [1895] 1 Ch 287 (CA), 322–23.
[3] ibid 322.

Smith LJ's is a good answer, but it makes the second question more pressing. If allowing damages in lieu permits the defendant to continue to violate the claimant's right, then why is this ever allowed? There is an answer to this question, but before we can get to it we must examine two challenges to the approach set out in *Shelfer v City of London*: the decision of the English Court of Appeal in *Miller v Jackson*[4] and of the High Court in *Dennis v Ministry of Defence*.[5]

B. *Miller v Jackson*[6]

As discussed in previous chapters, the defendant in *Miller v Jackson* ran a cricket club with a ground on which cricket had been played for over 70 years. The claimants had moved into a house on neighbouring land, previously farmland. Cricket balls were struck onto the claimants' land, frightening the claimants, exposing them to physical danger and damaging their house. As we saw, the majority held that the defendant was guilty of a nuisance. Here, however, we are concerned with the claimants' request for an injunction.

On this issue, the majority of the Court found for the defendant. As Lord Denning thought that no nuisance was committed, his conclusion that no injunction should be issued followed as a matter of course. For Cumming-Bruce LJ, however, who held that the defendant was committing a nuisance, matters were not so straightforward. As did Lord Denning, Cumming-Bruce LJ argued that the claimants ought to have known about the presence of the cricket club and were not being reasonable.[7] These arguments were also raised by Lord Denning, and have been dealt with in chapter six. Most significant here is that, according to Cumming-Bruce LJ, although the defendant was guilty of a continuing nuisance, respect for the public interest demanded that an injunction not be awarded. That position was also supported by Lord Denning.[8] We examine it now.

Cumming-Bruce LJ maintained:

> [O]n the facts of this case a court of equity must seek to strike a fair balance between the right of the plaintiffs to have quiet enjoyment of their house and garden without exposure to cricket balls occasionally falling like thunderbolts from the heavens, and the opportunity of the inhabitants of the village in which they live to continue to enjoy the manly sport which constitutes a summer recreation for adults and young persons . . . [A]s the judge found, [the female plaintiff] is reasonable in her fear that if the family use the garden while a match is in progress they will run risk of serious injury if a great hit happens to drive a ball up to the skies and down into their garden. It is reasonable to decide that during matches the family must keep out of the garden. The risk of damage

---

[4] *Miller v Jackson* [1977] QB 966 (CA).
[5] *Dennis v Ministry of Defence* [2003] EWHC 793, [2003] Env LR 34.
[6] This discussion proceeds on the basis that the defendant did not enjoy an easement in relation to the claimants' land. For the discussion of that matter, see ch 6, VI.
[7] *Miller v Jackson* [1977] QB 966 (CA), 988–89.
[8] ibid 981–82.

to the house can be dealt with in other ways, and is not such as to fortify significantly the case for an injunction stopping play on this ground.[9]

This passage clearly reveals what is at stake. The effect of the decision is to undermine the entitlement of the claimants to control the use of their property, thereby confiscating the claimants' property rights. What is more, the claimants' property rights were removed on the basis of interests possessed by the public – not, it must be stressed, by the defendant – that have no proper legal status whatsoever. If there were any doubt about this, it is removed by the following paragraph.

> [T]he plaintiffs . . . should accept [for example] the restrictions upon enjoyment of their garden which they may reasonably think necessary. That is the burden which they have to bear in order that the inhabitants of the village may not be deprived of their facilities for an innocent recreation which they have so long enjoyed on this ground.[10]

The claim is not that the result is unsupportable on policy grounds. Perhaps, for instance, had the defendant petitioned the local council to pass a bylaw protecting it from liability, the council ought to have granted its request. No stand is taken on that matter here. The point is that it cannot be right for a court to remove a party's legal entitlement in order to promote interests that have no legal basis. The claimants had a right to their land. The public had no right to use the cricket ground. The decision in *Miller v Jackson* is unjust.

C. *Dennis v Ministry of Defence*

The claimants were subject to extreme levels of noise from Harrier Jump Jets overflying their property operating from RAF Wittering. Buckley J held that this was sufficient to constitute a nuisance but maintained that, as the flights were conducted in order to secure the 'defence of the realm', consideration of the public interest demanded that an injunction not be awarded.[11]

In coming to this conclusion, Buckley J said:

> Where there is a real public interest in a particular use of land, I can see no objection in principle to taking that public interest into account, in one way or another, in deciding what is best to be done. Indeed, in effect that happens at present where use is authorised by statute . . . The difference in the instant case is that it is left to the common law to provide the answer, no statutory framework is present to assist. However, the public interest in question here, albeit very different, may be considered just as important [as in *Allen v Gulf Oil Refining Ltd*[12] and *Marcic v Thames Water Utilities Ltd*[13]], if not more

---

[9] ibid 988–89.

[10] ibid 989. And a question: Who are the 'they' in the passage 'which they may reasonably think necessary'?

[11] Strictly, as the defendant was the Crown, Buckley J considered only awarding a declaration. This need not concern us here, however.

[12] *Allen v Gulf Oil Refining Ltd* [1981] AC 1001 (HL).

[13] *Marcic v Thames Water Utilities Ltd* [2002] 2 All ER 55 (CA).

so. It could also be thought that the MoD's position, charged as it is with the defence of the realm, should be no less protected than commercial or other undertakings authorised directly by statute.[14]

This argument contains an error of a kind examined in the previous chapter.

The reason statutory authority negatives a claim in nuisance is not because it indicates that the legislature regards the defendant's activity as in the public interest. Though we must assume that, if the legislature authorises an activity, the legislature views the activity as in the public interest, that has no bearing on this area of the law. Rather, statutory authority shows directly that the defendant's activity cannot have been illegal. Cases involving statutory authority, then, provide no support for Buckley J's position.

Moreover, the judgment is an odd one. It is utterly convinced that the defendant's activities are in the public interest. As I am somewhat less impressed by the intonation of 'defence of the realm', I confess that this is far from clear to me.[15] But let us put that aside. What is of most interest now is that the conviction that the defendant's activity is socially beneficial seems coupled with the equally strong belief that, if an injunction were awarded, the MoD would have to cease its operations. But that is clearly wrong. If we accept that the defendant's activity was crucial for the 'defence of the realm', then we can be sure that, had an injunction been issued, the MoD would have been able to apply to the relevant public bodies for statutory protection. That would have meant that the public bodies would have been able to assess the public policy arguments in a forum to which all interested parties could have been invited. And that would have been the appropriate response.[16]

D. Damages in Lieu

On the face of it, the discussion of *Miller v Jackson* and *Dennis v Ministry of Defence* has made the outstanding question from I.A even harder to answer. If the criticism of the results in *Miller v Jackson* and *Dennis v Ministry of Defence* is that the Courts wrongly allowed the (non-right) interests of one group to trump the rights of the claimants, then how can an award of damages in lieu of an injunction ever be justified?

Given the thesis advanced here, there is only one possible answer. As the law of nuisance is concerned to prioritise property rights, damages may be awarded in lieu of an injunction when issuing an injunction would result in allowing the

---

[14] *Dennis v Ministry of Defence* [2003] EWHC 793, [2003] Env LR 34, [45].

[15] It is perhaps worth noting that the MoD was planning to move the relevant operations to the United States.

[16] This case is also interesting for another reason: its reliance on human rights arguments. What is most interesting about this is that it appears that these arguments made it easier, not harder, for Buckley J to fail properly to protect the claimants' private rights. This, I believe, is not an isolated example.

defendant's more fundamental right to be trumped by the less fundamental right of the claimant.

In order to illustrate this point, it is useful to examine the decision of the High Court of New Zealand in *Bank of New Zealand v Greenwood*.[17] The defendant built a shopping centre with an innovative design that included a glass frontage to a veranda. This frontage reflected sunlight into the claimants' properties, causing significant inconvenience to the customers and the people working in those buildings. The claimants maintained that this constituted a nuisance.

Hardie Boys J held that the defendant was guilty of a nuisance with respect to two of the three claimants. In regard to what I will call the third claimant, Hardie Boys J ruled that, as this party had venetian blinds fitted to the windows through which the light passed, and hence given that the glare could be eliminated by closing the blinds, no nuisance was committed.[18] The first two claimants, on the other hand, did not have blinds or any other convenient way of blocking the light.

The defendant maintained that the proper response was simply for the first two claimants to install blinds, curtains or the like and thereby place themselves in the position of the third claimant. But Hardie Boys J rejected this, saying 'as there would be no reason for either plaintiff to do anything were it not for the glare from the defendants' verandah, the argument does not impress me'.[19]

The key thing to take from this argument is that, according to Hardie Boys J, though the defendant was guilty of committing a nuisance vis-à-vis the first two claimants, this was a rather close-run thing. Had the claimants had curtains or blinds installed, the result would have been different.

The defendant also argued that the impact of liability would be considerable, not only for the defendant, but for owners of commercial buildings in general. To this, Hardie Boys J responded:

> To the extent that this is an appeal to set the public interest ahead of the private interests of the plaintiffs, then I regret that authority requires me to close my ears to it. Despite the valiant efforts of the cricket-loving members of the Court in *Miller v Jackson*, it has been made clear in *Kennaway v Thompson* that a long line of authority going back to *Shelfer v City of London Electric Lighting Company* . . . has maintained inviolate the principle that, in the words of Lindley LJ in the latter case, 'the circumstances that the wrong-doer is in some sense a public benefactor . . . [has not] ever been considered a sufficient reason for refusing to protect by injunction an individual whose rights are being persistently infringed.'[20]

What follows must be understood in the light of this comment. Though Hardie Boys J was right to reject the approach taken by the majority (on this issue) in *Miller v Jackson*, his determination to distance himself from that case led him to make one significant error.

---

[17] *Bank of New Zealand v Greenwood* [1984] 1 NZLR 525 (HC). See also *Jaggard v Sawyer* [1995] 1 WLR 269 (CA).

[18] *Bank of New Zealand v Greenwood* [1984] 1 NZLR 525 (HC), 533.

[19] ibid.

[20] ibid 535. Quoting from *Shelfer v City of London* [1895] 1 Ch 287 (CA), 316.

When turning to consider the appropriate remedy, Hardie Boys J began by remarking:

> The plaintiffs seek an injunction and not damages . . . Again despite the majority view in *Miller v Jackson* – which I hope it may not be impertinent to suggest may have been different if the defendant had been for instance a baseball club – it is clear that if an actionable nuisance of a continuing nature is established, the plaintiff is entitled to have the nuisance stopped, and not to be paid off in damages, for that would result in the Court licensing his wrongdoing: *Shelfer v City of London Electric Lighting Company, Kennaway v Thompson.*[21]

But the injunction awarded was more than a little curious.

> It seems to me that to require the defendants to take steps to eliminate the glare altogether would be to give the [first two claimants] more extensive relief than they are entitled to have. For as will be clear from the conclusion I have reached upon [the third claimant's] claim, I consider that the glare is not an actionable nuisance where it can reasonably be excluded by drawing venetian blinds. The provision of blinds . . . at the defendants' expense would thus satisfy the plaintiffs' rights and discharge the defendants' obligations. It would achieve these results at what is likely to be a much lower cost to the defendants, both in terms of money and detrimental effect. And it would avoid the possibility which might occur if the verandah had to be replaced, of the defendants being imposed with a burden quite out of proportion to the injury being done to the plaintiffs.[22]

Hardie Boys J further insisted that:

> To resolve the matter in this way is not of course to decide the case on the basis of relative costs to the parties, for clearly the plaintiffs should not have to pay anything. Nor is it an award of damages in lieu of an injunction.[23]

It is not possible to agree. This 'injunction' is an order, not to cease to commit the nuisance, but to pay the claimants money so that they, the claimants, will prevent the nuisance by blocking the light. That this is, in reality, damages in lieu of an injunction is surely clear when one realises that (taking the claimants' 'duty to mitigate' into account) an award of damages in lieu of an injunction would in the circumstances have amounted to exactly the same thing.

But this result was entirely appropriate. The mistake made by Hardie Boys J in this regard was to argue that the rejection of *Miller v Jackson* in favour of *Shelfer v City of London* entailed that the claimants were entitled to an injunction. That was wrong. *Shelfer v City of London* did not decide that damages in lieu of an injunction are never appropriate, nor is that proposition supported by *Kennaway v Thompson*. Thus, rejecting *Miller v Jackson* in favour of *Shelfer v City of London* does not require rejecting the possibility of awarding damages in lieu of an injunction. It requires insisting that damages will be awarded in lieu of an injunction on

---

[21] *Bank of New Zealand v Greenwood* [1984] 1 NZLR 525 (HC), 536.
[22] ibid.
[23] ibid.

the basis of the *Shelfer* rule only. In that light, we can see that Hardie Boys J's arguments for awarding his curious injunction would have been better employed as arguments in favour of the application of the *Shelfer* rule.

Recall that rule: damages can be awarded in lieu of an injunction if 'the injury to the plaintiff's legal rights is small', 'is one which is capable of being estimated in money', 'is one which can be adequately compensated by a small money payment', 'and the case is one in which it would be oppressive to the defendant to grant an injunction'.[24] These conditions are fulfilled by the facts in this case.

First, the injury to the claimant's legal rights was small. As Hardie Boys J noted, had the claimants had blinds or curtains in place, no action would have succeeded. In that regard, the interference was borderline.[25] Second, the claimants' injury was capable of being estimated in money: the amount needed to install blinds. Third, and for the same reason, the injury could adequately be compensated by a small money payment.

Finally, the case was one in which it would be oppressive to the defendant to grant an injunction,[26] as Hardie Boys J again demonstrated.

> [I]f the plaintiffs were granted their injunction, the cost to the defendants of any acceptable solution would be considerable. The simplest course would be to paint the glass, but that would quickly become unsightly, and would defeat the purpose of the design, as would replacing the glass with some opaque material. Other suggestions made by counsel, such as the provision of adjustable awnings or louvres, have considerable practical difficulties. The replacement of the verandah with one of different design would be expensive – perhaps costing up to $20,000.[27]

Hardie Boys J's analysis also reveals the basis for the *Shelfer* rule. The reason damages should be awarded in lieu of an injunction in the relevant circumstances is that, in those circumstances, the impact of an injunction on the defendant would result in a more fundamental curtailment of the defendant's property rights than allowing the activity to continue would with respect to the claimant's. In *Bank of New Zealand v Greenwood*, the solution that interfered in the least fundamental way with the parties' rights was the one Hardie Boys J adopted.[28]

These cases, then, have the following structure. The defendant performs an activity that has consequences that interfere with a more fundamental right in the claimant (hence there is a nuisance). But requiring the defendant to eliminate those consequences would interfere with a more fundamental right in the defendant. When this occurs, it is because the claimant is able to eliminate the interference in a way that is less intrusive than requiring the defendant to eliminate the nuisance. This is why the *Shelfer* rule focuses on both the extent of the claimant's injury and the degree of interference with the defendant were the injunction to be awarded.

[24] *Shelfer v City of London* [1895] 1 Ch 287 (CA), 322–23.
[25] *Bank of New Zealand v Greenwood* [1984] 1 NZLR 525 (HC), 533.
[26] See also *Jaggard v Sawyer* [1995] 1 WLR 269 (CA), 287–88.
[27] *Bank of New Zealand v Greenwood* [1984] 1 NZLR 525 (HC), 529.
[28] See also *Jaggard v Sawyer* [1995] 1 WLR 269 (CA).

Accordingly, the point of the *Shelfer* rule is to preserve equality between the parties in the unusual cases in which, though a nuisance has been created and thus must be remedied, the least intrusive way to do so is to require the defendant to provide the claimant with the means to do so.

II. Remoteness

Standard approaches to damages begin with a list of damage types – personal injury, property damage, economic loss, etc – and seek to categorise the circumstances in which recovery for each particular type of damage is available. In this regard, policy arguments are advanced in favour of or against particular species of recovery.

This is the inevitable consequence of beginning with an inadequate analysis of the basis of liability. As liability is said to rest on the unreasonableness of the defendant's use of his land, it seems to follow that, in principle, any loss suffered thereby ought to be recoverable. As that conclusion is unacceptable in practice, it becomes necessary to invent policy reasons – that is, reasons that do not relate to the basis of liability – to limit recovery. In short, the need to rely on policy is a sure sign of inadequate understanding. The approach advanced here is of a different order.

A. Remoteness and Nuisance

Chapter eight argued that nuisance liability should not depend on foreseeability. On the face of it, that approach generates the following difficulty. Some limit must be placed on liability for consequential loss in the law of nuisance, otherwise we would have indeterminate liability. Foreseeability is the tool that the law of negligence uses to provide such a limit,[29] and that concept currently performs the same role in the law of nuisance. If we remove it, indeterminate liability will result. In fact, however, this is not the case.

A nuisance is a use of land that interferes with a more fundamental use of another's. On this approach, recoverable damage is confined to the cost of removing the impediment to the claimant's use of land and the cost of the loss of that use. Two points in particular must be noted. First, if an injunction is awarded that eliminates the nuisance, then the first cost does not exist. Second, and more importantly, the claimant is entitled to recover the cost of the loss of the relevant use, not losses caused by the loss of the relevant use. *In that sense*, on the approach advanced here, recovery for consequential loss is not permitted.

---

[29] For my rejection of this view, see A Beever, *Rediscovering the Law of Negligence* (Oxford, Hart, 2007) ch 4 and the discussion below.

Imagine that a subsidence occurs on the defendant's land that causes soil to slide onto the claimant's land, blocking the claimant's access to the property. Here, the landslide prevents the claimant using his land in certain ways. She can therefore recover the cost of removing the soil so that she can again use the land, loss of amenity and so on. But imagine now that her complaint is that she was unable to get her car from the garage and in consequence missed an important meeting causing her significant economic loss. This is not recoverable. It is true that she missed the meeting as a result of her inability to use her land: her inability to get her car caused her to miss the meeting. But that is not the issue. She cannot recover because the meeting she missed was not a use of her land, and so, of course, not a use of her land more fundamental than the relevant use of the defendant's.

There is, therefore, no issue of indeterminate liability on this model. Liability is limited. And that limit is not arbitrary. It flows from the basic understanding of liability introduced in chapter three. It does not depend on policy arguments.

It is also important to stress that the reason the claimant in the example above is unable to recover is not because her loss was economic. The approach advanced here does not restrict recovery in terms of arbitrary categories of loss. Hence, there is no bar on the recovery of economic loss or, for that matter, personal injury. The sole issue is whether the damages claimed by the claimant are encompassed by the defendant's interference with the claimant's use of her land.

B. Remoteness in Nuisance and Negligence

In the law of negligence, a claimant who is wronged can recover for all reasonably foreseeable losses that result from that wrongdoing. Thus, if I negligently break your leg, you will be able to recover your lost earnings suffered as a result of not being able to work with a broken leg. On this picture, then, the claimant can recover consequential loss as the result of a wrong. Why not in the law of nuisance? In the example just examined, the claimant was wronged when the soil entered her property. Why, then, can she not recover for the consequences of that wrong?

The appropriate response to this difficulty is to maintain that the distinction between the laws of negligence and nuisance in this regard is apparent only. In fact, in the sense under discussion – though there are other senses available[30] – neither area of law permits consequential loss.[31]

Negligence liability rests on the defendant having exposed the claimant to an unreasonable risk. Thus, the defendant's liability is limited in terms of the scope of that risk. If I perform an action that places you at an unreasonable risk of injury

---

[30] eg *Hunter v Canary Wharf* [1997] AC 655 (HL), 706.

[31] Above and in A Beever, *Rediscovering the Law of Negligence* (Oxford, Hart, 2007) 243, I argued that it is wrong to place emphasis on the kind of loss that the claimant suffers. The same point is to be made here. The issue is not whether the loss is consequential or not. The issue is whether it is wrongly caused, ie whether it falls within the scope of the defendant's wrong.

by fire but, through some fantastic or far-fetched circumstances, I injure you by flooding, then I will not be liable in the law of negligence, as I was not negligent for causing you to be flooded.[32] But if I injure you by breaking your leg and you are unable to work as a result, then I am negligent for causing you to lose earnings. For instance, if your broken leg is caused by my negligent driving, then the risk associated with my activity is unreasonable not only because the activity might cause your leg to be broken but also because the activity might cause you to lose earnings as a result of having your leg broken. To put this as simply as possible, it would have made sense (though it would have been strangely precise) to have said to me 'Drive more carefully. You might injure that person and prevent her being able to work'. In other words, in this case, the lost earnings are not merely caused as a result of a wrong, they are wrongly caused. The loss lies within the scope of my wrongdoing. The loss is not, then, merely consequent upon a wrong.

Thus, we must distinguish between losses caused by a wrong and wrongful losses. A wrongful loss is a loss that lies within the scope of the defendant's wrong. Because one of the reasons I should not drive negligently is that I might prevent you being able to work, when I break your leg and you are unable to work, the associated losses are wrongful. They lie within the scope of my wrongdoing. But a loss caused by a wrong is merely a loss that results from a wrong. The flooding case is an example. It was wrong of me to place you at risk of fire and the action that created that risk caused you to be flooded, but my action was not wrongful because it placed you at risk of flooding. Your injury, then, does not lie within the ambit of my wrong. You suffered a loss as the result of a wrong but not a wrongful loss. Hence, you cannot recover.

Given the contours of the law of nuisance, the claimant who misses a meeting suffers a loss consequent on a wrong but that is not a wrongful loss. She cannot recover. Though the two areas of the law naturally operate on the basis of different principles, they are *ad idem* with respect to their understanding of remoteness.

---

[32] eg *Doughty v Turner Manufacturing Co Ltd* [1964] 1 QB 518 (CA). For discussion, see A Beever, *Rediscovering the Law of Negligence* (Oxford, Hart, 2007) ch 4.

13

Conclusion

Rightly understood, nuisance is a tort of strict liability. In that regard, it is more closely related to the law of trespass than to the law of negligence. It is particularly closely related to the law of trespass to property. But just as obviously, there are important differences. It is useful to examine the most important similarities and differences between these torts.

The law of negligence is concerned with the assessment of the defendant's conduct. It is called into play when the defendant has done something that has injured the claimant. As always, the law must seek to do justice as between the parties. As I have explained in detail elsewhere, it does so by adopting the objective standard of care, an approach that mediates between the interests of the parties by determining whether the defendant was negligent in accordance with a general standard of behaviour set for the community as a whole.[1] In this regard, the objective standard of care must be contrasted with a subjective standard, which would determine negligence in terms of the defendant's idiosyncrasies, thus privileging the position of that party, and strict liability, which would determine liability simply by asking whether the claimant was injured, privileging the position of that party. In that context, then, liability is appropriately fault based, where fault is understood in its familiar, objective sense.

Strict liability is appropriate in the law of trespass.[2] This is because, in these cases, the defendant has entered the space of the claimant without the claimant's consent, whether that space be the claimant's property or person. Fault here would not be appropriate. The entrance is itself wrongful, even if well motivated and done with care. This also explains why these torts require intention. The intention is a prerequisite for entering the claimant's space.

But this does not mean that one's ability to control the use of one's own space is absolute. If one uses one's space in a way that interferes with the space of another, then the law must find a way to prioritise such uses. That, as I have argued, is the purpose of the law of nuisance. This area of the law is appropriately strict, and appropriately ignores intention, as the issue is not the defendant's conduct but the significance of the use of the defendant's land vis-à-vis the claimant's. The law of nuisance is not concerned with conduct. It is concerned with prioritis-

---

[1] A Beever, *Rediscovering the Law of Negligence* (Oxford, Hart, 2007) ch 3.
[2] For the argument that trespass is strict, see A Beever, 'The Form of Liability in the Torts of Trespass' (2011) 40 *Common Law World Review* 378.

ing property rights. It is therefore a form of strict liability that ignores the state of the parties' minds.

Accordingly, though different forms of liability are found in the law of tort, that does not imply any lack of unity. Rather, each form of liability is called for by the need to do justice as between the parties in the circumstances pertinent to the relevant tort. The law is far from as systematic as one might have hoped, but it has worked out its own way consistently of doing justice as between the parties.

BIBLIOGRAPHY

Barker, K, Cane, P, Lunney, M and Trindade, FA, *The Law of Torts in Australia*, 5th edn (Melbourne, Oxford University Press, 2012).

Beever, A, *Rediscovering the Law of Negligence* (Oxford, Hart, 2007).

—— 'The Form of Liability in the Torts of Trespass' (2011) 40 *Common Law World Review* 378.

—— 'Our Most Fundamental Rights' in Robertson, A and Nolan, D (eds), *Rights and Private Law* (Oxford, Hart, 2011).

—— *Forgotten Justice: A History of Political and Legal Theory* (Oxford, Oxford University Press, 2013).

Beever, A and Rickett, C, 'Interpretive Legal Theory and the Academic Lawyer' (2005) 68 *MLR* 320.

Bohlen, FH, 'The Rule in *Rylands v Fletcher*' (1911) 59 *University of Pennsylvania Law Review* 298.

Byrd, BS and Hruschka, J, *Kant's Doctrine of Right: A Commentary* (New York, Cambridge University Press, 2010).

Campbell, D, 'Of Coase and Corn: A (Sort of) Defence of Private Nuisance' (2000) 63 *MLR* 197.

—— 'Gathering the Water: Abuse of Rights After the Recognition of Government Failure' (2010) 6 *Journal of Jurisprudence* 487.

Chambers, RS, 'Nuisance – Judicial Attack on Orthodoxy' [1978] *New Zealand Law Journal* 172.

Danto, AC, *The Philosophical Disenfranchisement of Art* (New York, Columbia University Press, 1986).

Deakin, S, Johnston, A and Markesinis, B, *Markesinis and Deakin's Tort Law*, 6th edn (Oxford, Clarendon Press, 2008).

Dworkin, R, *Taking Rights Seriously* (Cambridge, Mass., Harvard University Press, 1977).

Eekelaar, JM, 'Nuisance and Strict Liability' (1973) 8 *Irish Jurist* 191.

FitzPatrick, TM, 'Should Family Members have Title to Sue in Private Nuisance?' (1998) 6 *Torts Law Journal* 171.

Gearty, C, 'The Place of Private Nuisance in a Modern Law of Torts' [1989] *CLJ* 214.

Gordley, J, *Foundations of Private Law: Property, Tort, Contract, Unjust Enrichment* (Oxford, Oxford University Press, 2006).

Heuston, RFV, *Salmond on the Law of Torts*, 16th edn (London, Sweet & Maxwell, 1973).

Kant, I, 'The Metaphysics of Morals' in Gregor, M (ed), *Practical Philosophy* (Cambridge, Cambridge University Press, 1996).

—— *Critique of Pure Reason*, Guyer, P and Wood, A (trs) (Cambridge, Cambridge University Press, 1998).

—— *Critique of the Power of Judgment*, Guyer, P and Matthews, E (trs) (Cambridge, Cambridge University Press, 2000).

Lee, M, 'What is Private Nuisance?' (2003) 119 *LQR* 298.

McBride, NJ and Bagshaw, R, *Tort Law*, 2nd edn (Harlow, Pearson Education Ltd, 2005).

Murphy, J, 'The Merits of *Rylands v Fletcher*' (2004) 24 *OJLS* 643.

—— *The Law of Nuisance* (Oxford, Oxford University Press, 2010).

——, Witting, C and Goudkamp, J, *Street on Torts*, 13th edn (Oxford, Oxford University Press, 2012).

Newark, FH, 'The Boundaries of Nuisance' (1949) 65 *LQR* 480.

Neyers, JW and Diacur, J, 'What (is) a Nuisance?' (2011) 90 *Canadian Bar Review* 215.

Nolan, D, 'The Distinctiveness of *Rylands v Fletcher*' (2005) 121 *LQR* 421.

——'"A Tort Against Land": Private Nuisance as a Property Tort' in Robertson, A and Nolan, D (eds), *Rights and Private Law* (Oxford, Hart, 2011).

Ogus, AI and Richardson, GM, 'Economics and the Environment: A Study of Private Nuisance', [1977] *CLJ* 284.

Oliphant, K (ed), *The Law of Tort* (London, Butterworths, 2007).

Oliphant, K, 'Against Certainty in Tort Law', in Pitel, S, Neyers, J and Chamberlain, E (eds), *Tort Law: Challenging Orthodoxy* (Oxford, Hart, forthcoming 2013).

Penner, JE, 'Nuisance and the Character of the Neighbourhood' (1993) 5 *Journal of Environmental Law* 1.

Posner, RA, 'A Theory of Negligence' (1972) 1 *JLS* 29.

Rogers, WVH, *Winfield and Jolowicz on Tort*, 18th edn (London, Sweet & Maxwell, 2010).

Searle, JR, *Intentionality: An Essay in the Philosophy of Mind* (Cambridge, Cambridge University Press, 1983).

Seavey, WS, 'Mr Justice Cardozo and the Law of Torts' (1939) 39 *Columbia Law Review* 20.

——'Nuisance, Contributory Negligence and Other Mysteries' (1952) 65 *Harvard Law Review* 984.

Stevens, R, 'Non-Delegable Duties and Vicarious Liability' in Neyers, JW, Chamberlain, E and Pitel, SGA (eds), *Emerging Issues in Tort Law* (Oxford, Hart, 2007).

—— *Torts and Rights* (Oxford, Oxford University Press, 2007).

Stone, M, 'Legal Positivism as an Idea About Morality' (2011) 61 *University of Toronto Law Journal* 313.

Weinrib, EJ, *The Idea of Private Law* (Cambridge, Mass., Harvard University Press, 1995).

——'Poverty and Property in Kant's System of Rights' (2003) 78 *Notre Dame Law Review* 795.

Weir, T, *An Introduction to Tort Law*, 2nd edn (Oxford, Oxford University Press, 2006).

Winfield, PH, 'Nuisance as a Tort' [1931] *CLJ* 189.

INDEX